Building Empathy in Children through Community Connections

Taking a unique approach, which highlights lived experience and engagement with community, this book guides the reader on how to create learning environments in which children are encouraged to develop relationships, build meaningful connections, and take action which contributes to the wellbeing of their own communities.

Through evaluations and feedback from participating professionals, as well as children's learning in the form of artworks and photos, *Building Empathy in Children through Community Connections: A Guide for Early Years Educators* highlights how community partnership programs between children and community groups builds empathy and wellbeing in early childhood. Drawing on extensive research and professional experience in psychology and early childhood, it provides details of various community connections programs and considers the ways in which early learning settings can engage with their communities as they meet the requirements and objectives of the curriculum. Each chapter provides practical advice on implementation as well as take home messages intended to encourage and enable community engagement.

Demonstrating how young children can develop empathy through building community connections, this book is a vital resource for early childhood educators as well as parents and those working in community programs and early childhood settings.

Erica Frydenberg is Associate Professor and Principal Research Fellow (Honorary) in psychology in the Melbourne Graduate School of Education, University of Melbourne, Australia.

Janice Deans is Associate Director Early Childhood Education, University of Melbourne, Australia.

Rachel Liang is Honorary Research Fellow, Melbourne Graduate School of Education, University of Melbourne, Australia

Building Empathy in Children through Community Connections
A Guide for Early Years Educators

Erica Frydenberg, Janice Deans
and Rachel Liang

LONDON AND NEW YORK

Cover image: © Getty Images

First published 2023
by Routledge
4 Park Square, Milton Park, Abingdon, Oxon OX14 4RN

and by Routledge
605 Third Avenue, New York, NY 10158

Routledge is an imprint of the Taylor & Francis Group, an informa business

© 2023 Erica Frydenberg, Janice Deans, Rachel Liang

The right of Erica Frydenberg, Janice Deans, Rachel Liang to be identified as authors of this work has been asserted in accordance with sections 77 and 78 of the Copyright, Designs and Patents Act 1988.

All rights reserved. No part of this book may be reprinted or reproduced or utilised in any form or by any electronic, mechanical, or other means, now known or hereafter invented, including photocopying and recording, or in any information storage or retrieval system, without permission in writing from the publishers.

Trademark notice: Product or corporate names may be trademarks or registered trademarks, and are used only for identification and explanation without intent to infringe.

British Library Cataloguing-in-Publication Data
A catalogue record for this book is available from the British Library

Library of Congress Cataloging-in-Publication Data
Names: Frydenberg, Erica, 1943– author. | Deans, Jan, author. | Liang, Rachel (Rachel Pui-Tak), author.
Title: Building empathy in children through community connections : a guide for early years educators / Erica Frydenberg, Janice Deans and Rachel Liang.
Description: Abingdon, Oxon ; New York, NY : Routledge, 2022. | Includes bibliographical references and index.
Identifiers: LCCN 2022008741 (print) | LCCN 2022008742 (ebook) | ISBN 9781032081434 (hardback) | ISBN 9781032081427 (paperback) | ISBN 9781003213147 (ebook)
Subjects: LCSH: Early childhood education–Psychological aspects. | Community and school. | Empathy in children.
Classification: LCC LB1139.23 .F79 2022 (print) | LCC LB1139.23 (ebook) | DDC 372.21–dc23/eng/20220425
LC record available at https://lccn.loc.gov/2022008741
LC ebook record available at https://lccn.loc.gov/2022008742

ISBN: 9781032081434 (hbk)
ISBN: 9781032081427 (pbk)
ISBN: 9781003213147 (ebk)

DOI: 10.4324/9781003213147

Typeset in Bembo
by Newgen Publishing UK

Contents

List of Figures ix
List of Tables xi
Foreword by Susanne Garvis xii
Acknowledgements xiv

Introductory Remarks 1

PART I 3

1 Children as Active Participants in their Community 5
   Introduction to Community Connections 5
   Positive Psychology – as a Basis for Flourishing and Building Empathy 9
   Positive Education in the Preschool Years 9
   Ecological Systems Theory 10
   Theory of Cognitive Development 12
   Socio-Cultural Theory of Development 13
   Concluding Remarks 14
   Take Home Messages 14
   References 15

2 Social Emotional Curriculum Objectives in Early
   Childhood Education 17
   Introduction to Social Emotional Learning in Education 17
   Building Strong Foundations in the Early Years 19
   SEL as a Basis for Early Years Curriculum 20
   Attachment Theory 22
   Self-Regulation 23
   Emotional Intelligence 24
   The Role of Language 25
   Concluding Remarks 26
   Take Home Messages 27
   References 27

3 The Foundation for Community Connections: Empathy and Associated Constructs   31
Introduction 31
Contact Theory 32
Foundational Emotional Skills 33
The Role of the Teacher 39
Social Learning 40
Prosocial Skills 42
Program Implementation and Evaluation 43
Concluding Remarks 44
Take Home Messages 44
References 45

4 Artistic Meaning Making in Early Years Education: Children's Voices Expressed through Drawing, Painting, and Narrative   49
Playful Artistic Meaning Making 49
Perezhivanie *and Multidimensional Thinking 51*
The Significance of Arts Education 52
Semiotic Meaning Making 55
The Voices of Children as Expressed through the Arts 56
Active Citizenship through Drawing, Painting, and Narrative 58
Concluding Remarks 60
Take Home Messages 60
References 60

PART II   65

5 Children Developing Empathy, Care, and Concern for the Environment: Education for Sustainable Development in the Early Years   67
HARRIET DEANS

Introduction 67
Ecocentric Curriculum within an Education for Sustainable Development (ESD) Framework 68
The Wall-less Classroom 70
The Role of the Teacher in Enacting the Principles of ESD 71
ESD Wall-less Classroom Curriculum and Learning Objectives 72
Designing and Implementing a Stepping Out Program 77
Stepping Out Program and the ESD Learning Domains 78
Teaching and Learning in the Cognitive, Socio-Emotional and Behavioural Learning Domains 85

Tools for Teaching across the Learning Domains 85
Concluding Remarks 95
Take Home Messages 96
References 96

6 Children as Global Citizens: Children's Voices Expressed
through Drawing, Painting, and Narrative   99
   Introduction 99
   Collaborative Global Partnerships through Child Art Exhibitions 99
   The Promotion of Child Voice through Art Exhibitions 101
   Associazione L'Eta Verde 103
   The Interdependence Hexagon Project 107
   Reflection on Children's Learning through the Hexagon Project 112
   Concluding Remarks 113
   Take Home Messages 113
   References 113

7 Friends on the Farm: Reciprocal Relationship Building
with People with Special Needs   115
   Introduction 115
   The Background to the Project 117
   About the Participants 119
   More about the Children and their Teachers 119
   More about the Adults and the Disability Development Staff 120
   Artistic Community-Based Projects 121
   The Children's Farm 122
   The Art Program 122
   The Journal – Reflecting-in-and-on-Action 123
   The Outcomes of the Lived Experience 125
   Concluding Remarks 127
   Take Home Messages 127
   References 128

8 Building Intergenerational Connections: The Social and
Emotional Benefits of Intergenerational Programs   130
   Introduction 130
   The Need and the Opportunity 131
   Across the Globe 131
   Theoretical Underpinnings 134
   Empathy and Intergenerational Program (IGP) 135
   Concluding Remarks 142
   Take Home Messages 143
   References 143

viii   Contents

PART III   147

9   The COPE-Resilience Program: A Guide to Successful
    Connections Building Activities at Early Childhood
    Programs   149
    Introduction 149
    *A Less Discussed Area in Implementing Early Childhood
        SEL Programs: The Role of the Teacher 150*
    *Cultivating Empathic Capacity: Quality of Educator–Child Relationship
        Matters 151*
    *Creating a Community of Prosocial Learners and Fostering Skills
        Development 152*
    *Theory in Action: Process of Socialization and Embodiment
        of COPE-R 153*
    Creating your own Connections Building Activities 164
    International Adaptation 165
    Concluding Remarks 165
    Take Home Messages 166
    References 166

10 Community Connections   169
    Bringing it Together 169
    The International Focus 172
    The Challenges of 2020–2021 174
    Final Remarks 178
    References 178

    Index   180

Figures

1.1	A community of learners	7
1.2a, b	Spaces and resources that inspire focused engagement, creative thinking, and problem solving	8
1.3	An integration of cognitive, ecological system and socio-cultural theories of development	11
2.1a, b	Self-portraits by ELC children: a personalized symbol that represents the child's inner world of feelings and sense of belonging	21
2.2	Children collaborating on a piece of artwork	22
3.1	Core skills from the CASEL framework	31
3.2	Children expressing their care for environment in art form	36
3.3	Children stepping outside of their classroom and exploring the environments close to where they live and learn	36
3.4	Teacher facilitating group discussion on being a good listener	38
4.1	In the future there will be flying cars	58
5.1	Ecocentric curriculum	69
5.2	Wall-less classroom	70
5.3	Role of the teacher	72
5.4	Cognitive learning domain photo examples	81
5.5	Socio-emotional learning domain photo examples	82
5.6	Behavioural learning domain photo examples	83
5.7	3-year-old drawing-tellings	86
5.8	4-year-old drawing-tellings	87
5.9	Journaling in pairs	87
5.10	3-year-old journaling examples	88
5.11	4-year-old journaling examples	89
5.12	Thinking routines "See, Think, Wonder"	92
5.13	Mind-mapping children's ideas captured by ELC teachers	94
5.14	Teacher documentation: children's narratives and descriptive words	95
6.1	If I were a forest	104
6.2	Maybe your heart is a star	106
6.3	Children's drawing of the Heart of an Iceberg	106

6.4	A story by children from the ELC: The Iceberg's Heart	106
6.5	ELC Children's creation for the 2015 Hexagon Project on the theme of Natural Habitat	109
6.6a,b	ELC Children's creation for the 2019 Hexagon Project on the theme of Transforming Conflict	109
6.7	"Koalas need homes to live so they won't become extinct." – ELC Children's creation for the 2020 Hexagon Project on the theme of Diversity	110
6.8	"Bees help plants grow and make honey." – ELC Children's creation for the 2020 Hexagon Project on the theme of Diversity	110
6.9	The exhibition: the leather back turtle is endangered – ELC Children's creation for the 2020 Hexagon Project on the theme of Diversity	110
7.1	Children and adults with special needs engaging in Friends on Farm	118
7.2	Friends on Farm activity	120
7.3	Artmaking creations	121
7.4	Nature-inspired art-making	123
8.1	A child sharing his favourite book with one of the neighbours and handing her a cup of tea	136
8.2	Children invited the neighbours to visit the ELC community	137
9.1	Circle time: Tuning in to ourselves to start the day	156
9.2	Children's artwork to exploring different feelings	157
9.3	Children's art creation demonstrating empathy towards nature	158
9.4	Early Years Coping cards: getting hurt/feeling sad	159
9.5	Children's drawing: How to care for the environment	160
9.6	Mindful in May excursion: cloud and star gazing	161
9.7	Children drawings: what kind of heart do you have?	161
9.8	Children's drawing of listening with the whole body	163
9.9	Voice level chart	164
9.10	Children's creation of hand mandala	165
10.1	ELC children's drawings of wearing masks	175
10.2	ELC children's drawings of washing hands	176
10.3a,b	ELC children's drawing-tellings during the pandemic	176
10.4	Children's drawing for *Then and Now: Out of the Birdcage*	177

Tables

2.1	The CASEL framework in an educational context	18
3.1	Terms that are aligned with empathy and used interchangeably by class teachers	40
5.1	Example of wall-less classroom curriculum	73
5.2	Key indicators for ESD learning domains 3–5 Years	79
5.3	Examples of children's learning during the Stepping Out Program in the cognitive, socio-emotional, and behavioural learning domains	84
8.1	Sample of activities for each of the focus areas in the 2019 IGP program	137
9.1	COPE-R sessions: objectives and learning experiences	154

Foreword

As a parent of a young child during COVID, I took great delight in reading this important contribution the book *Building Empathy in Children through Community Connections: A Guide for Early Years Educators* makes to the field of early childhood education. Now, more than ever, there is a need for early childhood educators to be confident and capable in building children's empathy, especially with children who may have had remote learning and extended periods in isolation. As part of COVID recovery in education, community will help lead the re-establishment of important relationships for young children's learning.

By placing social emotional learning as the foundation of child development, young children are able to be supported and participate in all areas of their learning and development. When educators understand theories and important child development research, they are able to plan effective learning opportunities with young children. These learning opportunities are regularly reviewed and evaluated to always provide optimal learning environments that support teaching and learning.

In this book, a wide range of examples of programs are given to show connections with and across community and empathy with environmentally sustainable development, global citizenship, reciprocal relationships and intergenerational programs. A key feature is the COPE-resilience program that specifically focuses on the role of the educator, quality interactions, and the importance of pro-social behaviour. With programs, examples are also given that allow the grounding of reflective practice to become actively known. Reflective practice is an important tool for early years educators to explore new ways of working and also reflect on their own practices. The examples given provide opportunities for reflection across a variety of early years context and start to develop strong foundational understandings of the role of educators to support social and emotional development.

The COPE-R program in Chapter 9 is an exemplary example of bringing everything discussed together to create a strong theory-rich program for social and emotional learning. Evidence is shared of the program's implementation in a Melbourne early childhood setting, where a safe and supportive learning environment is created. A key feature is also the modelling associated with empathic behaviours in which children and families can learn together with the educator.

Effective communication behaviours are also encouraged and modelled to create a high-impact learning environment. This suggests strong foundations for social and emotional development and promotes the embodying of long-term SEL concepts.

Given the large base of evidence on the importance of social and emotional development, the book is foundational in building theory and practice within early childhood education settings. I hope that, as my young daughter continues through her schooling journey, she and her friends are able to meet educators who have read and been able to implement practices and ideas from the book. Through such changes to practice, early childhood education can truly support all young learners and their families and provide the very best start for all children.

Understanding the importance of developing empathy through community programs is the key.

Professor Susanne Garvis,
Chair of Department of Education,
Swinburne University of Technology
Jan 11, 2022

Acknowledgements

The purpose of this volume is to highlight the numerous community-related projects which have been undertaken by the University of Melbourne's Early Learning Centre. The centre is a research and demonstration preschool catering for children aged between 3 and 5 years.

As the reader progresses through the chapters it becomes clear that countless ELC and community leaders along with child and adult participants have made the projects come to life before reaching the pages of this book. Thus, it is a challenge to acknowledge all the many participants, students, teachers, parents, community personnel who have contributed to projects described.

Nevertheless, there are some people who have made outstanding contributions including:

> Natalie Jones, Victoria Ryle, Anne Ferguson, and Leah Raymond for their dedication to the development of the Friends on the Farm project described in Chapter 7.
> Suzana Klarin, Dominic Belvedere, Avis Gardner, Harriet Deans, and Louise Saxton for their artistic contributions to the multiple Association L'Eta Verde and Interdependence Hexagon Projects.
> Rei Otsuki, Sophia Stirling, Esther Wong, and Kylie Payman for their design, implementation, and development of the Intergenerational Program described in Chapter 8;
> Harriet Deans, with her colleague Margaret Bakes, developed the Stepping Out Program described in Chapter 5. and
> Suzana Klarin who championed the COPE-Resilience Program described in Chapter 9.

As the projects span more than a decade there have been hundreds of children and parents involved in the various programs and their work is reflected in the many images and drawing-tellings scattered throughout the text.

There have also been numerous postgraduate educational psychology students who have conducted research at the ELC during the decade and used various approaches to evaluate the programs described in the book. Emily Kirsh, Michelle Guneratne, and Joanne Alana Banks were involved in the intergenerational program which they evaluated; Danielle Soliman investigated empathy, Monique Alexander, the team who were involved in COPE-Resilience program, including, those who developed the first iteration of the COPE-R program, Neisha Kiernan, Danielle Kaufman, Chelsea Cornell, and Prishni Dobee as well as Marissa Wu who has recently taken SEL and the program to Taiwan. And Nathan McNamara who in 2021 provides additional evaluations to the Stepping Out Program.

With thanks, deep appreciation, and gratitude to teachers, children, and families of the University of Melbourne's Early Learning Centre.

Introductory Remarks

This book has been organised in three sections.

Part I focuses on the things that matter when we are infusing the development of empathy and wellbeing into the early years' classroom practices with a focus on the notion of community participation, engagement, and contribution. There is an emphasis on the rights of the child and the theories that explain child development. We also focus on social emotional learning (SEL), an essential part of which is the development of empathy through respectful caring relationships with people and environments. Optimum development depends on emotions, the associated language, understandings, and emotion regulation. The key mode of teaching and learning in this environment is through the arts, both visual, auditory, and sensory. These are on show in Part II.

Part II is where we focus on programs such as an arts-based program with adults with disability, an intergenerational program, and a program focusing on environment and sustainability which can be used as an exemplar of the key elements that can be integrated into almost any early childhood programs. In Chapter 6 a range of projects, many that are shared with international communities, are presented. The chapters outline and detail various programs that have been implemented to encourage the reader to consider the ways in which early learning settings can engage with their communities as they meet the requirements and objectives of the curriculum in their particular context.

Part III brings it all together. It illustrates with one program, COPE-Resilience, the skills that are focused on developing empathy and good citizenship. Although that program is not singularly focused on community participation it has embedded in it the skills that are so useful for a community connections project and it too can be used as an exemplar for skill development. Part III is where key examples are presented with the objective of helping educators bring these practices into their classrooms.

The challenges of 2020/2021 meant teachers had to adapt to remote learning when required and utilize the opportunity to focus on the here and now, such as the wearing of masks. The children's responses are reflected in their art works.

All in all children, parents, and educators belong in communities where connections can be developed and deepened to be educative and meaningful for all concerned. The early learning setting is an ideal vehicle for making those connections. This volume has been conceived as a resource and is intended to provide inspiration and encouragement for the reader to engage with their communities.

Part I

1 Children as Active Participants in their Community

Introduction to Community Connections

In 2021 as the world was recovering from a global pandemic and people were looking with hope and anticipation to a better future the importance and opportunities afforded by education in the early years was readily recognized in the developed world. We strive to have children grow into good citizens who engage in prosocial behaviours and are empathetic towards their environment and all living things within it. Early childhood settings provide unique possibilities for establishing learning environments where children can develop these skills through becoming active participants in their communities in a range of ways and in a range of locales. The settings range from the natural environment through to the lived one where there is engagement with peers, adults, and those who are distinctively different in their modes of living. Diverse environments provide opportunities for children to have unique experiences that expand their horizons and skill development in the social emotional domain.

Early childhood experiences can influence a sense of community in children, adolescents (Hasford et al., 2016), and beyond. In general terms early childhood education programs aim to produce children who have a strong sense of identity, who are connected with and contribute to their world, who have a strong sense of wellbeing, are confident and involved learners, and are effective communicators. Numerous studies have followed children through the teenage years and into late adolescence and early adulthood. The studies have focused on programs such as the Abecedarian Project (Campbell et al., 2002), the Mother–Child Home Program (Levenstein et al., 1998), the Perry Preschool Program (Berrueta-Clement et al., 1984), the Chicago Child–Parent Centers (Reynolds et al., 2001), and the Better Beginnings, Better Futures program (Peters et al., 2010). These studies have shown various positive impacts of early childhood development programs on a variety of adolescent outcomes, including community participation (Janzen et al., 2010), prosocial practices, positivity, and connections with the community (Hasford et al., 2016).

The early learning experiences described in this volume are framed by a guiding philosophy that frames curriculum requirements and is underpinned by a range of educational and psychological theories. Schools are being asked

DOI: 10.4324/9781003213147-3

not to focus exclusively on numeracy and literacy or the precursors of them but place an emphasis on social and emotional learning. How we deal with the world from an emotional and relational perspective impacts all that follows. The requirements are articulated in curriculum documents and are presented in Chapter 2.

First, there are some well accepted principles that guide early childhood education, namely the rights of the child. The human rights charter, the United Nations Convention on the Rights of the Child (UNCRC) (UN, 1989), acknowledges the right of children to be heard and consulted on matters that affect them. In particular Article 12 of the Convention notes that:

> State parties shall assure to the child who is capable of forming his or her own views the right to express those view freely in all matters affecting the child, the views of the child being given due weight in accordance with the age and maturity of the child.
>
> (UNCRC, 1989)

Throughout this volume, where programs conducted in the early learning setting are described or referenced, teachers have been influenced by the arts and utilize the arts to encourage, support, and guide children to independently express their ideas and understandings. Over time the arts take a central role in their learning and development.

Article 13 expands on Article 12 and intersects with it to endorse the important role of the arts in the lives of children. It states:

> The child shall have the right to freedom of expression; this right shall include freedom to seek, receive and impart information and ideas of all kinds, regardless of frontiers, either orally, in writing or in print, in the form of art, or through any other media of the child's choice.
>
> (UN, 1989)

Furthermore Article 14 (UN, 1989) recognizes and promotes the rights of the child to participate freely in play and in cultural life and the arts. It highlights the importance of children being provided with opportunities to engage in learning that supports their personal expression through art-making and community involvement. When young children are given an opportunity to express their views, they develop a sense of autonomy and self-determination (Lansdown, 2004; Lloyd-Smith & Tarr, 2000; Tobin, 2005).

The Code of Ethics of Early Childhood Australia (ECA, 2006), which was developed to inform and guide the professional behaviour and decision-making processes of all early childhood professionals, also endorses the principles advocated within the UNCRC (UN, 1989). It highlights the importance of learning that supports open-ended inquiry, focused engagement, ongoing development, and shows respect for children's capacities to self-direct their learning. ELC teachers recognize that children's contributions take many forms, and it is within the artistic domain that they demonstrate their abilities to expand understandings of their physical and social worlds.

Secondly, there is a philosophy that underpins the programs that are presented in this volume which is based on an image of children as creative, capable individuals who are intrinsically motivated to explore and discover their world. Through active engagement in free and structured imaginative play children employ a range of complex networks of abilities, interests, and symbolic languages. Engagement in diverse forms of play fosters the development of a spirit of curiosity experimentation and discovery, with children being supported to develop their thinking and understandings, fine and gross motor skills, language, personal and social awareness, emotional wellbeing, and creativity.

To realize the potential of all children the learning environment is nurturing, secure, and stimulating-play-based; it promotes happiness and a desire to learn. At the core of the philosophy is a commitment to the establishment of a dynamic culture of thinking where children and teachers explore "big ideas" that promote and sustain long-term enquiries. The philosophy incorporates the idea of the social construction of knowledge, which relies on the establishment of relationships between children and teachers and children and children. It also recognizes that children mature at different rates and have preferred styles of learning. Teachers prioritize the establishment of an emotionally secure foundation to support each child's developing sense of self and empathy for others. Relationships between children and children, children and teachers, and teachers and families are nurtured, with the aim being to create a community of learners (e.g. Figure 1.1) who embark on mutually beneficial and exciting learning journeys.

Within this philosophy the arts play a central role in helping children to be involved in independent decision-making, expressive and aesthetic communication, and collaborative learning. Also, the principles of Education

Figure 1.1 A community of learners.

for Sustainability underpin a unique pedagogical framework that supports children's learning in, about, and for the environment. Through the community connections programs, children and teachers engage in learning beyond the early learning setting, stepping out regularly to explore the natural environment and the wider community. The ELC, where the programs have been developed, is located on the lands of the Wurundjeri people and so the inclusion of Australian First Nations perspectives is considered integral to these outwardly focused experiences. Also, the philosophy recognizes the significance of presenting an inclusive and welcoming environment, one that reflects and promotes diversity and challenges bias through the inclusion of carefully considered resources and learning that promotes perspective-taking and thinking about difference.

Sensory-rich learning environments are established to stimulate curiosity and a sense of wonder. These environments are valued for their capacity to organize, to promote choices, to stimulate deep involvement, and to support the development of respectful relationships between individuals and materials. Learning experiences, routines, and resources are presented in such a way as to stimulate sensory perception and open-ended play, encourage creative thinking, and enhance opportunities for collaborative learning (see Figure 1.2a,b).

The primary aim for children in the early learning setting is for them to develop their understandings of the world in which they live through the development of broadly based knowledge, skills, and attitudes that enable them to take the prerequisite steps in preparation for lifelong learning. Well qualified teachers draw on resources to design, adapt, implement, and evaluate innovative and challenging programs that reflect the most contemporary early childhood theory and research which are articulated in curriculum guidelines.

The key guiding principles that inform practices described in this volume are underpinned by well-established psychological and educational theories as to how and what children learn. Front and centre in each of the programs is the

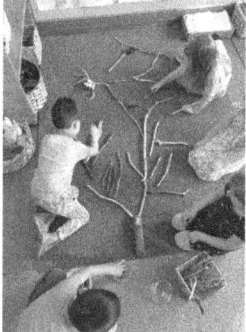

*Figure 1.2*a,b Spaces and resources that inspire focused engagement, creative thinking, and problem solving.

notion of building empathy and caring for others. The development of empathy underpins community connections and is well guided by the positive psychology movement that has at its core the notion of caring for all living things, including the environment that we live in, and showing gratitude as part of our shared humanity.

Positive Psychology – as a Basis for Flourishing and Building Empathy

At a child level, positive psychology is about bringing up children who are engaged with the world around them, who retain curiosity to explore their environment, and gain satisfaction when they accomplish a task. The aim is for children not only to be willing to engage in challenging activities but also to be able to engage with and relate to others, to show gratitude, and to appreciate their surroundings. While positive psychology emphasizes the important experience of positive emotions, it does not imply that we are not interested in also identifying and labelling negative emotions. We learn to appreciate the good through negative experiences and losses. However, generally it is through positive emotional experiences that we broaden and build our personal resources for living the good life.

Positive Education in the Preschool Years

Positive Education as defined by Martin Seligman, the founder of the positive psychology movement, and colleagues (2009) is an education for both traditional skills and for happiness. It aims to address the gap between what we all want for our children, namely happiness, positive physical, and mental health, versus the traditional focus on academic achievement as a measure of success in school. It is not a focus on mental health instead of academic achievement but on mental health in order to give students the opportunity for learning. Optimal learning is thus holistic, progressing simultaneously in areas of health, cognition, personal and social development, and wellbeing.

Schools are increasingly urged to provide students with opportunities not only to grow academically, but also to become caring, responsible, and productive members of society (White & Waters, 2015). A key aspect of achieving this in the early years is through teaching valuable life skills that assist early years learners to strengthen their relationships, build positive emotions, enhance personal resilience, promote mindfulness, and encourage a healthy lifestyle (Frydenberg et al., 2020). A focus on holistic well-being is one of the major learning outcomes for the early years that education can offer children. It provides a strong foundation on which they can build a successful life as caring, responsible, and productive members of society.

In addition to having a pervasive philosophy that respects the rights of the child, there are a range of foundational and contemporary educational and psychological theories that guide educational practice, such as the socio-cultural theory of development and ecological systems theory, along with attachment theory and self-regulation and emotional intelligence. Contemporary theories that relate to positive psychology and positive education can be construed both as empirically grounded theories or philosophical orientations that are complementary and consistent with the programs outlined in this volume.

Children's sense of agency and empathy development is supported not only by providing them with choices and options but also by listening with respect to their voice, specifically their words and their ideas in relation to their lived experiences. Conceptual approaches to the rights of children and their participation in their communities frame how we engage with children and in turn provide opportunities for them to engage with communities outside the early learning setting.

Child development in a general sense is underpinned by long-established theoretical understandings of how children develop cognitively and the context in which that development occurs.

Ecological Systems Theory

Throughout the late 1970s and 1980s, Bronfenbrenner (1979) proposed the model "Ecological Systems Theory" which views human development as an interaction between the individual and their environment. The model arose due to a lack of focus about the role of context in theories of human development up until that time.

The five ecological systems for child development described by Bronfenbrenner include:

1. Microsystem: The small, immediate environment within which the child lives and interacts such as family, caregivers, their school, and/or day care centre.
2. Mesosystem: The interactions between different parts of a child's microsystem, e.g. between parents and the school; between parents and peers.
3. Exosystem: The people and organizations that indirectly affect the child, e.g. parents' workplace arrangements, the neighbourhood.
4. Macrosystem: The largest and the most external layer of the context within which a child is embedded but which still has a great impact on a child's development. This includes the economy, societal beliefs, cultural values and practices, governance of laws, and freedom.
5. Chronosystem: How a person and his/her environment changes over the life course, as well as socio-historical circumstances, such as the growing economic equalities.

In the mid-1980s, in response to research starting to over-emphasize context and ignore development, Bronfenbrenner (1994) presented his "Bioecological Systems Theory".

Children as Active Participants in their Community 11

This theory is based on the Process-Person-Context-Time (PPCT) model:

- Process: Proximal processes or the interaction between a person and their environment as the primary mechanism for development.
- Person: The role of the individual and their personal characteristics (e.g. age, sex, gender, physical, or mental health) play in social interactions with their environment and consequently their proximal processes.
- Context: The five ecological systems (as above) serve as the context for an individual's development.
- Time: The influence micro-time (events during the proximal processes), meso-time (extent of the processes, e.g. a few days or over the course of weeks or years) and macro-time (the chronosystem) have on a child's development.

The bioecological systems model adds to our understanding of human development by highlighting how both the person and the environment influence one another bidirectionally, and the implications for early years research, practice, and policies.

It is important to consider the individual in their context and at the same time the individual's cognitive and emotional development needs to be kept in focus (see Figure 1.3).

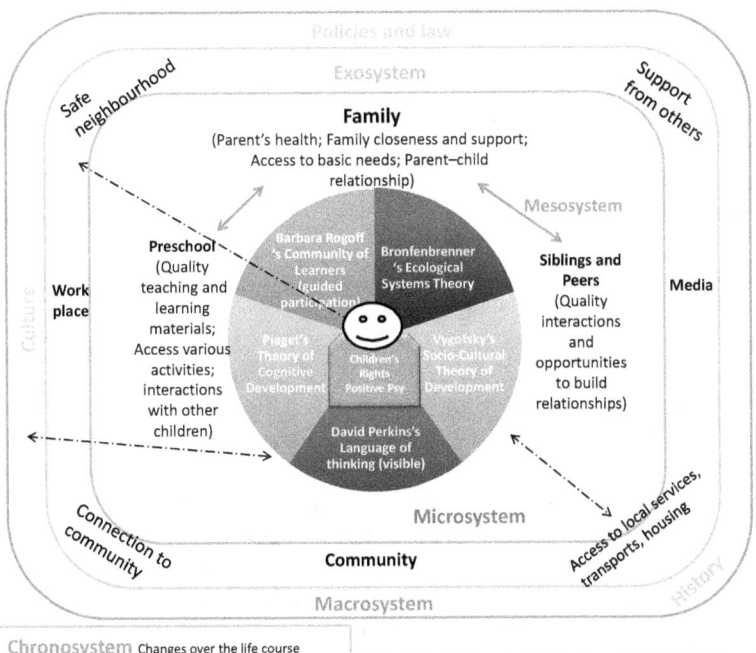

Figure 1.3 An integration of cognitive, ecological system and socio-cultural theories of development. An earlier version of this figure appeared in Frydenberg, Deans, & Liang (2020, p. 26) and is reproduced with permission.

Theory of Cognitive Development

Piaget (1952) viewed children as active learners, with their development and knowledge based on their experiences and interactions with the world. The child actively constructs their understanding of their world through exploring and interacting with the environment. These understandings are a set of mental representations of the world, which he called schema, that the child uses both to understand and to respond to situations. In addition to perceiving children as active learners, he proposed four discrete stages of child development; with each stage explaining the processes and mechanisms employed to assist the development of the child's cognitive skills by building more numerous and elaborate schemas.

These four stages of cognitive development with an indication of the age at which the average child would reach each stage include:

- *Sensorimotor (birth–2 years old):* The infant learns about the environment through responding to sensory stimuli through motor actions. The child acquires knowledge and understanding through physically interacting with the object (e.g. looking, touching, grabbing).
- *Pre-Operational (2–7 years old):* Children begin to understand symbolic meaning as opposed to the physical and concrete observations made in the previous stage. During this stage, children begin to use symbols in a more organized and logical manner.
- *Concrete Operational (7–11 years old):* Children's thinking becomes more flexible and logical. While children's learning mainly comes through actions, their ability to think in more abstract ways increases. This stage marks the understanding that quantities remain the same even if they change in shape or are different in appearance.
- *Formal Operations (11–15 years old):* The child/adolescent gains the ability to think hypothetically and uses abstract ideas, resulting in a more effective manner of thinking. Adolescents begin to have conversations about abstract topics in a meaningful manner.

According to Piaget (1952), each child goes through the stages in the same order through processes of assimilation (i.e. modifying new information to fit existing schemas), accommodation (i.e. restructuring schemas so that the new information can fit in better), and (dis)equilibration (i.e. a state of mental (im)balance). Children's ability to learn is determined by biological maturation which allows adults to interact with children in an appropriate manner related to their cognitive developmental ability. The key implication of Piaget's theory on education and learning is that teachers should create an environment that facilitates active exploration and learning by discovery for the children rather than direct tuition.

However, Piaget's theory underestimated young children's ability in some areas and his theory did not consider the role culture and education play in promoting cognitive development. Other theorists (Rogoff, 1990; Vygotsky, 1962) have identified a more flexible progression by children through their developmental stages that is linked to socio-cultural context. Children's higher order of thinking can be promoted through modelling and observation as well as through first-hand experience. Thus, the stages are not restricted in what is possible or rigidly fixed but, most importantly, opportunity can enhance progression and promote cognitive development.

Socio-Cultural Theory of Development

Vygotsky (1962) laid the groundwork for the "Socio-Cultural Theory of Development" which emphasizes the social and cultural origins of development. Vygotsky considered that social process such as interacting with parents, caregivers, peers, and the culture forms the basis for children's learning. The essential role of social interactions in learning means cognitive and linguistic development can differ between different cultures. Vygotsky believed in the powerful role of language acquisition in shaping children's thoughts and growing cognitive capabilities. He suggested children's first utterances with peers or adults are for the purpose of communication. These utterances then become private speech, i.e. how children talk to themselves while carrying out a difficult cognitive task, and once mastered they develop internalized "inner speech" as they become more capable of working on their own without help from a caregiver or parent. Inner speech is suggested to allow the development of more advanced cognitive abilities such as executive functioning.[1]

Additionally, the concept of zone of proximal development (ZPD) places emphasis on social interaction, such as adult guidance and peer collaboration, to support children to "stretch" their level of skills and knowledge development in accomplishing tasks which they cannot yet understand or perform on their own. The adult and the child's interactions through scaffolding (targeted assistance) have also been shown to have significant influences on the child's learning by progressively extending the ZPD. The key implication of this theory for parents and educators is that providing children with experiences which are in their ZPD can encourage and advance their learning and understanding of the world and the community that they are embedded within.

Barbara Rogoff (2003) took her theoretical inspiration from the work of Vygotsky, recognizing the centrality of social interaction and the cultural tools that are brought into practice. Being both a psychologist and an anthropologist by training she brought the perspectives from both disciplines to understand how culture and context intersect in the learning process. Also emphasizing the simultaneity of individual and cultural processes she eliminates the nature–culture

---

1 Executive functioning is a group of mental processes that enable us to plan, focus attention, remember instructions, and manage multiple tasks at the same time (Center on the Developing Child, 2020). It is controlled by the prefrontal cortex of the brain which acts as a control panel that orchestrates our thoughts and our actions.

dichotomy (Mey, 2005, p. 96). Inspired by Vygotsky's ZPG she writes about apprenticeship which can be termed "guided participation" (Mey, 2005, p. 97). Her work went on to extend the thinking about learning as part of the social and cultural processes. Much of her work has focused on children's participation in community life, which she calls Intent Community Participation. Whilst she comments that this approach is less prevalent in western communities she acknowledges that it is more likely to occur in the preschool setting, which is indeed from where the collection of Community Connections projects described in this volume emanate and reflect communities in practice in a particular early childhood setting.

Rogoff summarized the key aspects of her programs namely: learners are incorporated into endeavours where there are expectations to contribute, learners belong and are eager to contribute, they are collaborative, there is flexible leadership, and feedback is provided.

Whilst the programs outlined in this volume illustrate learning in action and communities of practice that are underpinned by a positive approach to human development, the ideas developed by David Perkins and his team at Harvard University also contribute to the work. Perkins' focus is on making thinking visible (Ritchhart & Perkins, 2008). He makes the point that thinking goes on "under the hood" but is not readily made visible as part of the learning process. There are techniques to be encouraged or, as he describes it, as a language of thinking that is deliberately put into action, such as, for example, setting up hypotheses, considering evidence, perspective taking, possibilities, and imagination. When it comes to the early childhood setting the questions are more straightforward: *"What if", What if not, How else could this be done, What's going on here? What makes you say so?* Perkins describes these as "thinking routines". These are the very teaching approaches that bring to life the projects described in this volume as children play, draw, interact, and describe. We are able to capture their thinking as well as their tangible outputs.

Concluding Remarks

Cognitive development occurs as children progress through their stages of physical and emotional development. How that progression occurs is very directly linked to the educational and socio-cultural context. The environments that these contexts establish, how they respect the rights of the child, and the curriculum they offer are all critical contributors to helping children to flourish and become good citizens of their communities. Some researchers like those who have followed young children through to their adolescent years are able to endorse the benefits of programs that engage children in practices that contribute both to their optimum psycho-social development and to their citizenship.

Take Home Messages

- Early childhood provides an opportunity for creating community connections and the educational environment can take a lead in this regard.

- The United Nations Convention on the Rights of the Child (UNCRC) (UN, 1989) acknowledges the right of children to be heard and consulted on matters that affect them.
- The arts play an important part in providing a vehicle for children to express their thoughts and ideas.
- Positive psychology through the vehicle of positive education provides a framework for focusing on strengths and what children can do rather than what they can't do.
- Jean Piaget's theory of cognitive development highlights the ages and stages of cognitive development. All children do not progress through these stages at the same rate and stage.
- Lev Vygotsky's socio-cultural theory and Barbara Rogoff's "community of learners" are foundational theories which address the context in which learning takes place and how children learn from others, be they children or adults.
- Bronfenbrenner's ecological systems theory addresses the relationships between children and their settings – home, school, or the wider community.
- Barbara Rogoff emphasizes the interactions between communities and their learners.
- David Perkins and the Harvard group focus on the responses to questioning that bring to life the children's outputs.

References

Berrueta-Clement, J. R., Schweinhart, L. J., Barnett, W. S., Epstein, A. S., & Weikart, D. P. (1984). *Changed lives: The effects of the Perry Preschool Program on youths through age 19.* Ypsilanti, MI: HighScope Press.

Bronfenbrenner, U. (1979). *The ecology of human development: Experiments by nature and design.* Cambridge, MA: Harvard University Press.

Bronfenbrenner, U. (1994). Ecological models of human development. *International Encyclopedia of Education,* Vol. 3, 2nd Ed. Oxford: Elsevier.

Campbell, F. A., Ramey, C., Pungello, E. P., Sparling, J. J., & Miller-Johnson, S. (2002). Early childhood education: Young adult outcomes from the Abecedarian Project. *Applied Developmental Science, 6,* 42–57.

Center on the Developing Child. (2020). https://developingchild.harvard.edu

Early Childhood Australia (2006). *Early Childhood Australia's Code of Ethics,* ACT: Early Childhood Australia.

Frydenberg, E., Deans, J., & Liang, R. (2020). *Promoting Well-Being in the Pre-school Years.* London: Routledge.

Hasford, J., Loomis, C., Nelson, G., & Pancer, S. M. (2016). Youth narratives on community experiences and sense of community and their relation to participation in an early childhood development program. *Youth & Society, 48*(4), 577–596. https://doi.org/10.1177/0044118X13506447

Janzen, R., Pancer, S. M., Nelson, G., Loomis, C., & Hasford, J. (2010). Evaluating community participation as prevention: Life narratives of youth. *Journal of Community Psychology, 38,* 992–1006.

Lansdown, G. (2004). Participation and young children. *Early Childhood Matters, 103*, 4–14.

Levenstein, P., Levenstein, S., Shiminski, J. A., & Stolzberg, J. E. (1998). Long-term impact of a verbal interaction program for at-risk toddlers: An exploratory study of high school outcomes in a replication of the Mother-Child Home Program. *Journal of Applied Developmental Psychology, 19*, 267–285.

Lloyd-Smith, M., & Tarr, J. (2000). Researching children's experiences: A sociological perspective. In A. Lewis & G. Lindsay (Eds.), *Researching Children's Perspectives* (pp. 59–69). Buckingham: Open University Press.

Mey, I. (2005). The cultural nature of human development. *Journal of Linguistic Anthropology, 15*(2), 290–291.

Peters, R. D., Bradshaw, A. J., Petrunka, K., Nelson, G., Herry, Y., Craig, W. M., … Rossiter, M. D. (2010). The Better Beginnings, Better Futures project: Findings from grade 3 to grade 9. *Monographs of the Society for Research in Child Development, 75*, 1–176.

Piaget, J. (1952). *The origins of intelligence in children*. New York: Norton.

Reynolds, A. J., Temple, J. A., Robertson, D. L., & Mann, E. A. (2001). Long-term effects of an early childhood intervention on educational achievement and juvenile arrest: A 15-year follow-up of low-income children in public schools. *Journal of the American Medical Association, 285*, 2339–2346.

Ritchhart, R., & Perkins, D. (2008). Making thinking visible. *Educational Leadership, 65*(5), 57.

Rogoff, B. (1990). *Apprenticeship in thinking: Cognitive development in social context*. New York: Oxford University Press.

Rogoff, B. (2003). *The cultural nature of human development*. Oxford: Oxford University Press.

Seligman, M. E. P., Ernst, R., Gillham, J., Reivich, K., & Linkins, M. (2009). Positive education: Positive psychology and classroom interventions. *Oxford Review of Education, 35*, 293–311.

Tobin, J. (2005). A right to be no longer dismissed or ignored: Children's voices in pedagogy and policy making. [Electronic version.] *International Journal of Equity and Innovation in Early Childhood, 3*(2), 4–18.

United Nations (UNCRC). (1989). *Convention on the Rights of the Child*. Geneva: Office of the United Nations High Commissioner of Human Rights.

Vygotsky, L. (1962). *Thought and Language*. Cambridge, MA: MIT Press.

White, M. A., & Waters, L. E. (2015). A case study of "The Good School": Examples of the use of Peterson's strengths-based approach with students. *Journal of Positive Psychology, 10*(1), 69–76.

2 Social Emotional Curriculum Objectives in Early Childhood Education

Introduction to Social Emotional Learning in Education

Children transition through numerous communities throughout their childhood. The early learning setting is one such community that provides an opportunity for connection, belonging, and skill development. There is a growing recognition that the educational experience is more than learning formal skills generally known as the three Rs – reading, writing, and arithmetic. Thus, educational settings are increasingly being required to provide students with opportunities to focus on skills that help children become resilient, caring, and productive members of society (White & Waters, 2015). At the forefront of this growing awareness has been the work and influence of the United States initiative, Collaborative for Academic Social and Emotional Learning (CASEL). The collaborative has clearly articulated its goals and objectives and other countries have developed their own approaches to impacting Social and Emotional Learning (SEL).

CASEL (2013) defines SEL as:

> [T]he process by which children and adults acquire the knowledge, attitudes and skills to recognise and manage their emotions, set and achieve positive goals, demonstrate caring and concern for others, establish and maintain positive relationships, make responsible decisions [and] handle inter-personal situations effectively.

Australian Curriculum, Assessment and Reporting Authority's (ACARA, 2012) documentation refers to SEL in these terms:

> Students develop personal and social capability as they learn to understand themselves and others, and manage their relationships, lives, work and learning more effectively. This capability involves students in a range of practices including recognising and regulating emotions, developing empathy for and understanding of others, establishing positive and respectful relationships, making responsible decisions, working effectively in teams and handling challenging situations constructively.

There are several important common elements in these definitions. First, social and emotional learning consists of acquiring knowledge and developing skills. That implies the existence of two dimensions in SEL education: a cognitive dimension and a practical dimension. It has also been noted that the acquisition of cognitive capacity (knowledge) does not necessarily mean that a person will exercise good practice (skills) (McKown, 2015). It is in this gap between knowledge and skills that a third dimension, identified by CASEL, may prove decisive: attitude. Two British researchers Weare and Gray (2003) made the point that there is no definitive list of what constitutes emotional and social competence. They assembled a description of what it might consist of, noting that there were huge natural and social differences between people, and great variations in what was acceptable in different cultures. The application of the CASEL framework in the educational context that is described in this book is illustrated in Table 2.1.

The principles of CASEL are consistent around the globe. Nevertheless, the application in practice reflects the local context or setting. The CASEL principles are embedded in the activities described in Part II of this volume.

Table 2.1 The CASEL framework in an educational context

ACARA (2012) Area Description	Four interrelated elements of the personal and social capability learning continuum
Self-awareness	Developing personal and social capacities to: • recognize emotions • recognize personal qualities and achievements • understand themselves as learners • develop reflective practice
Self-management	Regulating emotional responses and to work independently. Students are to: • express emotions appropriately • develop self-discipline and set goals • work independently and show initiative • become confident, resilient, and adaptable
Social awareness	Learning to show respect for and understand others' perspectives, emotional states, and needs: • appreciate diverse perspectives • contribute to civil society • understand relationships.
Social management	Learning to interact effectively and respectfully with a range of adults and peers; Developing the ability to initiate and manage successful personal relationships, and participate in social and communal activities: • communicate effectively • work collaboratively • make decisions • negotiate and resolve conflict • develop leadership skills.

The CASEL researchers in the United States of America (2013) identified five core competencies to aim for in social and emotional education, which distilled many of the elements of social and emotional competence set out by Weare and Gray:

- Self-awareness
- Social awareness
- Self-management
- Relationship skills
- Responsible decision-making

ACARA adopted a similar list in the Australian Curriculum:

- Self-awareness
- Self-management
- Social awareness
- Social management

Generally speaking, SEL in the context of education refers to students' development and acquisition of skills to become more aware of their emotions and how to manage them so that they can make the most of their own lives by making responsible decisions, working towards their goals, and developing respectful and fulfilling relationships with peers and adults.

The call to embed SEL in the classroom in school settings is gaining traction. The primary school years are increasingly considered the prime intervention period as many mental health conditions are precipitated during high school (Schaps & Battistich, 1991). However, less focus has been given to the seminal development of social and emotional competencies during early childhood (Cornell et al., 2017). The opportunity for early socialization of skill development is key, as preschool is the first time for many children that structured social demands are placed on the child outside of the immediate home environment.

Building Strong Foundations in the Early Years

The benefits of SEL have been convincingly demonstrated. For example, Durlak and colleagues' (2011) study covered 270,034 students. They found as a result of the social and emotional interventions across those 213 sites that, compared to controls, SEL participants demonstrated significantly improved social and emotional skills, attitudes, behaviour, and academic performance that reflected an 11-percentile-point gain in achievement (p. 405). They went on to argue from this evidence that social and emotional development is an essential part of students' education. They also noted that SEL program designers typically are interested in promoting the *integration* (our emphasis) of emotion, cognition, communication, and behaviour (Crick & Dodge, 1994; Lemerise & Arsenio, 2000).

Durlak et al.'s (2011) findings add to the growing empirical evidence regarding the positive impact of SEL programs. This evidence includes the existence of compelling links between the acquisition of SEL competencies and improved school attitudes and performance (Zins et al., 2004). For example, students who are more self-aware and confident about their learning capacities try harder and persist in the face of challenges (Aronson, 2002). The foundations for a strong connection between social and emotional competence and educational success are laid in the early years.

SEL as a Basis for Early Years Curriculum

Given the growing evidence and appreciation that SEL is an important component of development, the CASEL framework from the USA and related concepts for social and emotional competencies have been incorporated into the early years curriculum guidelines in the international landscape.

Australia and New Zealand

The Australian Government's Belonging, Being, and Becoming in the early years framework contains five core learning outcomes that speak to SEL development in preschool children; "children have a strong sense of identity, children are connected with, and contribute to their world, children have a strong sense of well-being; children are confident learners, and children are effective communicators" (Commonwealth of Australia, 2009, p. 8). The New Zealand curriculum articulates "Children are supported to be confident and competent learners" (ERO, 2011).

What is common to these documents is the recognition of the individual and the opportunities that they need to be afforded in terms of relationship building, belonging, and the importance of community.

United Kingdom

The UK Curriculum (Department of Education, UK, 2017, p. 9) articulates the area of personal social and emotional learning and development:

> Personal, social and emotional development involves helping children to develop a positive sense of themselves, and others; to form positive relationships and develop respect for others; to develop social skills and learn how to manage their feelings; to understand appropriate behaviour in groups; and to have confidence in their own abilities p8. There is an ongoing judgement to be made by practitioners about the balance between activities led by children, and activities led or guided by adults.

The areas to focus on are detailed in the section on personal, social, and emotional development, namely:

Self-confidence and self-awareness: children are confident to try new activities and say why they like some activities more than others. They are confident to speak in a familiar group, will talk about their ideas, and will choose the resources they need for their chosen activities. They say when they do or don't need help.

Managing feelings and behaviour: children talk about how they and others show feelings, talk about their own and others' behaviour, and its consequences, and know that some behaviour is unacceptable. They work as part of a group or class and understand and follow the rules. They adjust their behaviour to different situations and take changes of routine in their stride. Figure 2.1a,b shows how children depict their inner world using self-portraits.

Making relationships: children play cooperatively, taking turns with others (e.g. Figure 2.2). They take account of one another's ideas about how to organize their activity. They show sensitivity to others' needs and feelings and form positive relationships with adults and other children. For example, before the age of 5 each child in the UK receives an EYFS Profile which is shared with parents and carers (Department of Education, UK, 2017, p. 11).

Europe and Beyond

Eight countries, namely, Chile, the Czech Republic, Denmark, Estonia, Italy, Poland, the Russian Federation, and the United States, participated in the first phase of the International Early Childhood Education Study (ECES) (IEA, 2021). Whilst policy uniformities were reported, there were variations. Generally, Early Childhood Education (ECE) expected outcomes were broad and included cognitive and non-cognitive learning outcomes, such as

*Figure 2.1*a,b Self-portraits by ELC children: a personalized symbol that represents the child's inner world of feelings and sense of belonging.

Figure 2.2 Children collaborating on a piece of artwork.

socio-emotional development, executive functioning, and child wellbeing (Bertram & Pascal, 2016).

There are several aspects of child development that are closely aligned with children's social emotional development. The first is related to self-regulation and the second is related to friendship and relationship building. Both oral language and play are critical vehicles through which self-regulation is developed, as is the important role of play in fostering relationship skill development. Self-regulation is about students understanding and regulating their own thoughts, behaviours, and emotions (Sinclaire-Harding et al., 2015). Children in the early years show capacity to self-regulate and develop their skills to do so. For example, the child who stops playing when asked even if they don't want to, begins to put away the toys when requested, shares with others, is not only compliant but likely to be able to regulate their thoughts and emotions to an age-appropriate extent. Those who can set goals, monitor, and evaluate their progress as they go are likely to be the children who succeed both at school and in life in general.

Various theoretical constructs contribute to children's social emotional learning and ultimate social emotional competence, which are fostered through the Community Connections programs. These are attachment theory, self-regulation, emotional intelligence, along with the role of language, as each of these has significant impacts from early childhood through to the adult years.

Attachment Theory

Attachment theory reflects the deep bonds that connect persons to one another across time and place. An early proponent of attachment theory, John Bowlby (1969) emphasized the importance of the relation between infants and their caregivers, particularly parents. Bowlby focused on the relationship between infants and their mothers in terms of social emotional and cognitive development. In recent times attachment theory has encompassed the relationships developed throughout the lifespan, often expressed in terms of belonging (Frydenberg et al., 2012). The critical period for developing attachments is 0–5 years. Hence the preschool years provide an important opportunity to build on those early relationships and prepare children for the school years. The skills of attachment and belonging include communication and language skills which underscore the COPE-Resilience program described in Chapter 9 but are less directly embedded in all aspects of the curriculum and feature in the programs described in Part II of this volume. Programs such as COPE-R concern emotion knowledge and practices and include self-regulatory processes. By exploring empathy and sharing and caring children learn to relate to others including peers. Whilst attachment is determined by a host of temperamental factors, including having an engaging predisposition, the interactions in the preschool setting provide opportunities for significant attachment and life-skill development.

Self-Regulation

Marc Brackett, the author of *Permission to feel* (Brackett, 2019) and the RULER program (Brackett et al., 2012) focuses on the development of emotions and how we recognize, understand, label, express, and regulate them. Emotions are at the core of our being and influence all our actions and reactions. At infancy it is about need for comfort and release from discomfort but beyond that it is about how emotions influence our relationship with others and our perceptions of the world. Whilst control or regulation of emotions is the most challenging of the RULER skills, it is teachable but dependent on the four previously learnt skills. In COPE-R we emphasize the recognition, understanding, labelling, and expression of emotions in age-appropriate ways and the development of self-regulation follows. Adults, such as parents and teachers, are core influencers, along with peers, hence the way each of us regulates our emotions to be the best calm selves will influence young children. Brackett encourages us to use the meta-moment, to stop and draw breath before responding, while other programs describe it as "stop, think and do" (Petersen & Adderley, 2002).

In simple terms self-regulation is about children being able to respond to their environments effectively as they adapt. Self-regulation, according to Bandura (1997), emphasizes that children can learn to regulate their thoughts and behaviours as well as their emotions. Children demonstrate these skills when they do as they are asked or when instructed. Whilst self-regulatory skills contribute to success in school they also contribute to success in life in general. Additionally, the link between oral language and self-regulation is readily evident, since lack of language skills often leaves the child frustrated and leads them to draw upon less helpful ways of communicating or releasing frustration.

In what has been called "dialogic" pedagogy children learn to argue and make their case in a discussion with explanations for their views. Both cognitive and social development are considered to be a way of increasing children's metacognitive abilities (Whitebread et al., 2015; Whitebread, 2018).[1] As children learn to label and talk about their feelings, emotion language is developed. Regulating emotions is reliant on emotional arousal, along with linguistic and cognitive control systems (Tizard & Hughes, 1984). These approaches are incorporated into the educational programs described in Part II of this volume. Attachment theories posit that children are inherently motivated to form attachments with adults such as parents, caregivers, or teachers. When these relationships are warm and reliable there is likely be a sense of belonging and wellbeing which in turn can be transformed into empathy and caring. At the core of these social emotional skills is executive functioning that relies on the development of working memory, flexible thinking, and emotional control.

A range of studies have shown that early self-regulation predicts long-term academic outcomes and emotional well-being more powerfully than any other aspect of children's development (e.g. Baumeister et al., 2002; Denham et al., 2012). Self-regulation can be achieved through promoting a positive emotional climate that supports and encourages children to develop a sense of autonomy and competence. For example, self-determination theory developed by Deci and Ryan (2008) highlights the benefit of giving children opportunities to establish goals, set up challenges, and engage in problem solving.

One approach is the notion of personal best (Martin & Elliot, 2016) or personal progress rather than social comparisons. A warm, responsive non-judgemental emotional climate, where children can be curious, do their best without comparing themselves to others, and where issues are discussed, develops the emotional wellbeing of learners.

The importance of social interactions in the early learning setting has been stressed convincingly by Howe (2010). The impact of friendships in the classroom has a powerful impact on both emotional and learning outcomes. There is a powerful role for teachers in the implementation of the curriculum to foster and monitor friendship skills as children engage in classroom practices and in community-related projects. The role of project design and peer-related activities provides opportunities to focus on all children, and particularly those at both ranges of the spectrum, those who are prone to being aggressive and less agreeable as well as those who are shy and anxious.

Emotional Intelligence

The concept of emotional intelligence or EI has been popularized since the mid-1990s by Daniel Goleman in his book *Emotional Intelligence* (1995). Some years earlier Salovey and Mayer described EI as "the ability to monitor one's own and others' emotions, to discriminate among them, and to use the information to guide one's thinking and actions" (Salovey & Mayer, 1990, p. 189).

---

1 Metacognitive skills are often referred to as "thinking about thinking"; that is, being able to approach tasks in an organized way.

That is, emotions can be recognized both in oneself and others, using cues that are verbal and non-verbal. Being able to regulate or manage emotions has been an important feature of EI and is closely linked to wellbeing (Mayer & Salovey, 1993; Mayer et al., 2008). Another aspect of EI is the ability to interact well with others utilizing emotional understandings and putting this information to work in daily interactions and communication. This is commonly referred to as social intelligence, which is highly linked to success in relationships and life in general. Social skills can be nurtured and improved, starting in the preschool years, which contributes to early school success (Denham et al., 2017). As with general intelligence some people are inherently more intelligent than others and the same is the case with EI. The important difference is that emotional intelligence can be developed, the earlier the better. Whilst much of the popular writing has been on the adult domain, it is readily acknowledged that the teaching of emotional intelligence and associated skills provides a significant opportunity in the early years when cognition and language development occur at such a rapid pace.

EI has often been considered to be anything that is not IQ. However, there is real science behind EI and "there is intelligence behind emotions" according to Brackett and his colleagues (Brackett et al., 2012). As noted earlier, Brackett developed the RULER program, with the acronym standing for recognition, understanding, labelling, expression, and regulation of emotions. The acronym covers all the elements that are important in EI. The emphasis in RULER as in COPE-R (see Chapter 9) is that there are cognitions (thoughts) and affect (feelings) and the two are interdependent. How we think affects how we feel and how we feel affects how we think. An additional element is that, if we can name it, we can "tame" it. Thus, there is an emphasis on learning to label emotions and subsequently develop the skills to manage them, that is, both to enhance and to regulate. EI can be developed and cultivated in the early years by teaching children to first become aware, take notice, and have the language to label emotions (Bailey et al., 2019). Emotional literacy is a core element of COPE-R as it is of RULER. Emotions are not inherently good or bad, it is about knowing when and how to utilize or regulate them. For example, feeling joy can be appropriate when something good has happened, such as receiving a gift, but not when someone is hurt. Alternatively, anger or frustration may be appropriate when one is being teased but not when receiving a gift. It is both what one thinks and how these emotions are expressed that matters, and that is coping. In the programs described in Part II emphasis is placed on the development of language to identify emotions and to articulate them.

The Role of Language

The role of language in children's development in general and relationship development more specifically is well established. Vygotsky (1962) considered language as one of the key drivers of both learning and relationships – social interactions are a means to engage with others, solve problems whilst language *per se* plays a significant part in the development of early metacognition (an ability to explain one's thinking) and self-regulation. Whitebread (2018) notes that several studies have directly linked early language development with later emerging aspects of self-regulation. For example, there was a found to be a strong relationship between vocabulary size at 14, 24, and 36 months and a range of observed self-regulatory behaviours, for example, the ability to maintain attention on tasks and to adapt to changes in tasks and procedures (Vallotton & Ayoub, 2011).

A powerful way to foster language development is the adult–child relationship. In that context there are benefits for children's development when adults follow the child's interests rather than their own agenda (Schaffer, 2004). This approach can be built into the community connections projects where adults can make available or initiate the activity and children then become the active contributors. The metacognitive processes that occur as an intrinsic part of these activities with "question and answer" dialogues have been labelled as the "visible" elements of learning (Hattie, 2009; Whitebread et al., 2015) as the processes of learning are made explicit.

In addition to the role of oral language in the teacher– and in the adult–child interactions, group work with peers provides opportunities for collaboration. Through the give and take in group work the development of self-regulation is fostered.

The conversations have "rules" of talk where views, opinions, and reasons are shared. Children can argue and give explanations for their thinking, thus showing that they are able to make gains in the way they argue their case and give explanations (Littleton et al., 2005). Whitebread et al. (2015) notes a study with Year 1 children (i.e. 5–6-year-olds) in the UK which showed that these types of activities enhanced the children's metacognitive abilities.

Informal play-based learning, pretend and dramatic play, games with rules, or games where children set the rules, provide opportunities for the development of self-regulation and lay the foundation for benefiting from more formal instruction in the later years. Nevertheless, stimulating environments where activities can engage the interests of the child are important features of an ideal learning environment. When this occurs in the context of social relationships such as those in the early learning setting there is opportunity for development in the social emotional domains (Sinclaire-Harding et al., 2015).

Concluding Remarks

In the course of developing young learners' social emotional competence in an early childhood setting, several community connections programs have been identified as useful vehicles for contributing to the development of children's empathy through the early childhood years in the context of the early childhood curriculum. Community connections programs can generally be acknowledged as coming under the generic umbrella of social emotional learning. They are underpinned by core theories of child development, such as socio-cultural development which is described in Chapter 1 and general attachment theory. Additional to the theories of cognitive development there is a focus on social cognitions and the importance of emotions and how to regulate them.

Take Home Messages

- Social emotional aspects of learning are acknowledged as important aspects of the educational curriculum. The Collaborative of Academic and Social Emotional Learning has articulated the core principles:
  - Self-awareness
  - Social awareness
  - Self-management
  - Relationship skills
  - Responsible decision-making.
- Australian *Belonging, Being, and Becoming* in the early years' framework contains five core learning outcomes, namely that children have:
  - a strong sense of identity
  - are connected with and contribute to their world
  - have a strong sense of wellbeing
  - are confident learners
  - are effective communicators.
- New Zealand curriculum highlights:
  - Children are supported to be confident and competent learners
- The UK Curriculum EYFS articulates that personal, social, and emotional development involves helping children to develop
  - a positive sense of themselves, and others
  - to form positive relationships and develop respect for others
  - to develop social skills and learn how to manage their feelings
  - to understand appropriate behaviour in groups
  - and to have confidence in their own abilities.
- When addressing these competencies other theories become of relevance such as
  - Attachment theory
  - Emotional intelligence
  - Self-regulation
  - The part that language plays in developing the social emotional skills.

References

Aronson, J. (Ed.) (2002). *Improving academic achievement: Impact of psychological factors on education*. New York: Academic Press.
Australian Curriculum, Assessment and Reporting Authority (ACARA). (2012). *General capabilities*. Retrieved from www.australiancurriculum.edu.au/generalcapabilities/personal-and-social-capability/introduction/introduction

Bailey, C. S., Rivers, S. E., Tominey, S. L., O'Bryon, E. C., Olsen, S. G., Sneeden, C. K., Peisch, V. D., Gal, D. E., & Brackett, M. A. (2019). Promoting early childhood social and emotional learning with Preschool RULER. Manuscript submitted for publication, Yale Child Study Center, Yale School of Medicine.

Bandura, A. (1997). *Self-efficacy: The exercise of control.* New York: W. H. Freeman/Times Books/Henry Holt & Co.

Baumeister, R. F., Leith, K. P., Muraven, M., & Bratslavsky E. (2002) Self-regulation as a key to success in life. In D. Pushkar, W. M. Bukowski, A. E. Schwartzman, D., M. Stack, & D. R. White (Eds.), *Improving competence across the lifespan.* Boston, MA: Springer. https://doi.org/10.1007/0-306-47149-3_9

Bertram, T., & Pascal, C. (2016). *Early childhood policies and systems in eight countries: Findings from IEA's Early Childhood Education Study.* Cham: Springer International Publishing. Retrieved from www.iea.nl/fileadmin/user_upload/Publications/Electronic_versions/ECES-policies_and_systems-report.pdf

Bowlby, J. (1969). *Attachment and loss,* Vol. 1: *Attachment.* New York: Basic Books.

Brackett, M. (2019). *Permission to feel: Unlocking the power of emotions to help our kids, ourselves, and our society thrive.* New York: Celadon Books.

Brackett, M. A., Rivers, S. E., Reyes, M. R., & Salovey, P. (2012). Enhancing academic performance and social and emotional competence with the RULER feeling words curriculum. *Learning and Individual Differences, 22*(2), 218–224. https://doi.org/10.1016/j.lindif.2010.10.002

Collaborative for Academic, Social and Emotional Learning (CASEL) (2013). *Social and emotional learning core competencies.* Retrieved from: www.casel.org/social-and-emotional-learning/core-competencies.

Commonwealth of Australia (2009) *Belonging, being and becoming: An early years learning framework for Australia.* Canberra: Commonwealth of Australia.

Cornell, C., Kiernan, N., Kaufman, D., Dobeee, P., Frydenberg, E., & Deans, J. (2017). Developing social emotional competence in the early years. In E. Frydenberg, A. Martin, & R. Collie (Eds.), *Social and emotional learning in Australia and the Asia-Pacific* (pp. 391–441). Singapore: Springer.

Crick, N. R., & Dodge, K. A. (1994). A review and reformulation of social information-processing mechanisms in children's social adjustment. *Psychological Bulletin, 115,* 74–101.

Deci, E. L., & Ryan, R. M. (2008). Self-determination theory: A macrotheory of human motivation, development, and health. *Canadian Psychology/Psychologie canadienne, 49*(3), 182–185. https://doi.org/10.1037/a0012801

Denham, S. A., Bassett, H. H., & Miller, S. L. (2017). Early childhood teachers' socialization of emotion: Contextual and individual contributors. *Child & Youth Care Forum, 46*(6), 805–824.

Denham, S. A., Bassett, H., Mincic, M., Kalb, S., Way, E., Wyatt, T., & Segal, Y. (2012). Social–emotional learning profiles of preschoolers' early school success: A person-centered approach. *Learning and Individual Differences, 22*(2), 178–189. https://doi.org/10.1016/j.lindif.2011.05.001

Department of Education, UK. (2017). *Early years foundation stage statutory framework (EYFS).* Retrieved from, https://assets.publishing.service.gov.uk/government/uploads/system/uploads/attachment_data/file/596629/EYFS_STATUTORY_FRAMEWORK_2017.pdf

Durlak, J. A., Weissberg, R. P., Dymnicki, A. B., Taylor, R. D., & Schellinger, K. B. (2011). The impact of enhancing students' social and emotional learning: A meta-analysis of school-based universal interventions. *Child Development*, *82*(1), 405–432. doi: 10.1111/j.1467-8624.2010.01564.x

Education Review Office (ERO). (2011). *Positive foundations for learning: Confident and competent children in early childhood services.* Retrieved from, https://thehub.swa.govt.nz/assets/documents/Positive-Foundations-for-Learning.pdf

Frydenberg, E., Deans, J., & O'Brien, K. (2012). *Developing everyday coping skills in the early years: Proactive strategies for supporting social and emotional development.* New York: Continuum Inc. Press.

Goleman, D. (1995). *Emotional intelligence.* New York: Bantam Books

Hattie, J. A. C. (2009). *Visible learning: A synthesis of over 800 meta-analyses relating to achievement.* London: Routledge.

Howe, T. R. (2010). International child welfare: Guidelines for educators and a case study from Cyprus. *Journal of Social Work Education, 46*, 425–443.

IEA. (2021). *International Early Childhood Education Study*, ECES. https://eces.iea.nl/

Lemerise, E. A., & Arsenio, W. F. (2000). An integrated model of emotion processes and cognition in social information processing. *Child Development, 71*(1), 107–118. https://doi.org/10.1111/1467-8624.00124

Littleton, K., Mercer, N., Dawes, L., Wegerif, R., Rowe, D., & Sams, C. (2005). Talking and thinking together at Key Stage 1. *Early Years* (Stoke on Trent)*, 2*, 167.

Martin, A. J., & Elliot, A. J. (2016). The role of personal best (PB) goal setting in students' academic achievement gains. *Learning and Individual Differences, 45*, 222–227.

Mayer, J. D., & Salovey, P. (1993). The intelligence of emotional intelligence. *Intelligence, 17*, 433–442.

Mayer, J. D., Roberts, R. D., & Barsade, S. G. (2008). Human abilities: Emotional intelligence. *Annual Review of Psychology, 59*, 507–536.

McKown, C. (2015). Challenges and opportunities in the direct assessment of children's social-emotional comprehension. In J. A. Durlak, C. E. Domitrovich, R. P. Weissberg, & T. P. Gullotta (Eds.), *Handbook of social and emotional learning: Research and practice* (pp. 320–335). New York: Guilford.

Petersen, L., & Adderley, A. (2002). *STOP THINK DO social skills training: Early years of schooling ages 4–8.* Camberwell, Victoria: ACER Press.

Salovey, P., & Mayer, J. D. (1990). Emotional intelligence. *Imagination, Cognition, and Personality, 9*, 185–211.

Schaffer, H. R. (2004). *Introducing child psychology.* Oxford: Blackwell Publishing.

Schaps, E., & Battistich, V. (1991). Promoting health development through school-based prevention: New approaches. In E. Goplerude (Ed.), *Preventing adolescent drug use: From theory to practice*, OSAP Prevention Monograph No. 8 (pp. 127–181). Washington, DC: US Department of Health and Human Services.

Sinclaire-Harding, L., Vuillier, L., & Whitebread, D. (2015). Neuroscience and early childhood education. In S. Robson & S. Quinn (Eds.), *The Routledge international handbook of young children's thinking and understanding* (pp. 199–214). London: Routledge.

Statutory framework for the early years foundation stage (EYFS). (2017). *Statutory framework for the early years foundation stage: Setting the standards for learning, development and care for children from birth to five.* Retrieved from: www.foundationyears.org.uk/files/2017/03/EYFS_STATUTORY_FRAMEWORK_2017.pdf

Tizard, B., & Hughes, M. (1984). *Young children learning.* London: Fontana.

Vallotton, C., & Ayoub, C. (2011). Use your words: The role of language in the development of toddlers' self-regulation. *Early Child Research Quarterly, 26*(2), 169–181. doi: 10.1016/j.ecresq.2010.09.002

Vygotsky, L. (1962). *Thought and Language.* Cambridge, MA: MIT Press.
Weare, K., & Gray, G. (2003) *What works in developing children's emotional and social competence and wellbeing?* London: Department for Education and Skills.
White, M. A., & Waters, L. E. (2015). A case study of "The Good School": Examples of the use of Peterson's strengths-based approach with students. *Journal of Positive Psychology, 10*(1), 69–76.
Whitebread, D. (2018). Quality in early childhood education: The contribution of developmental psychology. In M. Fleer & B. van Oers (Eds.), *International handbook of early childhood education.* Cham: Springer. International Handbooks of Education, DOI: 10.1007/978-94-024-0927-7_13
Whitebread, D., Pino-Pasternak, D., & Coltman, P. (2015). Making learning visible: The role of language in the development of metacognition and self-regulation in young children. In S. Robson & S. Quinn (Eds.), *The Routledge international handbook of young children's thinking and understanding* (pp. 199–214). London: Routledge.
Zins, J. E., Weissberg, R. P., Wang, M. C., & Walberg, H. J. (2004). *Building academic success on social and emotional learning: What does the research say?* New York: Teachers College Press.

3 The Foundation for Community Connections

Empathy and Associated Constructs

Introduction

The goal of the Collaborative for Academic and Social Emotional Learning (CASEL, 2021) as outlined in Chapter 2 includes the recognizing and managing our emotions, developing caring and concern for others, establishing positive relationships, making responsible decisions, and handling challenging situations constructively and ethically. These are prosocial skills that CASEL summarize as: establishing and maintaining relationships and being able to calm oneself in difficult situations, self-awareness, self-management, social awareness, relationship skills, and responsible decision-making (see Figure 3.1).

The idea of children and their communities being in close connection is not a new one. In 1987, Esta Borden noted that community connections work. Borden pointed out that Piaget told us that the child's relationship with the physical environment is the basis for developing a "rudimentary and intuitive" understanding of the world and how it works. Early childhood settings are

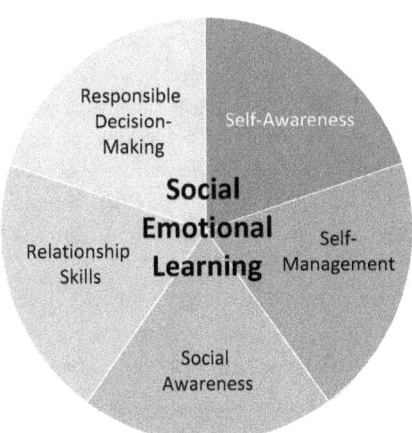

Figure 3.1 Core skills from the CASEL framework.

DOI: 10.4324/9781003213147-5

laboratories of learning where the teacher is a major catalyst. Every school is in a community and every community has members who are talented, resourceful, and caring and who can enrich children's social emotional learning and well-being. Early childhood educators are in a unique position to provide children with learning experiences that will enable them to deal with the futures that they may encounter in healthy and meaningful ways. Of particularly benefit is the cultivation of relational skills including empathy, caring, and politeness in the early years.

Contact Theory

By far the most relevant theory when it comes to community connections is contact theory, first developed by Gordon Allport in the 1950s. It works on the premise that contact between two groups can create understanding and reduce prejudice. The early iterations of the theory had specifications such as that the two groups had to be of equal status and share common goals. Over the years psychologists have expanded the criteria to include numerous aspects of the encounter to ensure that the contact would work. Thomas Pettigrew (2016), a research psychologist who conducted a meta-analysis[1] of 500 studies demonstrated that all that was required between two groups for greater understand was that they have contact (except in the most hostile and threatening situations). Of course, there was a better result if there were other conditions such as mutual goals, pleasurable activities, some preparation, and so on. Another major finding of Pettigrew was that it is not only a cognitive outcome, that is, we learn more about each other, but an emotional one, in that you learn to like each other.

Whilst contact theory has been most frequently adopted in intergenerational programs such as one described in Chapter 8, as in such programs there is a ready-made possibility of meeting contact theory criteria (Kuehne & Melville, 2014), contact theory is readily applicable in other settings where two groups are brought together, as is the case in many of the programs described in this volume. For example, equal group status occurs when adults and children are given active roles in the program in which they participate. Common goals can be established when there is a mutual goal of building relationships engaging participants' current abilities and interests. Finally, cooperation pertains to the physical setting and layout is critical for cooperation between, for example, intergenerational partners, the teacher, and children in environment or First Nations programs or meeting with disabled young adults (see Part II). For example, in the intergenerational program materials are arranged for pairs in close physical proximity to promote collaboration and teamwork to achieve a mutual goal (for instance in playing a game or engaging in a portrait lesson).

---

1 Meta-analysis is a quantitative, formal, epidemiological study design used to systematically assess the results of previous research to derive conclusions about that body of research.

Intergroup contact is more effective, and prejudice is ameliorated, when it facilitates mechanisms for friendship such as self-disclosure, which is best achieved through repeated contact. Pettigrew called this "opportunity for friendships" (Pettigrew, 2016).

Community Connections programs collectively have a focus on social emotional development of children, their wellbeing, and acquisition of skills to navigate the world. Clearly what underpins the programs in this volume is how we develop good citizens who care about the world around them and who contribute to the wellbeing of others. Thus, empathy is a core construct to consider.

Foundational Emotional Skills

Empathy

In simplest terms empathy is the ability to feel for another person. It is about being able to walk in another person's shoes, being able to see and feel the world from the other's perspective rather than relying exclusively on one's own experience. Empathy can be described as individuals being able to understand and interpret the behaviour of others, to anticipate what someone else might do and feel, and then to respond to them (Allison et al., 2011; Baron-Cohen & Wheelwright, 2004). It is about perspective taking and developing sympathy and compassion. From the outset the child bonds with an empathic caregiver and the foundations for a child's attachment to others is laid (Solms, 2017). Whilst some children and adults have a greater innate capacity for empathy than others, like all skills in the social emotional domain, the skills can be fostered and developed beginning in the early years and continued throughout the child's educational journey.

Thus, empathy is the ability to take another person's perspective, to visualize their inner world, and to reflect on their thoughts and feelings (Gillberg, 1992). Consequently, empathy forms an important part of social and emotional development in children and underpins important social skills (Beceren & Özdemir, 2019). Empathy fosters social interactions, self-regulation, and pro-social behaviours (Belacchi & Farina, 2012).

Empathy develops early, before a child can report on it. There are two aspects of empathy, the affective and the cognitive. Cognitive empathy is the ability to take the perspective of another from an intellectual or understanding point of view. Affective empathy is feeling what the other feels, whilst cognitive empathy is more about understanding how the other feels. While cognitive empathy comprises emotion recognition and perspective taking, emotional empathy includes the phenomenon of sharing feelings more adequately to another person's situation than to one's own. A relatively recent study revealed that emotional empathy development is complete in the preschool years, whereas cognitive empathy develops well into the school years (Schwenck et al., 2014).

There is a notion of global empathy when you can match the emotions of another, such as when an infant cries and another follows. As children approach

2 years of age, they can understand themselves and they start displaying empathy and recognition of the feelings of others (Frydenberg et al., 2012; Pedlow et al., 2004). Thus, at 2 years of age when the toddler actively offers help to another that is affective empathy.

By the third year of life the child becomes aware that feelings of another are different from their own. As children develop the capacity to regulate their emotions, empathic distress transforms to sympathy (Eisenberg et al., 2006). The more "primitive" responses give way to cognitive empathy. By late childhood children can process that the emotions of others may be due to circumstances rather than immediate events for individuals and groups and communities. Thus preschool (3–5 years) marks the emergence of cognitive empathy. By this age, children advance their cognitive flexibility to take others' perspectives and effectively reflect on situations impacting them. Some have found that empathy significantly increases in preschool before stabilizing, highlighting the preschool years as a critical stage to develop empathy (Taylor et al., 2013). Later (five years onwards), children become better at managing their own unpleasant feelings and can express compassion for others. As empathy progresses on a developmental continuum, children's empathy grows in parallel with their cognitive capacity and moral reasoning (Decety, 2011). As emotional empathy development is considered to be complete in the preschool years, whereas cognitive empathy continues to develop well into the school years (Schwenck et al., 2014), for the young child the development of empathy for others is ongoing (Feshbach, 1982, 2009) and contingent on developing cognitive and emotional skills that enable the child to not only assume the perspective of another person but also to be able to feel and understand the emotional state of the person or their experience. The recognition and naming of feelings also support the development of empathy for others (Denham & Burton, 2003). Thus, the skills relating to emotion language and self-regulation are important.

The question can be asked whether empathy is a trait or a skill that can be learnt. Since there is no conclusive evidence that swings to the one side or the other it is generally considered to be both. Some people are born with a greater propensity to be empathetic, and it is true from our research and that of others that girls are more inclined to be empathetic than boys (Kirsh et al., 2021). But what happens throughout the childhood journey and the education experience makes a difference. Daniel Goleman (2005) who popularized the concept of emotional intelligence describes empathy as "basically the ability to understand others' emotions". It is the capacity to put yourself in another's shoes. Empathy is a skill that can be developed. Whilst reflexive or affective empathy seems to come naturally, cognitive empathy is a skill that is developed over time and leads to success in life, such as having effective relationships, holding a job, or being able to parent effectively.

Empathy, like many human behaviours, is multifaceted. While cognitive empathy comprises emotion recognition and perspective taking, emotional empathy includes the phenomenon of having shared feelings to be able to more adequately respond to another person's situation than to one's own. Empathy has been considered as an emotional capacity to connect and share in others' feelings (Wondra & Ellsworth, 2015). As such, cognitive and affective empathy are both complex and difficult to distinguish without the other (Eisenberg et al., 2014). Thus, evidence indicates that empathy is a multidimensional construct with cognitive and affective components (Belacchi & Farina, 2012; Watt, 2007); generally, the two coexist and are interconnected.

Personality traits, temperament, and cultural norms contribute to the developmental of empathy. For example, children from collectivist cultures are considered to be better at perspective taking than those from more individualistic cultures (Decety & Meyer, 2008). Children who are high empathizers are likely to be high empathizers as adults (Christov-Moore et al., 2014). Therefore, the investment of effort to teach and develop empathetic skills yields high dividends. Empathy can be improved with dedication and practice (Olson, 2013). In the main, the programs described in this volume provide opportunities to foster the development of empathy.

Children with high levels of cognitive and affective empathy are less likely to bully or be bullied, and are more likely to intervene, mediate, or help in bullying situations (Van Noorden et al., 2015). On the other hand, preschool children low in cognitive empathy are more likely to have antisocial behaviour and conduct problems compared to children with higher empathy (Georgiou et al., 2018).

Empathy in Action

Empathy in action is about caring and sharing and includes engagement in prosocial behaviours (Carlo et al., 2015) that are voluntary and promote another's wellbeing. Researchers suggest that empathy embodies essential skills that precede self- awareness, cognitive perspective taking, and emotion regulation, which together drive prosocial actions (Eisenberg et al., 2006). Thus, one salient feature of empathy development is often the resultant prosocial behaviour (Carlo et al., 2015). It is well known that prosocial behaviour, that is, any voluntary action that aims to promote another's wellbeing, provides immense benefits to the individual and community (Warden & Mackinnon, 2003). Prosocial actions have been associated with greater self-confidence, more supportive relationships. Prosocial behaviour is associated with social emotional development and thus warrants promotion in the educational context.

Caring can be described as empathy in action. Early childhood educators in Nordic countries base their work on caring, creating an affirming and nurturing ethos (Fugelsnes, 2018). The underlying premise is that there is a reciprocal relation between children and adults, and as adults model these behaviours social learning takes place. Figure 3.2 illustrates a group of children collaborating on an artwork in clay that represents their care for the environment whilst Figure 3.3 shows taking learning outside of the classroom into nature.

The establishment of empathetic behaviours is important for moral reasoning and overall prosocial behaviour (Decety, 2011; Feshbach & Feshbach,

Figure 3.2 Children expressing their care for environment in art form.

Figure 3.3 Children stepping outside of their classroom and exploring the environments close to where they live and learn.

2009). Baron-Cohen and Wheelwright (2004) distinguish the cognitive from the emotional dimension of empathy (Frydenberg et al., 2012). Going beyond saying "I'm sorry" requires children to have an internal voice that tells them to act with kindness, consideration, respect, and fairness, often called the emergence of conscience (Smith, 2013). The foundations of conscience are compassion, sympathy, and empathy. And this is an intellectual experience that is accessible to 4-year-olds.

A comprehensive body of emotion language is helpful as a communication tool to advance social emotional learning (Brackett, 2019; Deans et al., 2017; Pang et al., 2018). Children as young as 3 have emotional understanding (EU) which is associated with recognizing and understanding one's own and another's emotions. The way children read, interpret, express, and understand various emotions are guided and affected by the expectations and rules of the culture and community in which they live (Ma et al., 2017). EU is underpinned by the theory of the mind (ToM) that posits that preschool children can appreciate inner states and can distinguish between true or false belief systems. EU in turn is considered to increase with prosocial behaviours such as helping and sharing (Eisenberg et al., 2006; Ornaghi et al., 2016).

Conscience

Whilst empathy is the concept that we often think about in relationship to emotions and emotional development, conscience is a related concept that emphasizes the cognitive aspects.

> Conscience is an internal voice that obliges us to act with kindness, respect and fairness – and make things right as best as we can .... The word conscience comes from the Latin *conscientia*, which means "knowledge within oneself, a moral sense." To have a mature conscience is to know what is right and wrong and to govern one's actions by the shared principles that strengthen the human community.
> (Smith, 2013, p. 76)

Conscience, like empathy, must have a catalyst to flourish and that is done through the care and guidance of loving adults like parents, teachers, or other caring adults. Like empathy the critical period for this development in the first three years of life is affirmed by Smith (2013) when the brain structures necessary for interpreting social events, experiencing compassion, or making decisions are being shaped and connected between the limbic system of the brain and the prefrontal cortex. As Smith explains, the foundations of conscience are compassion, sympathy, and empathy. Compassion is when there is an awareness of the emotions of another along with wanting to provide help; sympathy puts compassion into action when a child hugs a child who is hurt or has lost something; and empathy is the intellectual experience that involves both the perception and the understanding. With empathy the emotional centres of the brain connect to the thinking part, especially the prefrontal cortex. Thus, the foundations of conscience are compassion, sympathy, and empathy.

The stages of the development of conscience are linked to development, much like that outlined in Chapter 1:

- In the first year of life infants respond to attention and pleasure with cooing, gurgling, and laughter,
- By one year they can react to sounds of another's distress.
- By 18 months they can try and comfort a loved one.
- By 2 years of age, they can articulate what the other is feeling, such as indicating that the baby is sad.
- At 3 they can understand how another is feeling.
- At 4 years they can distinguish how two people may react to the same situation differently.

38 Part I

Figure 3.4 Teacher facilitating group discussion on being a good listener.

All the good practices of adult–child relationships contribute to the development of conscience and caring, such as when adults show respect, listen, engage with children at eye level, show attention, affection and caring when appropriate, and share in the fun, laughter, and humour. Additionally, showing compassion and forgiveness when called for includes, for example, modelling saying sorry with understanding. Figure 3.4 shows a teacher facilitating group discussions on how to be a good listener.

Open Communication

The ability to communicate is an essential life skill for all children in the 21st century and becomes of increasing importance as children proceed through the school years. The universal communication skills include listening, being able to be assertive, and problem solving. Each are life-skills that are common across the age groups and are taught both to parents and teachers as well as children (Frydenberg, 2015).

Research shows that improved communication skills lead to better outcomes in learning, behaviour, and confidence (Bain et al., 2015). Much of the classroom practice incorporates communication skills through the classroom environment, where there are displays of children's work that can elicit discussion, reading stories that involve discussion, and activity tables where children collaborate and talk whilst working on their activities. The researchers also highlight the value and importance of engaging parents in open communication when they bring the children to school or when they collect them. Additionally, keeping parents informed as to what is happening in a program, such as those described in subsequent chapters, including the COPE-Resilience program, the intergenerational program, disability programs, and environment or Indigenous programs encourages ongoing family conversations.

Politeness

Whilst some consider that children's acquisition of politeness is generally at the age of 5 or later (Pedlow et al., 2004) children can be socialized into politeness earlier. Exposure to verbal forms such as thank you, please, I am sorry is a feature of English and this appears in other cultures by the age of 3 in the form of greetings, polite expression, and language (Nakamura, 2006). So, it is both language and nonverbal acts that form the expression of kindness (Huebscher et al., 2019).

For example, there is the teaching of the concept of *nunchi* to children in Korea – the subtle art and ability of sensing and gauging what other people are thinking and feeling, and then responding appropriately. According to author Euny Hong in her book *The power of nunchi: The Korean secret to happiness and success* (2019), *nunchi* – translated directly from Korean to English as "eye measure" – is a mixture of tact, savoir-faire, perceptiveness, and an eye for social situations, all rolled up in an instinctive sense of how to read any given encounter and respond in order to build trust, harmony, and connection in a collective culture. Hong gave examples in her book of how this concept is instilled in the early years through parenting and socializing. "We've been here forever! I'm hungry!" the son complains. A Korean mother won't respond with, "Oh, you poor thing! I'm sorry. Here, I have some grapes in my purse that can hold you over." Instead, she'll say, "Take a look at everyone else waiting in line, just like you. Now do you think you're the only person in this queue who is hungry?" This concept of *nunchi* has existed in Korea for centuries and coincides with the central principles of Confucianism: respect for elders, treating others with consideration in all circumstances, and acting or speaking with caution.

Thus, when it comes to the teaching of social emotional skills, the role of the cultural context is all important, as is the role of the teacher as the conveyor and interpreter of that context. In sum, all these behaviours can be considered as foundations of relational skills for children to develop into compassionate, empathic, and authentic human beings who can relate, engage, and build strong connections with one another in the communities they live in and in the broader world context.

The Role of the Teacher

When it comes to the teaching and development of social and emotional skills the teacher is front and centre in the early childhood setting, both from a direct instruction perspective and an indirect one that fosters ideal child development through modelling of the teacher's values, skills, and understandings. And this is of utmost importance. It includes exhibiting care and empathy. Whilst in the broadest sense empathy is about caring and sharing there are a range of terms and constructs that are complementary and sometimes used interchangeably which contribute to the nurturing of empathy (see Table 3.1, Eisenberg et al., 2006, p. 646).

Table 3.1 Terms that are aligned with empathy and used interchangeably by class teachers

Empathy	Ability to understand another's emotions
Emotional Intelligence	Understanding one's own emotions and that of others
Conscience	An internal voice that obliges us to act with kindness, respect, and fairness
Caring	Caring behaviours that indicate concern for the well-being of others, such as comforting, cooperating, helping, and sharing
Prosocial skills	Voluntary behaviour intended to benefit another

In addition to core theories outlined in Chapters 1 and 2, namely, the sociocultural theory of development of Vygotsky and Rogoff, ecological systems theory of Bronfenbrenner, Bowlby's attachment theory, emotional intelligence, and the theoretical underpinnings of positive psychology, SEL programs have generally focused on direct instruction. SEL programs have their roots in programs that focused on clinical interventions. Indeed, when we conducted a review of the literature on the evaluation of SEL (Frydenberg et al., 2017) we found that the evaluation tools were those used in clinical practice. However, as the field has progressed it has become clear that there is a growing emphasis on social cognitive variables such as social learning theory and information-processing models, along with differential emotion and attachment theories and an emphasis on self-regulation (Bierman & Motamedi, 2015).

In the first instance the classroom must promote a positive emotional climate within the context of self-determination theory (Deci & Ryan, 2008). Within the classroom climate the rights of the child are a given, the climate is warm, responsive, and non-judgmental, where strengths rather than incapacities are focused on. The classroom is where adults establish the programs that are under consideration, but children's interests are followed, which is an effective way of fostering language development (Schaffer, 2004). Children set their own challenges, assess their own progress rather than making social comparisons, and encourage positive feelings in relation to their tasks. This fosters positive feelings about themselves as learners, and establishes wellbeing, a good precursor to empathy.

Social Learning

The aspects of cognition and learning that are emphasized in SEL programming is that children learn through observation, imitation, and through instruction. Teachers demonstrate and illustrate helpful behaviours through storytelling, acting and drawing, and group discussions. The social information processing models that have emerged since the 1980s focus on perceptions utilizing encoding and interpreting social cues, social goals, and social problem solving. These are highly relevant skills when it comes to community connections and participation of learners in the early childhood settings. More recently there has been a growing emphasis on the part that emotions play and how young people become aware of their emotions, learn to label them, and regulate their emotions in a socially appropriate way.

Children's social experiences in classrooms, with adults, and peer friendships have a powerful impact on academic, social, and wellbeing outcomes (Howe, 2010). Children learn through play and language as they interact with others, as Vygotsky pointed out that children engage in tasks through their hands and their eyes with the help of their speech (Vygosky, 1978).

Empathy is a skill that leaders such as teachers require in this complex world where diversity is a given in most settings, where children come from a range of settings from which they bring diverse cultural experiences. Indeed, in many cases children come from families that are different from those that are experienced by teachers (Maude et al., 2009, 2011). The modern family comes in many configurations; no individual can experience first-hand the numerous contemporary variations. In many communities there are single-parent families, same-sex parents, a blend of cultures and backgrounds.

It can be argued that empathy helps professionals such as teachers to become more effective (Gerdes & Segal, 2011). There are numerous ways that empathy in the context of community can be enacted in a school setting. First, by enacting an inclusive philosophy, teachers can engage in meaningful connections with families; listening more than talking, celebrating cultural holidays such as Ramadan, can be a source of professional satisfaction (Peck et al., 2015). There is a general call out for empathy training in the preservice years by those who believe that it is possible to train and enhance empathy practices (Feshbach & Feshback, 2009; Decety & Jackson, 2004).

Prosocial skills, defined as "caring behaviours that indicate concern for the well-being of others, such as comforting, cooperating, helping and sharing", are to be encouraged (Hollingsworth & Winter, 2013, p. 1759). When teachers were surveyed, they reported that social emotional behaviour and skills are more important than developmental skills. Friendships are important. Prosocial skills can be fostered through pretend play. Teachers are also able to set up situations to foster friendships both in the classroom and in the playground. These friendship groups in turn can be encouraged to engage in prosocial practices individually or collectively.

Whilst emotional intelligence is foundational, when it comes to empathy training more specifically, a teacher's own philosophy and values regarding a range of issues around inclusiveness and culture have been considered by Peck and colleagues (2015) in the process of preparing culturally responsive practitioners. Empathy can be considered as an essential component of the human condition (Hojat, 2007). When 24 female participating teachers, 15 of whom identified as Caucasian, from a preschool setting (children ages 3–5 years) were interviewed over a two-year period, the extensive data highlighted the importance of seeing inclusion as a philosophy, being relaxed and balanced, accepting and responding to family culture. The modelling of empathy both to students and parents is critical to being able to teach empathy in the classroom and impact the development of empathy within the family (Smith, 2013).

The foundations of good educational practice are the values and beliefs of teachers. Several researchers have shone a light on how to assess and develop teachers' beliefs and values to influence best practice. Emotional intelligence (EI) is a core skill required for lifelong success in all situations. The term was first coined by Salovey and Mayer in 1990 and popularized by Daniel Goleman in 1995 to highlight that EI contrasts with IQ, not being a fixed trait but one that can be developed. At its heart is the understanding of one's own emotions and that of others. In one study Kremenitzer (2005) challenged early childhood teachers to systematically assess their own emotional intelligence skills using self-reflective journaling. The skills that they were focused on were:

1) The ability to perceive and appraise the expression of emotion with questions like "am I good at identifying how I am feeling or how my students are feeling?"
2) The ability to assess or generate feeling that help you think better such as, "am I good in identifying swings in myself and others?"
3) Understanding and analysing emotions with reflective questions such as, "am I good at finding the right word(s) to express my feelings?"
4) Reflective regulation of emotions with questions such as "am I able to self-regulate my behaviour even in the most difficult of circumstances?"

The teacher is encouraged to keep a reflective journal for several weeks and the process is likely to make them hyperaware of their emotional reactions and practices, in the expectation that the individual will derive benefits for themselves as well as impact the development of these skills in their students in an age-appropriate way. This is an excellent preparation for running Community Connections programs.

Prosocial Skills

When it comes to prosocial skills the definition offered by Eisenberg, Fabes, and Spinrad (2006) as voluntary behaviour intended to help another emphasizes the charitable aspects of the behaviour. Children are often made to apologize and say sorry, which is quite different from the spontaneity of a child showing caring and concern for another. The caring and concern can take many forms, which in a preschool setting it is often manifested through sharing, showing compassion for another, helpfulness, or hugging a peer. Children who showed these qualities in the early years were found to be more prosocial in the primary school grades (Eisenberg et al., 2006) and a study by Eisenberg et al., (1999) that followed children through to adulthood found that these prosocial skills remained 19 years later. Additionally, children who demonstrate prosocial skills were found to be the most cognitively ready for school (Bierman et al., 2009).

Although there are genetic influences in prosocial tendencies in preschoolers, as demonstrated in twin studies of children brought up in different families (Knafo & Plomin, 2006), the influences are small. It is more likely to be the experiences of the child and the role models, including parents and teachers, that determine the development of prosocial practices. In this regard children who have healthy strong attachments with key adults in their family are likely to bring to the early childhood setting a range of prosocial practices. Teachers also have an opportunity to provide an environment of warm secure attachments, which are often described as belonging. Teachers have a wide range of opportunities to model empathic behaviour in numerous ways. Listening attentively, responding with warmth, showing kindness and consideration, not only in their classrooms but also to each other in the peer context as they interact with colleagues. Greeting, meeting, and supporting families provides opportunities for modelling both to children and parents what is good practice. These skills are part of a teacher's everyday practice in the social emotional domain.

In the community connections programs showcased, all those qualities described in Table 3.1 are highly promoted, sometimes directly, such in programs like COPE-Resilience, Friends on the Farm, through the intergenerational programs, or indirectly where the expectation is that the child will learn from observing the practices of the adult. From the countless programs and articles written for teachers on this topic, the aim is to promote:

- Building a sense of community in the classroom, e.g. tea ceremony, doing group projects where collaborations are important (see Figure 3.1), group displays showing artworks, e.g. Boorai – The Children's Art Gallery project (see Chapter 10);
- Using the teachable moments;
- Using displays of photographs showing how children work together;
- Acknowledging prosocial behaviour when you see it, i.e. "catch a kid doing something good";
- Encouraging friendships amongst children who are less likely to spontaneously choose to work with each other;
- Having reasons for classroom rules – explaining the rules shows respect for the child;
- Responding to situations that arise;
- Scaffolding children's efforts – a term from Vygotsky (1978) that denotes taking a child to the next level of understanding or practice by giving them a helping hand;
- Engaging families in the learning process – sharing with parents what the teacher is doing brings them on the journey and multiplies the outcomes, acknowledging individual and cultural differences that families bring;
- Giving children with behavioural challenges one-to-one time, showing care and respect.

Program Implementation and Evaluation

In each of the programs described in Part II of this volume the above values feature within the goals and purposes. A common feature across all programs is the evaluation component within early childhood programs which takes multiple formats. Teachers kept extensive systematic records of their classroom practice and progress was generally seen in developmental terms, as illustrated in Chapter 5 where the 3-year-old and the 5-year-old children demonstrate very clear progression in terms of drawing and describing their learning outcomes. On many occasions teachers and parents completed evaluative questionnaires and children likewise were regularly involved in an interactive format. Ultimately teacher, parent, and child recording of outcomes provides an excellent indication of progress in any sphere of early years educational practice. In addition, quantitative and qualitative research was undertaken as a way of ensuring the triangulation of children's responses with those of the teachers and the parents. In conducting mixed methods research it has been possible to use more comprehensive quantitative evaluations of outcomes that use tools to measure, for example, empathy, coping, and strengths and difficulties (McNamara, 2021).

Concluding Remarks

Early childhood curriculum guidelines generally focus on the attainment of age-appropriate literacy and numeracy skills and the development of concept knowledge through experience in language, mathematics, science, music, art, dance, drama, literature, social and cultural studies, and technology. These significant areas of focus are complemented by those aspects of learning and development related to children's sense of self and wellbeing, with an emphasis on social emotional learning and prosocial practices that make children connected to and contributors to their world.

Take Home Messages

- Contact theory is underscored by the premise that if there is contact between two groups it can create understanding and reduce prejudice.
- Empathy is about caring about the people around you; it is about caring in action.
- Bonding with a critical other in the early years (see attachment theory in Chapter 2) lays the foundations for empathy.
- Empathy is multifaceted and can be developed in the first five years of life and continues to develop subsequently.
- Empathy fosters social interactions.
- Affective empathy is feeling what the other feels whilst cognitive empathy is more about understanding how the other feels.
- Numerous concepts are associated with empathy, such as developing conscience or displaying politeness.
- The role of the teacher is paramount both in design and delivery of curriculum and through facilitating social learning and being a role model when fostering the development of skills relating to empathy.

References

Allison, C., Baron-Cohen, S., Wheelwright, S., Stone, M., & Muncer, S. (2011). Psychometric analysis of the Empathy Quotient (EQ). Personality and *Individual Differences*, *51*(7), 829–835. https://doi.org/10.1016/j.paid.2011.07.005

Allport, G. W. (1950). Prejudice: A problem in psychological and social causation. *Journal of Social Issues*, *6*, 4–23. https://doi.org/10.1111/j.1540-4560.1950.tb02175.x

Bain, J., James, D., & Harrison, M. (2015). Supporting communication development in the early years: A practitioner's perspective. *Child Language Teaching & Therapy*, *31*(3), 325–336. https://doi.org/10.1177/0265659015596795

Baron-Cohen, S., & Wheelwright, S. (2004). The empathy quotient: An investigation of adults with Asperger syndrome or high functioning autism, and normal sex differences. *Journal of Autism and Developmental Disorders*, *34*(2), 163–175.

Beceren, B., & Özdemir, A. (2019). Role of temperament traits and empathy skills of preschool children in predicting emotional adjustment. *International Journal of Progressive Education*, *15*(3), 91–107. https://doi.org/10.29329/ijpe.2019.193.7

Belacchi, C., & Farina, E. (2012). Feeling and thinking of others: Affective and cognitive empathy and emotion comprehension in prosocial/hostile preschoolers. *Aggressive Behavior*, *38*(2), 150–165. https://doi.org/10.1002/ab.21415

Bierman, K. L., Torres, M. M., Domitrovich, C. E., Welsh, J. A., & Gest, S. D. (2009). Behavioral and cognitive readiness for school: Cross-domain associations for children attending Head Start. *Social Development* (Oxford), *18*(2), 305–323. https://doi.org/10.1111/j.1467-9507.2008.00490.x

Bierman, K. L. & Motamedi, M. (2015). SEL programs for preschool children. In J. A. Durlak, C. E. Domitrovich, R. P. Weissberg, & T. P. Gullotta (Eds.), *Handbook of social and emotional learning: Research and practice* (pp. 135–150). New York: Guilford Press.

Borden, E. J. (1987). The community connection: It works. *Young Children*, *42*(4), 14–23.

Brackett, M. (2019). *Permission to feel: Unlocking the power of emotions to help our kids, ourselves, and our society thrive*. New York: Celadon Books.

Carlo, G., Padilla-Walker, L. M., & Nielson, M. G. (2015). Longitudinal bidirectional relations between adolescents' sympathy and prosocial behavior. *Developmental Psychology*, *51*(12), 1771–1777. https://doi.org/10.1037/dev0000056

Christov-Moore, L., Simpson, E., Coudé, G., Grigaityte, K., Iacoboni, M., and Francesco, P. (2014). Empathy: Gender effects in brain and behavior. *Neuroscience Biobehavior Review*, *46*, 604–627. http://doi: 10.1016/j.neubiorev.2014.09.001

Collaborative for Academic, Social and Emotional Learning (CASEL). (2021). *Social and emotional learning core competencies*. Retrieved from: www.casel.org/social-and-emotional-learning/core-competencies.

Deans, J., Klarin, S., Liang, R., & Frydenberg, E. (2017). All children have the best start in life to create a better future for themselves and for the nation. *Australasian Journal of Early Childhood*, *4*, 78.

Decety, J. (2011). The neuroevolution of empathy. *Annals of the New York Academy of Sciences*, *1231*, 35–45.

Decety, J., & Jackson, P. (2004). The functional architecture of human empathy. *Behavioral and Cognitive Neuroscience Reviews*, *3*(2), 71–100.

Decety, J., & Meyer, M. (2008). From emotion resonance to empathic understanding: A social developmental neuroscience account. *Development and Psychopathology*, *20*, 1053–1080.

Deci, E. L., & Ryan, R. M. (2008). Self-determination theory: A macrotheory of human motivation, development, and health. *Canadian Psychology/Psychologie canadienne*, *49*(3), 182–185. https://doi.org/10.1037/a0012801

Denham, S. A., & Burton, R. (2003). *Social and emotional prevention and intervention programming for pre-schoolers*. Dordrecht: Kluwer Academic/Plenum Publishers.

Eisenberg, N., Fabes, R. A., & Spinrad, T. L. (2006). Prosocial development. In W. Damon & R. Lerner (Eds.), *Handbook of child psychology, social, emotional, and personality development* (Vol. 3, pp. 646–702). Chichester: John Wiley.

Eisenberg, N., Fabes, R. A., Shepard, S. A., Guthrie, I. K., Murphy, B. C., and Reiser, M. (1999). Parental reactions to children's negative emotions: Longitudinal relations to quality of children's social functioning. *Child Development, 70,* 513–534. https://doi.org/10.1111/1467-8624.00037

Eisenberg, N., Spinrad, T. L., & Morris A. (2014). Empathy-related responding in children. In M., Killen & J. G. Smetana (Eds.), *Handbook of moral development* (pp. 184–207). Mahwah, NJ: Lawrence Erlbaum Associates.

Feshbach, N. D. (1982). Sex differences in empathy and social behavior in children. In N. Eisenberg (Ed.), *The development of prosocial behavior* (pp. 315–338). New York: Academic Press.

Feshbach, N. D., & Feshbach, S. (2009). Empathy and education. In J. Decety & W. Ickes (Eds.), *The social neuroscience of empathy* (pp. 85–98). Cambridge, MA: MIT Press.

Frydenberg, E. (2015). *Families coping: Effective strategies for you and your child*. Canberra: Australian Council for Educational Research (ACER Press).

Frydenberg, E., Deans, J., & O'Brien, K. (2012). *Developing everyday coping skills in the early years: Proactive strategies for supporting social and emotional development*. New York: Continuum Inc. Press.

Frydenberg, E., Liang, R., & Muller D. (2017) Assessing students' social and emotional learning: A review of the literature on assessment tools and related issues. In E. Frydenberg, A. Martin, & R. Collie (Eds.), *Social and emotional learning in Australia and the Asia-Pacific: Perspectives, programs and approaches* (pp. 55–82). Singapore: Springer. https://doi.org/10.1007/978-981-10-3394-0_4

Fugelsnes, K. (2018). Reciprocal caring in ECEC settings. In E. Johansson, A. Emilson, & A.-M. Puroila (Eds.), *Values education in early childhood settings: Concepts, approaches and practices* (pp. 187–198). Cham: Springer.

Georgiou, G., Kimonis, E., & Fanti, K. (2018). What do others feel? Cognitive empathy deficits explain the association between callous-unemotional traits and conduct problems among preschool children. *European Journal of Developmental Psychology, 16,* 1–21. http://doi.org/10.1080/17405629.2018.1478810.

Gerdes, K. E., & Segal, E. (2011). Importance of empathy for social work practice: Integrating new science. *Social Work, 56*(2), 141–148.

Gillberg, C. (1992). Autism and autistic like conditions: Subclasses among disorders of empathy. *Journal of Child Psychology Psychiatry, 33,* 813–842. https://doi.org/10.1111/j.1469-7610.1992.tb01959.x

Goleman, D. (2005). *Emotional intelligence*. New York: Bantam Books.

Hojat, M. (2007). *Empathy in patient care: Antecedents, developments, measurements, and outcomes*. New York: Springer Science+Business Media.

Hollingsworth, H., & Winter, M.K. (2013). Teacher beliefs and practices relating to development in preschool: Importance placed on social–emotional behaviours and skills. *Early Child Development and Care, 183*(12), 1758–1781. https://doi.org/10.1080/03004430.2012.759567

Hong, E. (2019). The power of nunchi: The Korean secret to happiness and success. *Publishers Weekly, 266*(34), 117. Retrieved: www.cnbc.com/2019/11/15/how-kor ean-parents-raise-smart-successful-kids-best-kept-secret.html

Howe, D. (2010), The safety of children and the parent–worker relationship in cases of child abuse and neglect. *Child Abuse Review, 19*, 330–341. https://doi.org/10.1002/car.1136

Huebscher, I., Garufi, M., & Prieto, P. (2019). The development of polite stance in preschoolers: How prosody, gesture, and body cues pave the way. *Journal of Child Language, 46*(5), 825–862. https://doi.org/10.1017/S0305000919000126

Kirsh, E., Frydenberg, E., & Deans, J. (2021). Benefits of an intergenerational program in the early years. *Journal of Early Childhood Education Research, 10*(2), 140–164.

Knafo, A., & Plomin, R. (2006). Parental discipline and affection and children's prosocial behavior: Genetic and environmental links. *Journal of Personality and Social Psychology, 90*(1), 147–164. https://doi.org/10.1037/0022-3514.90.1.147

Kremenitzer, J. (2005). Emotional intelligence in teacher education. *Focus on Teacher Education, 5*, 6–7.

Kuehne, V. S., & Melville, J. (2014). The state of our art: A review of theories used in intergenerational program research (2003–2014) and ways forward. *Journal of Intergenerational Relationships, 4*, 317.

Ma, X., Tamir, M., & Miyamoto, Y. (2017). A socio-cultural instrumental approach to emotion regulation: Culture and the regulation of positive emotions. *Emotion, 18*, 138–152. https://doi.org/10.1037/emo0000315

Maude, S., Brotherson, M. J., Summers, J., Erwin, E., Palmer, S., Peck, N. F., et al. (2011). Performance ethnography: A strategy to link research to professional development in inclusive early childhood teacher preparation. *Journal of Early Childhood Teacher Education, 32*, 355–366.

Maude, S., Hodges, L., Brotherson, M. J., Hughes, K., Peck, N., Weigel, C., et al. (2009). Critical reflections on working with diverse families: Culturally responsive professional development strategies for early childhood and early childhood special educators. Multiple Voices for Ethnically Diverse Exceptional *Learners, 12*(1), 38–53.

McNamara, N. (2021). Social and emotional learning through an environmental education program: An evaluation of the Learning in Nature Program. Unpublished master's thesis, University of Melbourne.

Nakamura, K. (2006). The acquisition of linguistic politeness in Japanese. In M. Nakayama, R. Mazuka, & Y. Shirai (Eds.), *The handbook of East Asian psycholinguistics*, Vol. 2: *Japanese* (pp. 110–115). Cambridge: Cambridge University Press.

Olson, G. (2013). *Empathy imperiled: Capitalism, culture, and the brain*. Cham: Springer Science + Business Media. https://doi.org/10.1007/978-1-4614-6117-3

Ornaghi, V., Pepe, A., & Grazzani, I. (2016). False-belief understanding and language ability mediate the relationship between emotion comprehension and prosocial orientation in preschoolers. *Frontiers in Psychology, 7*, 1534. https://doi.org/10.3389/fpsyg.2016.01534

Pang, D., Frydenberg, E., Liang, R., & Deans, J. (2018). Improving coping skills and promoting social and emotional competence in pre-schoolers: A 5-week COPE-R program. *Journal of Early Childhood Education Research, 7*(2), 1–31.

Peck, N. F., Maude, S. P., & Brotherson, M. J. (2015). Understanding preschool teachers' perspectives on empathy: A qualitative inquiry. *Early Childhood Education Journal, 43*, 169–179. https://doi.org/10.1007/s10643-014-0648-3

Pedlow, R., Sanson, A., & Wales, R. (2004). Children's production and comprehension of politeness in requests: relationships to behavioural adjustment, temperament and empathy. *First Language, 24*(3), 347–367.

Pettigrew, T. F. (2016). In pursuit of three theories: Authoritarianism, relative deprivation, and intergroup contact. *Annual Review of Psychology, 67*, 1. https://doi.org/10.1146/annurev-psych-122414-033327

Salovey, P., & Mayer, J. D. (1990). Emotional intelligence. *Imagination, Cognition and Personality, 9*(3), 185–211. https://doi.org/10.2190/DUGG-P24E-52WK-6CDG

Schaffer, H. R. (2004). *Introducing child psychology*. Oxford: Blackwell Publishing.

Schwenck, C., Göhle, B., Hauf, J., Warnke, A., Freitag, C. M., & Schneider, W. (2014). Cognitive and emotional empathy in typically developing children: The influence of age, gender, and intelligence. *European Journal of Developmental Psychology, 11*(1), 63–76. https://doi.org/10.1080/17405629.2013.808994

Smith, C. A. (2013). Beyond "I'm sorry": The educator's role in preschoolers' emergence of conscience. *Young Children, 68*(1), 76.

Solms, M. (2017). Empathy and other minds: A neuropsychoanalytic perspective and a clinical vignette. In V. Lux & S. Weigel (Eds.), *Empathy: Epistemic problems and cultural-historical perspectives of a cross-disciplinary concept* (pp. 93–114). Basingstoke: Palgrave Macmillan/Springer Nature. https://doi.org/10.1057/978-1-137-51299-4_4

Taylor, S. J., Barker, L. A., Heavey, L., & McHale, S. (2013). The typical developmental trajectory of social and executive functions in late adolescence and early adulthood. *Developmental Psychology, 49*, 1253–1265. https://doi.org/10.1037/a0029871

Van Noorden, T. H., Haselager, G. J., Cillessen, A. H., & Bukowski, W. M. (2015). Empathy and involvement in bullying in children and adolescents: A systematic review. *Journal of Youth and Adolescence, 44*, 637–657. http://doi.org/10.1007/s10964-014-0135-6

Vygotsky, L. S. (1978). *Mind in society: The development of higher psychological processes*. Cambridge, MA: Harvard University Press.

Warden, D., & Mackinnon, S. (2003). Prosocial children, bullies and victims: An investigation of their sociometric status, empathy and social problem-solving strategies. *British Journal of Developmental Psychology, 21*(3), 367–385. https://doi.org/10.1348/026151003322277757

Watt, D. (2007). Toward a neuroscience of empathy: Integrating affective and cognitive perspectives. *Neuro-Psychoanalysis, 9*(2), 119–140. https://doi.org/10.1080/15294145.2007.10773550

Wondra, J. D., & Ellsworth, P. C. (2015). An appraisal theory of empathy and other vicarious emotional experiences. *Psychological Review, 122*(3), 411–428. https://doi.org/10.1037/a0039252

4 Artistic Meaning Making in Early Years Education

Children's Voices Expressed through Drawing, Painting, and Narrative

At a national and global level there is an established recognition of the importance of the early years for children's learning and development. Research indicates that children who participate in enriched play-based learning programs are more likely to be successful throughout life, hence the focus by governments on ensuring that quality education and care programs are available for all children. The current world into which children are born is filled with new challenges, uncertainties, ambiguities, and new technologies, all of which tend to distract children from the essence of what it is to be human. With this somewhat sobering idea in mind, this chapter focuses on the importance of play-based artistic meaning making as an expressive medium for young children to give voice to their understandings of the world they live in as well as their creative ideas for the future.

Playful Artistic Meaning Making

Slade (1995, p. 2) states, "one of the great gifts of life is to know how to play" and for all humans the universal experience of play fulfils a basic need for individuals to adapt to the world, to learn about the self and others, and to learn and realize their potential through experience. Much has been written about the importance of play and its benefits in relation to young children's learning and, although there is some controversy surrounding the pros and cons of teaching through play, the concept of play-based learning is widely accepted and documented in early childhood literature (Anning et al., 2004; Docket & Fleer, 1999; Paley, 2005), having been originally endorsed by the well-known early philosophers and educators Jean-Jacques Rousseau (1712–1778), Friedrich Froebel (1782–1852), and Maria Montessori (1870–1952). Within early childhood education "learning through play" is the phrase frequently used to describe a particular pedagogical approach to teaching and learning. It has been defined in the Early Years Learning Framework (DEEWR, 2009) as "a context for learning through which children organize and make sense of their social worlds as they engage actively with people, objects and representations" (p. 46). Drawing on developmental psychology as an overarching theoretical framework, play is seen as a basis for the development of early childhood curriculum and pedagogy.

Play is defined as a meaningful, joyful activity that children willingly choose to participate in, which involves physical, cognitive, and communicative efforts in both social and cultural contexts (Docket & Fleer, 1999). Most scholars would agree that it is through play that much of children's learning and understandings is achieved, with play providing a way for children to make sense of their natural, social, physical, and material worlds. As such, play can be viewed as a tool for meaning making through which construction of knowledge and understandings is achieved through broadly based interaction in a variety of physical and social contexts.

The idea of linking play with the arts is not new. A number of authors (Eisner, 2002; Matthews, 1994; Maranović-Shane & Beljanski-Ristić, 2008; Sansom, 2011; Stinson, 1993; Wright, 2007a,b) have noted the integral relationship that exists between the two, recognizing that they share similar attributes when it comes to exploratory and imaginative sensory processing. As Eisner (2002, p. 4) states:

> The arts have an important role to play in refining our sensory system and cultivating our imaginative abilities. Indeed, the arts provide a kind of permission to pursue qualitative experience in a particularly focused way and to engage in the constructive exploration of what the imaginative process may engender. In this sense, the arts in all their manifestations are close in attitude to play.

Vygotsky (1978) is widely regarded by contemporary early childhood educators as the most significant and forward-thinking theorist on play (Holmes & Geiger, 2002; Roopnarine et al., 1998, 2000). He believed that play represented an interactive social form of imagination and was integral to development during the early years, providing the foundation for broadly ranging skills essential for holistic growth. Play was identified as being rule-bound and essentially social in character supporting children to fulfil a range of social and emotional needs, providing a means of deferring immediate gratification and practising both internal and externally imposed self-regulation. Vygotsky (1978) noted that play provides the vehicle for children to behave more maturely than at other times and the memorable quotation "in play a child always performs above his average age, above his daily behaviour: in play it is as though he were a head taller than himself" (p. 110), draws attention to the importance of play for children's growth and development. Vygotsky (1978, p. 96) also identified play as "a novel form of behaviour liberating the child from constraints", an idea that resonates with free-flowing and spontaneous explorations and expressive communications through the arts.

Governed by innate natural curiosity and a desire to explore and learn about the world, children demonstrate a significant capacity to live in and through their playing. Play is acknowledged to be a creative act and early childhood scholars believe that it is through play that much of children's learning is achieved. As noted in the Early Years Learning Framework: Belonging, Being, and Becoming (DEEWR, 2009, p. 15):

> Play provides opportunities for children to learn as they discover, create, improvise and imagine. When children play with other children, they create social groups, test out ideas, challenge each other's thinking and build new understandings. Play provides a supportive environment where children can ask questions, solve problems, and engage in critical thinking. Play can expand children's thinking and enhance their desire to know and learn. In these ways play can promote positive dispositions towards learning. Children's immersion in their play illustrates how play enables them to enjoy being.

From this perspective, a strong relationship between play and artistic activity is further affirmed with the improvisational processing of ideas, forms, colours, shapes, materials, sounds, and movements, having the capacity to produce new interpretations or impressions. Through play children have ongoing opportunities to "self-scaffold" their learning, enlivening, and enlarging their imaginations, to find out what they need to "know next through self-initiated problem-solving/finding and through implicitly drawn connections for self-discovered meaning-making" (St John, cited in Connery et al., 2010, p. 66).

In his writings about children's imagination and creativity, Vygotsky (1978) introduced the notion of the circular path of imagination. This process is understood to involve the filtering of lived experience through imaginative embodied processing that combines and recombines elements of the experience, to create an artistic product such as an image, music, dance, or story. According to Vygotsky, for the circular path to be completed, both intellectual and emotional factors need to be involved. It is at this point that a clear relationship between play, creativity, and artistic endeavour is identified, with imaginative musings and fantasy being fundamental to the experience. As further justification for the importance of play-based learning Vygotsky (1978, pp. 102–103) states:

> Though the play–development relationship can be compared to the instruction–development relationship, play provides a much wider background for changes in needs and consciousness. Action in the imaginative sphere, in an imaginary situation, the creation of voluntary intentions, and the formation of real-life plans and volitional motives – all appear in play and make it the highest level of preschool development.

Perezhivanie and Multidimensional Thinking

Within the construct of learning through play, the phenomenon of *perezhivanie* (intensely emotionally lived experience in a social situation) is identified (Vygotsky, 1978). Through the course of making complex and dynamic connections between the key psychological processes of thinking, imagining, and creating, the young child transforms information from the material and social world of lived experience, constructing knowledge into understandings and making meaning across a variety of contexts and codes or symbol systems. This construct provides a frame for thinking that acknowledges that the child is in a dialectical relationship with the environment and his or her thinking-emotions. Vygotsky's concept of the environment was extended "beyond the physical to include social and affective activity, products of cultural development such as speech and other symbol systems, and social systems and formations" (Kozulin et al., 2003, p. 135). As such, *perezhivanie* describes the complex internal synthesis of thought and emotion and its transformation into multidimensional meaning making activity that culminates in semiotic expressions that demonstrate understandings/and or involvement in the world.

As previously outlined, Vygotsky's theory highlights the link between play, conceptual understandings, and creative imagination within the social world of the child. It also describes the mutual influence and coexistence of scientific (i.e. formal, or conceptual) and everyday (i.e. experiential) concepts in children's learning. Vygotsky (1978) described how children learn every-day or spontaneous concepts through experience, and gradually, through open-ended exploratory play across modes and language exchange, they develop and reconceptualize these into more formal concepts. Bruner (1966) proposed that children use three modes of symbolic representation: enactive representation (action based), iconic representation (image-based), and symbolic representation (language based) to develop understandings of their world. Such a paradigm draws attention to the notion of "learning through discovery", a tenet that underpins contemporary early childhood pedagogy and is at the heart of children's multidimensional expressive communications.

The Significance of Arts Education

It is widely understood that the arts provide humanity with unique ways of making meaning of experience or "knowing" about the world, and in all cultures, they provide important ways of expressing and representing ideas, emotions, values, and spiritual beliefs. Representational practices across modes fulfil a basic human need to communicate and, as such, the arts are legitimately grouped as a key area of human learning and activity. Through art, people across age groups bring their thinking and imaginative dreaming into a form of reality. Through the creative manipulation of a range of symbols individuals are enabled to construct and deconstruct, shape, and reshape, revise and revision their personal and hidden and subjective lives (Abbs, 2003). Hence the arts provide a powerful tool for accessing abstract parts of lived experience, bring to the surface thoughts, feelings, and emotions that are given a new and unique form.

Eisner (2002) speaks about the arts as a means of allowing individuals to explore their personal "interior landscapes" and thus, from this perspective, engagement in the arts can be viewed as a way of tapping into felt emotion, providing a range of expressive and communicative modalities for responses to lived and felt experience.

In the 1930s eminent scholar John Dewey introduced a series of revolutionary educational ideas and theories which fundamentally changed approaches to teaching and learning across all years of education. In what became known as the Progressive Education Movement, Dewey drew attention to the importance of learning from life experience, taking a "hands on" approach to teaching and learning. Experimentation was central to the idea, with human life experiences being recognized for their capacity to support human learning, growth, and development. In his seminal work *Art as experience*, Dewey (1934) argues that aesthetic experience is the highest form of human interaction, there being no essential gap between aesthetic experience and other forms of experience. He notes that the arts are not just add-on luxuries of education, but important expressions of that which makes the educational experience worthwhile. He recognizes the arts as the main means by which individuals achieve a focused and enhanced appreciation for lived experience; their purpose, being pleasurable, offers individuals an opportunity to concentrate on first-hand flexible explorations that expand thinking and understanding.

Within educational settings experimentation and exploration are central to teaching and learning through the arts where the purpose is for children to discover ways of articulating their experience, representing it through multiple modes, and finding new ways to express their ideas, emotions, values, and cultural beliefs. Through engagement in the arts, children learn to take risks, to be imaginative, to question, to explore alternative solutions and extend their limits, and to develop, practise, and refine techniques with the expressed purpose of communicating and sharing and their opinions. As noted within the Australian National Curriculum (ACARA, 2012, p. 2):

> The arts have the capacity to engage, inspire and enrich all students, exciting the imagination and encouraging them to reach their creative and expressive potential ... they provide opportunities for students to create, share and communicate ideas, emotions, experiences, and imagination.

Eminent scholar Eliot Eisner (2002, p. 24) notes:

> a major aim of arts education is to promote the child's ability to develop his or her mind through the experience that the creation of perception of expressive form makes possible. In this activity sensibilities are refined, distinctions are made more subtle, the imagination is stimulated, and skills are developed to give form to feeling.

Recent research has identified the arts as symbol systems or modes of communication that are used in organized ways through cultural practices to express and communicate meanings (ACARA, 2012; DEEWR, 2009). From this perspective several eminent scholars (Cassirer, 1953; Eisner, 2002; Gardner, 1983; Goodman, 1976; Langer, 1953;Vygotsky, 1978) have investigated symbol systems as a distinctive feature of human cognition offering an insight into the link between the biological and cultural, namely "the nervous system with its structures and functions and the culture with its roles and activities" (Gardner, 1983, p. 301). Thus, for the young child, symbolization or artistic expression offers a way of perceiving and constructing understandings of lived experience and is recognized for the role it plays in supporting thinking and meaning making.

It is widely understood that young children's learning is based on sensory explorations and relies on active and physical engagement with the world (Piaget, 1953). Eisner (2002, p. 2) acknowledges that humans are "sentient creatures born into a qualitative environment in and through which they live", and he places great emphasis on the relationship between sensory or perceptual experience and thinking, citing the senses as the first avenues to consciousness. He describes cognition as a generic process of coming to know the world through the senses and identifies the arts as playing an important role in refining the sensory system and cultivating imaginative and expressive capabilities. Hence, it is recognized that the learning process for the young child is dependent on sensory input and involves complex neurological perceptual activity, which stimulates the abstraction of a wide range of sensory concepts that are made available from the environment. It is through the abstraction of each of the sensory modalities that concepts are formed (Piaget, 1953; Taylor, 1988).This process depends upon a constructive use of cognition, with concepts being formed and then joined with other concepts, enabling the child to make sense of the environment, use symbols to express understandings, predict probability patterns, and regulate a wide range of interactions with the world and people in it. Eisner (2002, p. 2) believes that it is this process of construction and abstraction that is at the root of art and forms the basis of thinking and knowing, pointing out that:

> The sensory system does not work alone; it requires for its development the tools of culture: language, the arts, science, values and the like.With the aid of culture we learn to create ourselves.

As Eisner (2002, p. 100) states, "the senses feed ideas, and ideas focus one's senses" and with this idea in mind, the child draws on the information coming in from the senses and uses this as a starting point for the construction of knowledge, which in turn is expressed through a variety of symbolic modes. Through the arts, thoughts, feelings, ideas, and imaginings, are recognized for the important role they play across a variety of contexts and modes to enable unique personal interpretations or ways of making meaning of the natural and built environment and the social world in which the child lives.

Semiotic Meaning Making

To highlight young children's artistic and expressive communications as meaning-making tools, an overview of the value of semiotics in early childhood education is provided. Semiotics is the study of signs (a sign being something that stands for something else) of all kinds, hence the field of semiotics looks at "meanings and messages in all their forms and in all their contexts" (Innis, 1985, p. 8). Put simply, Danesi (2020, p. x) notes semiotics as "an academic discipline that studies what is a critical feature of human sapience – the capacity to create and use signs as words and symbols for thinking, communicating, reflecting, transmitting and preserving knowledge". Within the early childhood arts education domain, semiotics is understood to be the capacity of children to use a variety of symbolic languages (drawing, painting, music making, dancing, and spoken language) all of which possess differing functions and offer different ways of thinking and interpreting experience, which leads to the preservation of knowledge. As such, the arts offer a variety of ways to construct understandings about the world, allowing children to view, feel, and hear the world in unique and refreshing ways.

Vygotsky (1978), in his examination of the thinking and speaking process, wrote extensively about how semiotic mediation employs both physical and psychological signs or cultural tools which serve as carriers of cultural thought to support meaning making. Vygotsky (1978, p. 249) described artistic meaning making as "the social technique of emotion, a tool for society which brings the most intimate and personal aspects of our being into the circle of social life". He identified that thinking was enhanced by the interplay of a range of mediating tools, both psychological and material. These he argued are mutually linked and yet separate in the child's intellectual, social, emotional, and cultural development. As Connery, (cited in Connery et al., 2010, p. 87) notes, "signs, including gestures, movements, words and visual symbols, provide an efficient means of mediating generalizations". Drawing and painting, when combined with narration, provide the young child with readily accessible semiotic tools for "investigating, deciphering, documenting and explaining the what, why and how" (Wright, 2007a, p. 12) of lived experience.

It could be argued that children have an innate need to engage in creative activities to help them to come to understand more fully or even unravel what it means to be human. The central motivation for the young child to engage in artistic explorations is to find out how understandings can be further advanced, how ideas can be blended, connections made between disciplines, findings deciphered, and discourses commenced through communications that can be externally shared. Hence drawing, painting, narratives, making installations, dancing and music making, and in fact any other imaginative activity that the child wishes to engage in, provide the means for semiotic meaning making. Creative problem solving and interpretation is given a position of importance, as information alone has little meaning unless there is interpretation. From this perspective children engaging in interdisciplinary modes of inquiry, that is, linking the visual graphic with narrative and/or words, provide an authentic expression of child voice that enables communication that can be interpreted for its meaning by those other than the child.

The Voices of Children as Expressed through the Arts

Recent literature (Conklin Thompson, 2005; Clark & Moss, 2001; Dahlberg & Moss, 2005; Rinaldi, 2006) draws attention to the importance of teachers listening to children's voices and perspectives. The catalyst of this trend has been the highly influential human rights charter, the United Nations Convention on the Rights of the Child (UNCRC) (UN, 1989) which recognizes the right of children to be heard and consulted on matters that affect them. Of relevance is Article 12 of the Convention, which states, as quoted in Chapter 1, that the child is capable of having views and has the right to state them and be given recognition for these views according to the age and maturity of the child.

This Article has had a significant impact on how early childhood professionals view the capacities of young children to independently express their ideas and understandings and to take an active role in their learning and development and to be recognized as "social actors in their own lives" (Page, 2000, p. 20). Intersecting and expanding upon Article 12 is Article 13, which endorses the importance of children having the opportunity to express their ideas in a variety of ways. It was also noted in Chapter 1 that the child has the right to "seek and impart information and ideas of all kinds" both orally and in written form or through art as the child's medium of communication.

Thus Articles 12, 13, and 14 (UN, 1989) recognize the rights of the child to participate freely in play, the arts, and the cultural life, acknowledging that opportunities and supports need to be provided.

The United Nation's General Comment No. 7 "Implementing child rights in early childhood" (UNCRC et al., 2006) provides further support for practices that acknowledge children as "persons in their own right … as active members of families, communities and societies, with their own concerns, interests and points of view" (p. 3). General Comment No. 7 also draws attention to the significance of adult and child relationships and the impact that they have on helping young children to make sense of the world they live in and to participate in that world and actively construct their lives. In the broadest sense the principles articulated in the UN Convention honour the right of children to a healthy, happy, and productive childhood that encompasses educational opportunity that supports the holistic development of the child's personality, abilities, and mental and physical talents to their fullest potential (UN, 1989: Article 29).

Embedded within the principles of the Convention is an image of the child as strong, competent, and capable and a social actor (UNCRC et al., 2006) in his or her own right who can articulate concerns, interests, and points of view (Clark & Moss, 2001). Such a view challenges traditional ideas that young children are too naive and immature to effectively contribute to decisions that are made about them or to be central protagonists in the learning process. This enlightened image of the child highlights the capacities of young children to construct valid meanings about the world and their place in it; a position that supports the notion of children as "active agents" who are capable of influencing and directing their own learning and making an impact on the environment (Limber & Flekkøy, 1995). It also affirms the significance of children's artistic explorations and expressions and specifically the many possibilities that are contained within the concept of children's art for public presentation. Many authors have commented that, when young children are given an opportunity to express their views, they develop a sense of autonomy and self-determination (Hatch et al., 2002; Lansdown, 2001; Lloyd-Smith & Tarr, 2000; Tobin, 2005), and from this perspective the presentation of children's thoughts and understandings as expressed through their art and narrative provide a powerful semiotic tool for the expression of voice.

The Code of Ethics of Early Childhood Australia (ECA, 2006), which was developed to inform and guide the professional behaviour and decision-making processes of all professionals involved in the provision of early childhood services to children aged between birth and 8t years of age, also endorses the principles advocated within the UN Convention (UN, 1989). It highlights the importance of learning that supports open-ended inquiry, focused engagement, ongoing development, and shows respect for children's capacities to self-direct their learning and to join with teachers and peers to take risks in communicating responses to the world in which they are living. Children's communications within the artistic domain demonstrate their abilities and capacities to not only grapple with complex world issues but also to be able to speak out about the physical, social, and cultural worlds they inhabit. Trevarthen (1998, p. 97) explains this phenomenon:

> Young children ... are adept at expressing communicable ideas by means of signs, gestures, postures, vocalizations that are situated in a negotiated context of inter-subjectivity – well before they can say words with their mother tongue. Their awareness of reality and learning is aesthetic, dramatic and moral because it is built through communication with the motives and emotions of other persons. Provided that they can maintain relationships of trust and understanding, there is no reason why this learning cannot be carried out with many persons outside the family, and groups of other children offer a particularly rich context for testing feelings and ideas.

From this discussion it is evident that young children display an inherent interest in creating and expressing through various modes and the recognition of this desire highlights artmaking as a fundamental aspect of human cognition. The ideas of Loris Malaguzzi (1997) shed further light on the young child's capacity to communicate through what have been metaphorically labelled "the hundred

Figure 4.1 In the future there will be flying cars.

languages of children". The highly acclaimed Reggio Emilia philosophy draws attention to the image of the child:

> who from the moment he is born, is so eager to be part of the world that he actively employs a complex (and still not fully appreciated) network of abilities, learning strategies, ways of organizing relationships, and creating maps for personal, interpersonal, social, cognitive, affective, and even symbolic orientation.
>
> (Malaguzzi, 1996, p. 10)

The Reggio Emilia philosophy incorporates the idea that young children communicate using many different languages for expressive communicative purposes. Children are acknowledged as having "a hundred ways of knowing, feeling and understanding" (Malaguzzi, 1996, p. 1) and it is through the utilization of graphic and performing arts that they build knowledge and concepts and find avenues to express emotions, feelings, and many other things that cannot be qualified through other means of communication.

Through both the enactive mode (representing thoughts through motor responses) and the iconic mode (graphically representing mental images through drawing and painting, children can represent both everyday experience and a range of "big ideas" (Perkins, 2014) such as creative problem solving for more sustainable future or even more abstract ideas such as the meaning of peace and harmony. Figure 4.1 shows children's ideas for *Flying cars in the future*.

Active Citizenship through Drawing, Painting, and Narrative

As previously noted, young children are naturally drawn to sensory-based explorations of their environment using a range of modalities including the cognitive, playful, expressive, communicative, relational, imaginative, and symbolic. As time passes, children become increasingly competent at linking symbolic representations with language and when this skill develops the child can competently reflect on and express personalized patterns of thinking.

With the support of adults, children can make meaningful and relational connections with a wide range of subject matter that includes speculation through symbols and spontaneous comment about their physical, social, and cultural worlds. Embedded within this concept is the image of child as active citizen who seeks a sense of belonging and demonstrates a willingness to be part of community through various participatory means. When provided with regular opportunities to spend time with others collaborating and communicating with peers, teachers, family, and community members, children learn to understand and trust the human person for its difference and its uniqueness and, more importantly, children are empowered to play an active part in community life.

During the early childhood years young children's thinking is flexible, imaginative, and linked to both a playful realm of fiction and to more serious concrete understandings about the world. Rogoff (1994) describes the active and meaningful participation of children and teachers in the learning process where the three-foci involvement of intrapersonal, interpersonal, and cultural-historical-institutional influences work together to support learning. She has termed this "a community of learners"; an approach that highlights the value of collaborative participation in shared experiences where each participant is valued for the knowledge, skills, and experience they bring.

Wright (2010, p. 10) speaks about future-conscious teachers who aim to:

> equip children to become autonomous and active creators of the future, through skills such as adaptability, imagination, fantasy, altruism, sensitivity towards others, decision making, empathy, an interest in other cultures and abilities in communication, problem solving and lateral thinking.

With this aspiration in mind meaning making through drawing and accompanying narration is a means by which children can achieve many of the values and practices cited above. It is well known that, when children are supported to engage in reflective thinking through these modes, children come to not only know that focus aids understanding, by bringing into play analysis, synthesis, and evaluation of experience. To reflect is to recall, review, and relate and, for the young child, having the opportunity to focus thinking about an experience can result in a deeper level of engagement in the learning process. Furthermore, drawing and narration have been noted widely (Burkitt et al., 2005; Docket & Perry, 2005; Wright, 2010, 2014) as activities that young children readily participate in to express their views, imaginative musings, and understandings of their personal worlds of experience.

Dewey (1934) described artmaking, or thinking in symbols, as one of the most sophisticated modes of thinking. It brings into play a creative process that enables the outpourings of personal experience, thought, and imaginative problem solving. This ability to capture a personally meaningful moment through graphic symbolization sheds light on the young child's focus, interests, intention, mood, and emotions (Matthews, 1994; Trevarthen, 1998; Wright, 2007a, 2007b, 2014), opening another window into the nature of the child's experience. Drawing when combined with verbal narration affords a mutually beneficial integration of thinking and feeling modalities. Cox (2005) notes that "talk and drawing interact with each other as parallel and equally transformative processes" (p. 123) work in tandem to help children crystallize their understandings.

Concluding Remarks

In summary, young children show an innate and courageous propensity to express themselves naturally and readily through the arts. Government policy and educational discourse acknowledge the importance of learning which has the capacity to provoke expressive meaning making. It highlights that it is through teaching and learning through the arts that children can attune and integrate their cognitive, physical, emotional, and social capacities and align their states of mind with life-worthy learning content (Perkins, 2014) that leads to deeper understandings of what it means to be a member of a democratic society where the social, cultural, and ethical insights of individuals are valued and celebrated.

Take Home Messages

- There is a strong relationship between play and artistic activity which is integral to children's early years development.
- Learning through discovery using different modes of symbolic representation is at the heart of children's multidimensional expressive communications (action-based, language-based, image-based).
- Children have an innate need to engage in creative activities to help them to come to understand more fully what it means to be human.
- Arts education (arts, thoughts, feelings, ideas, and imaginings) enables children to make meaning of the natural and built environment and the social world in which they live.
- Children are capable of having views on "big ideas" and have the right to state them and be given recognition for these views according to age and maturity of the child.

References

Abbs, P. (2003) *Against the flow: Education, the arts and postmodern culture*. London: Routledge Falmer.
ACARA *Australian Curriculum, Assessment and Reporting Authority* (2012). Retrieved March 2012, from www.acara.edu.au/default.asp.
Anning, A., Cullen, J. & Fleer, M. (2004). *Early childhood education: Society and culture*. London: Sage.

Bruner, J. (1996). *The culture of education.* Cambridge, MA, and London: Harvard University Press.
Burkitt, E., Barrett, M., & Davis, A. (2005). Drawings of emotionally characterized figures by children from different educational backgrounds [Electronic version]. *Journal of Art and Design Education. 24,* 71–83.
Cassirer, E. (1953). *Philosophy of symbolic forms.* New Haven, CT: Yale University Press.
Clark, A. & Moss, P. (2001). *Listening to young children: The mosaic approach.* London: National Children's Bureau Enterprises.
Conklin Thompson, S. (2005). *Children as illustrators: Making meaning through art and language.* Washington, DC: National Association for the Education of Young Children.
Connery, C., John-Steiner, V. P., & Marjanović -Shane, A. (Eds.) (2010). *Vygotsky and creativity: A cultural-historical approach to play, meaning making, and the arts.* New York: Peter Lang Publishing.
Cox, S. (2005). Intention and meaning in young children's drawing. *Journal of Art and Design Education, 24*(2), 115–125.
Dahlberg, G. & Moss, P. (2005). *Ethics and politics in early childhood education.* London: Routledge Falmer.
Danesi, M. (2020). *The quest for meaning: A guide to semiotic theory and practice.* 2nd Ed. Toronto: University of Toronto Press.
DEEWR Department of Education, Employment and Workplace (2009). *Belonging, being and becoming: The Early Years Learning Framework for Australia.* Canberra: Commonwealth Copyright Division.
Dewey, J. (1934). *Art as experience.* New York: Capricorn Books.
Docket, S. & Fleer, M. (1999). *Play and pedagogy in early childhood: Bending the rules.* Southbank, Victoria: Harcourt Brace.
Docket, S., & Perry, B. (2005). Children's drawings: Experiences and expectations of school [Electronic version]. *International Journal of Equity and Innovation in Early Childhood, 3*(2), 77–89.
Early Childhood Australia (2006). *Early Childhood Australia's code of ethics.* Canberra: Early Childhood Australia.
Edwards, C., Gandini, L., & Forman, G. (Eds.) (1998). *The hundred languages of children: The Reggio Emilia approach to early childhood education.* Westport, CT: Ablex.
Eisner, E. (2002). *The arts and the creation of the mind.* New Haven, CT: Yale University Press.
Gardner, H. (1983). *Frames of mind: The theory of multiple intelligences.* New York: Basic Books.
Goodman, N. (1976). *Languages of art: An approach to a theory of symbols.* Indianapolis, IN, and Cambridge: Hackett Publishing Co.
Hatch, J. A., Bowman, B., Jordan, J. J., Lopez Morgan, C., Diaz Soto, L., Lubeck, S., Hyson, M. (2002). Developmentally appropriate practice: Continuing their dialogue [Electronic version]. *Contemporary Issues in Early Childhood, 3*(3), 439–457.
Holmes, R., & Geiger, C. (2002). The relationship between creativity and cognitive abilities in preschoolers. In J. L. Roopnarine (Ed.), *Conceptual, social-cognitive, and contextual issues in the fields of play* (Vol. 4, pp. 127–148). Westport, CT: Ablex.
Innis, R. (Ed.). (1985). *Semiotics: An introductory anthology.* Bloomington, IN: Indiana University Press.
Kozulin, A., Gindis, B., Ageyev, V. S., & Miller, S. M. (Eds.). (2003). *Vygotsky's educational theory in cultural context.* Cambridge: Cambridge University Press. https://doi.org/10.1017/CBO9780511840975
Langer, S. K. (1953). Virtual powers. In *Feeling and form: A theory of art developed from philosophy in a new key* (pp. 169–187). New York: Charles Scribner's Sons.

Lansdown, G. (2001). *Promoting children's participation in democratic decision-making*. Florence: United Nations Children's Fund.
Limber, S. P., & Flekkøy M. G. (1995). The U.N. Convention on the Rights of the Child: Its relevance for social scientists. Social policy report. *Society for Research in Child Development, 9*(2), 1–15.
Lloyd-Smith, M., & Tarr, J. (2000). Researching children's experiences: A sociological perspective. In A. Lewis & G. Lindsay (Eds.), *Researching Children's Perspectives* (pp. 59–69). Buckingham: Open University Press.
Malaguzzi, L. (1996) The hundred languages of children: Narrative of the possible. *Catalogue of the "Hundred Languages of Children" Exhibition, Reggio Emilia*, Comune di Reggio Emilia, Italy.
Malaguzzi, L. (1997). The experiences of the municipal infant toddler centres and preschools of Reggio Emilia, International Winter Institute, 12–18 January, The Loris Malaguzzi International Center, Italy.
Maranović-Shane, A., & Beljanski-Ristic, L. (2008). From play to art–from experience to insight. *Mind, Culture and Activity, 15*, 93–114.
Matthews, J. (1994). *Helping children to draw and paint in early childhood*. London: Hodder & Stoughton.
Page, J. (2000). *Reframing the early childhood curriculum: Educational imperatives for the future*. London: Routledge Falmer.
Paley, V. (2005). *A child's work: The importance of fantasy play*. Chicago, IL: University of Chicago Press.
Perkins, D. (2014). *Future wise. Educating our children for a changing world*. San Francisco, CA: Jossey-Bass.
Piaget, J. (1953). *The origin of intelligence in children*. New York: International University Press.
Rinaldi, C. (2006). *In dialogue with Reggio Emilia: Listening, researching, and learning*. New York: Routledge.
Rogoff, B. (1994). Developing understanding of the idea of communities of learners. *Mind, Culture and Activity, 1*(4), 209–229.
Roopnarine, J. L, Lasker, J., Sacks, M., & Stores, M. (1998). The cultural context of children's play. In O. N. Saracho & B. Spodek (Eds.), *Multiple perspectives on play in early childhood education* (pp. 194–219). Albany, NY: State University of New York Press.
Roopnarine, J. L., Shin, M., Donovan, B., & Suppal, P. (2000). Sociocultural contexts of dramatic play: Implications for early education. In K. A. Roskos & J. F. Christie (Eds.), *Play and literacy in early childhood* (pp. 205–230). Mahwah, NJ: Lawrence Erlbaum.
Sansom, A. N. (2011). *Movement and dance in young children's lives: Crossing the divide*. New York: Peter Lang Publishing, Inc.
Slade, P. (1995). *Child play: Its importance for human development*. London: J. Kingsley Publishers.
Smith, A. B. (2002). Interpreting and supporting participation rights: Contributions from sociocultural theory. *International Journal of Children's Rights, 10*, 73–88.
Stinson, S. (1993) Dance for young children. Finding the magic in movement. Reston, VA: American Alliance for Health, Physical Education, Recreation and Dance.
Taylor, M. (1988). The development of children's understanding of the seeing–knowing distinction. In J. W. Astington, P. L. Harris, & D. R. Olson (Eds.), *Developing theories of mind* (pp. 207–225). New York: Cambridge University Press.

Tobin, J. (2005). A right to be no longer dismissed or ignored: Children's voices in pedagogy and policy making [Electronic version]. *International Journal of Equity and Innovation in Early Childhood, 3*(2), 4–18.

Trevarthen, C. (1998). The child's need to learn a culture. In M. Woodhead, D. Faulkner, & K Littleton (Eds.), *Cultural worlds of early childhood* (pp. 87–101). London: Routledge.

United Nations. (1989). *Convention on the Rights of the Child*. Geneva: Office of the United Nations High Commissioner of Human Rights.

UN Committee on the Rights of the Child, United Nations Children's Fund & Bernard van Leer Foundation. (2006). *A Guide to General Comment 7: 'Implementing Child Rights in Early Childhood'*. The Hague: Bernard van Leer Foundation.

Vygotsky, L. (1978). *Mind in society. The development of higher psychological processes.* Cambridge, MA: Harvard University Press.

Wright, S. (2007a). Graphic-narrative play: Young children's authoring through drawing and telling. *International Journal of Education and the Arts, 8*, 1–28.

Wright, S. (2007b). Young children's meaning-making through drawing and "telling": Analogies to filmic textual features. *Australian Journal of Early Childhood, 321(4)*, 37–48.

Wright, S. (2010). *Understanding creativity in early childhood meaning making and children's drawing.* Washington, DC: Sage.

Wright, S. (2014). The art of voice: The voice of art – understanding children's graphic-narrative-embodied communication. In D. Machin (Ed.), *Visual communication* (pp. 515–534). Frankfurt: DeGruyter.

Part II

5 Children Developing Empathy, Care, and Concern for the Environment

Education for Sustainable Development in the Early Years

Harriet Deans

Introduction

This chapter focuses on the relationship between children, the environment, and society and how Education for Sustainable Development can support children's growing prosocial skills such as empathy, care and concern for all living and non-living things. Examples of environmental and community-based practices are showcased in this chapter to illustrate the important role of the teacher in supporting children to step out, find out, and speak out about matters of environmental and societal concern.

Education for Sustainable Development (ESD) in the Early Years

The importance of teaching Education for Sustainable Development (ESD) in the early years has been recognized at local, national, and international levels (ACECQA, 2016; ACARA, 2020; UNESCO, 2020) and government guidelines and policy documents have endorsed ESD as a key priority area, recommending that environmental curriculum content be embedded into the teaching and learning of children in the early years (UNESCO, 2014). There has also been a growing interest in the design and implementation of curriculum guidelines and learning objectives that recognize and value ESD as a prominent area of study for young children, with a focus on learning that encompasses "stepping out, finding out and speaking out" (Deans & Deans, 2018, p. 88) about matters of environmental interest and concern. As noted by the United Nations (1992) education is central in promoting ESD, as it is seen as "critical for achieving environmental and ethical awareness, values and attitudes, skills and behavior consistent with sustainable development, and for effective public participation in decision-making" (Agenda 21, paragraph 36.3).

ESD in early childhood education has been informed by the growing understanding that children are in a stage of development where they establish the knowledge and skills associated with lifelong learning. Therefore, actively participating in their learning around issues relating to the environment and society leads to understandings of and actions taken for a sustainable future. ESD as a key element of quality early childhood education involves multiple

DOI: 10.4324/9781003213147-8

dimensions of learning, including those connected to the cognitive, socio-emotional, and behavioural domains (UNESCO, 2019). The transformative actions necessary for young children to build sustainable relationships with nature begin when these dimensions of learning are enacted at the experiential level. Here, ESD becomes "citizenship in action" (UNESCO, 2019, p. 5), a concept where children are seen to have a right to be involved in past, current, and future environmental realities, issues, and concerns (UNESCO, 2020).

Around the world, ESD has become a strong and central learning paradigm, and whole-of-school approaches to environmental and sustainability-oriented programs are becoming more prominent. ESD is viewed as a "cross-cutting topic in the school curriculum" (UNESCO, 2014, p. 88) and is an important framework to support children's lifelong learning skills, specifically connected to children's moral and ethical foundations (UNESCO, 2015, p. 37). Exposing children to real-world ESD experiences, ideas, and concepts, both inside and outside of the classroom, fosters prosocial, empathetic, caring, and respectful behaviours and attitudes, which are all necessary for children to become problem seekers, problem solvers, and action takers (Perkins 2014), connected to the realities of an ever-changing world.

Defining Education for Sustainable Development (ESD)

Education for Sustainable Development (ESD) is a lifelong learning process that focuses on a futures-oriented, holistic, and transformational cycle of learning (UNESCO, 2020), with particular attention paid to the care, protection, and restoration of environments, including all living and non-living things. A framework for teaching ESD in the early years connects to the Sustainable Development Goals (SDGs) (UNESCO, 2017). These goals integrate environmental, societal, cultural, and the economic content areas of study, with an aim to create a more ecologically and socially just world (AESA, 2014) through awareness-raising and action-taking practices. These central pillars of ESD connect to learning outcomes that focus on empowering children to become responsible global citizens and pedagogy and learning environments that are inquiry driven and learner focused and, which value first-hand experiential learning. ESD is connected and related to several educational terms including environmental education, education for sustainability, climate education, global citizenship, and peace education, all of which value learning around real-world, big ideas.

Ecocentric Curriculum within an Education for Sustainable Development (ESD) Framework

It is in the early years when children develop the skills, attitudes, and knowledge that they will take with them into later life. Therefore, early childhood education has an important role to play in embedding values that foster a positive relationship with natural and built worlds. ESD, being a significant overarching learning paradigm in the early years, supports children's holistic development, including the cognitive, socio-emotional, and behavioural domains. The curriculum design behind ESD empowers children to make informed and important decisions around environmental and societal protection, restoration, and preservation and, through this process, aims to equip children to become global citizens. Additionally, the learning outcomes of ESD in the early years include "core competencies such as critical and systemic thinking, collaborative decision-making, and taking responsibility for the actions of present and future generations" (UNESCO, 2019).

Although it is recognized that learning in, about, for, and from the environment (Palmer, 1998) is highly significant in supporting the aims of ESD and children's overall growth and development, recent literature states that exploration in the natural world has become less common, and now requires thoughtful planning by teachers in the early years (O'Brien, 2009; Warden, 2010) *to step out* of the classroom. Figure 5.1 presents an Ecocentric Curriculum

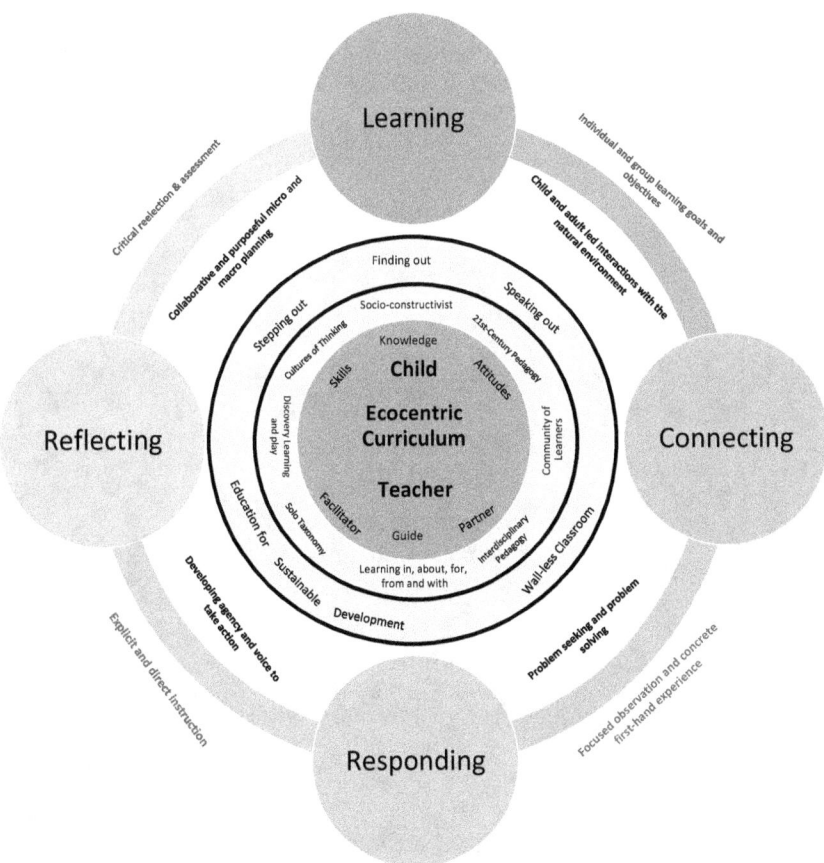

Figure 5.1 Ecocentric curriculum.

that conceptualizes ESD in the early years, highlighting the important relationship between the child and the teacher, the guiding pedagogy, context, and objectives relative to the creation of a Wall-less Classroom and Stepping Out Program. This cycle includes the process of connecting, responding, reflecting, and learning in the natural environment and local community; that leads to the overall growth in children's knowledge, awareness, and action.

The Wall-less Classroom

The Ecocentric Curriculum highlights the important role of the teacher in creating a "Wall-less Classroom" that takes children outside of the preschool environment to interact first-hand with the natural earth elements and urban landscape and, in doing so, extending the children's current understandings and knowledge of the natural and built worlds (Figure 5.2). The Wall-less Classroom creates a synergy between the indoor and outdoor learning environments and includes pedagogy, goals and objectives, experience, and learning; all of which align with the process of ESD. The Wall-less Classroom also draws attention to the importance of embedding ESD into a whole-of-school approach, leading to the overall process of stepping out, finding out, and speaking out (Deans & Deans, 2018).

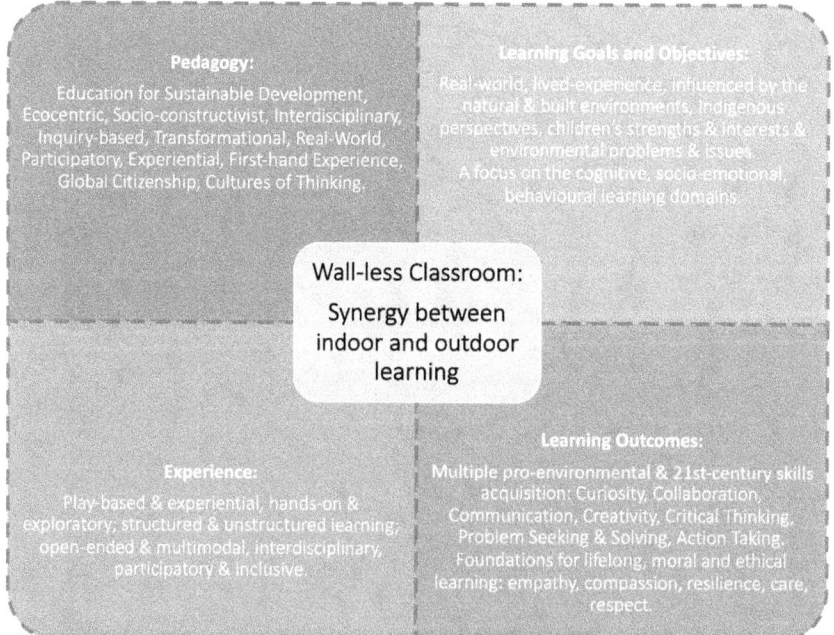

Figure 5.2 Wall-less classroom.

The Role of the Teacher in Enacting the Principles of ESD

The role of the early childhood teacher to guide and facilitate learning in an ESD curriculum is critical in ensuring that children are encouraged as future citizens to take individual and collective participatory action in social and environmental change. Teaching for sustainability includes pedagogical approaches connected to ESD, socio-constructivist theory (Vygotsky, 1978), interdisciplinary and transformational learning, inquiry and participatory learning, and real-world and global citizenship education. The value of these approaches allows children to contribute more effectively to a sustainable world and what it means to be an active agent of change in the community. Within this context, teachers have a key role to play in the design, implementation, enactment, and evaluation of ESD curricula and therefore an important position in developing programs that are:

- Influenced by the natural and built environments, First Nations perspectives, and children's strengths and interests (cognitive, socio-emotional, and behavioural domains).
- Play-based and experiential, hands-on and exploratory, structured and unstructured, open-ended and multimodal, and participatory and inclusive.
- Supporting learning outcomes of multiple pro-environmental 21st-century skill acquisition including curiosity, collaboration, communication, creativity, critical thinking, problem solving, and action taking.

The co-construction of knowledge within ESD supports flexible relationships between children and their peers, children and their teachers, teachers and their colleagues, children and their families, and teachers and families. The role of the teacher is to first build an understanding of what it means to embed ESD in the early years and how to best enact the principles behind ESD and Ecocentric Curriculums in their context. Secondly, teachers are required to support children to step out and actively participate in the natural local environment and to construct knowledge and behaviours of care and appreciation for the natural world. The third step relies on the teacher facilitating and guiding peer-to-peer interactions in the natural environment and to empower children to collaboratively research and find out about the natural world. The final step involves exercising the children's agency to speak out and enact change in relation to a range of issues related to sustainability. This includes the transfer of knowledge into the children's families and broader community. The following stages require learning of ESD both inside and outside of the classroom, with teachers bringing intentionality and purpose to their planning, teaching strategies, and experiences (Figure 5.3). This ensures ESD is appropriately embedded into the whole-of-school curriculum and supports a holistic and transformational approach to teaching and learning, inevitably creating the Wall-less Classroom.

72 Part II

Figure 5.3 Role of the teacher.

The above process involves several additional stages that are completed by the teacher in consultation with children, colleagues, local environmental community members, and draws on government/policy documents including:

- Developing a whole-of-school approach and framework of ESD.
- Designing a Wall-less Classroom underpinned by an Ecocentric Curriculum and learning objectives (Table 5.1) supported by ESD and connected to the SDGs; the local social and environmental context; children's learning domains and the areas prescribed in government early learning frameworks (Victorian Early Learning and Development Framework). Wall-less classroom learning objectives are enacted in both the indoor and outdoor environments (Classroom and Stepping Out Programs).
- Designing a Stepping Out Program guided by the Ecocentric Curriculum including documentation related to long-term goals and learning intentions, weekly teaching and learning experiences, curriculum evaluations, designing for future learning opportunities, specific locations, and risk.

ESD Wall-less Classroom Curriculum and Learning Objectives

Integrating an ESD Wall-less Classroom curriculum into the early years takes careful consideration and planning by teachers and curriculum makers. A Wall-less Classroom curriculum is a comprehensive learning system that focuses on learning in, about, for, from, and with the environment and society, while connecting to specific SDGs; the cognitive, socio-emotional, and behavioural domains of learning; learning outcomes connected to a chosen early years framework and guiding questions and learning outcomes to assess and support children's thinking and doing. With the characteristics of the 21st-century child also in mind, a multiplicity of modes for teaching and learning are employed,

Table 5.1 Example of wall-less classroom curriculum

Learning Outcome (connected to SDGs)	Guiding Questions	Learning Objectives For the children to:
Identity SDG 3: Good Health and Wellbeing SDG 4: Quality Education SDG 5: Gender Equality SDG 16: Peace, Justice, and Strong Institutions	How do I learn? Where do I learn best? What makes me feel confident, peaceful, focused? How do I feel empowered and included?	- Engage in group singing (example songs: *Love for the Green Earth, We've Got the Whole World in Our Hands, The River is Flowing, Hurt No Living Thing*) and "acknowledgement of country'" - Show empathy towards each other and the environment through eco-card making and letter writing *(provocation: Children's Book – Dear Earth)*. - Engage in small group dramatic play experiences with native animal soft puppet, to develop awareness of protection for animals and all living things (learn to show empathy and inclusive practices). - Explore Indigenous stories *(provocation: Children's Book – Respect/Welcome to Country)* to foster children's understanding of identity, respect, belonging, empathy, connection, care for the environment.
Community SDG 3: Good Health and Wellbeing SDG 6: Clean Water and Sanitation SDG 16: Peace, Justice, and Strong Institutions SDG 17: Partnerships for the Goals	What is community? What matters to you? What is environment? How do you show respect and care and empathy? What is your hope for the future?	- Share stories from home that connect to the natural environment (bird sightings, plant identification, patterns in nature, changes in weather, bike/active transport). - Become aware of the power of collaboration and the metaphor "Ripple Effect": create an installation and experiment with creating ripples in river/water to represent the global ripple effect and how one idea can influence many and create change. - Define eco-words: "community", "empathy", "care", "respect", "cooperation", and "environment" and discuss examples from the children''s lived experience. - Engage in the global movement connected to the Climate Crisis *(provocation: Children's Book: Greta and the Giants)* and create action posters connected to observations made during the Stepping Out Program. - Identify and explore the characteristics of the 7 seasons of the Kulin nation through story and outdoor observation. - List the birds of the local river environment and create a short story/poem to understand the importance of preserving their habitat.

(continued)

Table 5.1 Cont.

Learning Outcome (connected to SDGs)	Guiding Questions	Learning Objectives For the children to:
Wellbeing SDG 3: Good Health and Wellbeing SDG 16: Peace, Justice, and Strong Institutions	How do I feel? What do feelings look like? How can I manage my emotions? What makes me feel happy/angry/calm etc?	- Engage in choir experiences, dance specialist classes, and feelings role play scenarios that support combined gross and fine motor development. - Recognize and identify feelings in self, other, living, and non-living things and list language (calm, angry, sad, happy, joyous, surprised, peaceful, etc.) and strategies for different feelings (e.g. smelling a flower, looking at clouds, taking a deep breath, dancing). - Explore colour mixing to create shades of green and the feelings/emotions or natural experiences associated with each colour. Paint a green patchwork painting representing the environment. - Use clay and natural materials to create patterns and symbols that represent care and respect for the natural environment. - Understand the importance of plant health for human health through researching, growing, and nurturing native plant species and how to protect them.
Learning SDG 3: Good Health and Wellbeing SDG 6: Clean Water and Sanitation SDG 11: Sustainable Cities and Communities	What can I discover? How can I find out? What is research? How do I engage actively in projects?	- Engage in group-time verbal and non-verbal experiences: Indigenous culture and history connected to seasons, community, storytelling; Feelings/Emotions Exploration; Eco-word exploration: Ripple Effect; Dear Earth Letters and Cards; Climate Crisis Action Statements; Birds of the River; See, Think, Wonder Thinking Routine. - Engage in fine-motor experiences: Ripple artworks, Dear Earth cards and letters; Climate Crisis Action Words and Drawings, Clay Symbols. - Science experiences: research, observe and photograph native plant growth (hypothesising and measuring the diverse growth of the seedlings; list animals that might live in them); track changes in seasons; create an emotional barometer; colour mixing shades of green at the easel that connect to the environment. - Mathematics experiences: ripples (counting, size); tree growth (measuring), bird identification (counting, mapping).

Table 5.1 Cont.

Learning Outcome (connected to SDGs)	Guiding Questions	Learning Objectives For the children to:
Communication SDG 5: Gender Equality SDG 11: Sustainable Cities and Communities SDG 13: Climate Action	*How can I actively listen and respond to others? How can I share my ideas? How can my ideas create change?*	- Actively participate in group discussions (see Learning) and Singing (see Identity). - Engage verbally and non-verbally in science, mathematical and literacy experiences (Indigenous culture and history connected to seasons, community, storytelling; Feelings/Emotions Exploration; Eco-word exploration: Ripple Effect; Dear Earth Letters and Cards; Climate Crisis Action Statements; Birds of the River; See, Think, Wonder Thinking Routine; Mind-mapping. - Engage in pretend play to explore feelings and expressing emotions.
Sustainability SDG 7: Affordable and Clean Energy SDG 11: Sustainable Cities and Communities SDG 12: Responsible Consumption and Production SDG 13: Climate Action	*What do I see, think, wonder? How can I care for the environment? What can I change to reduce my impact?*	- Actively participate in the Stepping Out Program; being aware of the goals and responsibilities during the program – connect to the Journals/Thinking Routines/ Drawing-Tellings; collect natural materials to show the diversity found in nature and to create symbols for caring for the environment (COPE-R). - Develop children's eco-literacy: "caring for the environment" and moving to "action statements for the environment" – who/what/why/ how? (Climate Crisis). - Research, observe and photograph native plant growth (hypothesizing and measuring the diverse growth of the seedlings; list animals that might live in them). - Share stories of eco-living from home (e.g. growing plants, riding bikes, recycling, etc.). - "Green" the outdoor Dolls House using recycled collage materials/ drawings to create green walls of native plants, solar panels, water tanks, and insect hotels.

(continued)

Table 5.1 Cont.

Learning Outcome (connected to SDGs)	Guiding Questions	Learning Objectives For the children to:
The Arts SDG 4: Quality Education SDG 11: Sustainable Cities and Communities SDG 13: Climate Action SDG 15: Life on Land	How can I express my understanding? What materials can I use to share my ideas?	- Engage in group singing (example songs: *Love for the Green Earth, We've Got the Whole World in Our Hands, The River is Flowing, Hurt No Living Thing*) and "acknowledgement of country". - Explore painting at the easel: exploring "Greening", interest led painting and colour mixing representative of different shades of green. - Engage in singing and movement experiences (dance, yoga, and music) that connect to curriculum and individual interests. - Explore video experiences connected to the climate crisis (e.g. plastic cleanup, school strike, animal conservation) and complete drawing-tellings. - Observe the season changes in the natural environment and take photographs of interesting characteristics identified (Stepping Out Program). - Create action posters/signs connected to individual Climate Crisis ideas. - Design eco symbols using clay as natural materials.
Outdoors SDG 7: Affordable and Clean Energy SDG 11: Sustainable Cities and Communities	How can I explore freely? How can I be visible? How can I move my body?	- Explore the garden and create a drawing that reconceptualise the garden to represent a Native Plant Garden. - Observe the changes in season in the natural environment and take photographs of interesting characteristics identified. - Explore light and shadow in the environment and observe the body and its form in the outdoors. - Use chalk to create eco symbols and messages of care and respect for the environment on the pavement (Climate Crisis). - Research, observe, and photograph native plant growth (hypothesizing and measuring the diverse growth of the seedlings; list animals that might live in them). - "Green" the outdoor Dolls House using recycled collage materials/drawings to create green walls of native plants, solar panels, water tanks, and insect hotels.

including visual, audio, gestural, tactile, and spatial. Through this design, children can actively participate in their learning with the aim to develop a deeper understanding of earth's systems, connection to the natural world, and the skills necessary for a sustainable frame of mind.

Designing and Implementing a Stepping Out Program

Program Outline

The University of Melbourne Early Learning Centre's Stepping Out Program is a unique program that has been designed and implemented for children aged 3–5 years, aiming to put into action an Ecocentric Curriculum, while also creating a Wall-less Classroom that responds to the educational aims of ESD outlined thus far. The Stepping Out Program is offered as part of the mainstream kindergarten program on two mornings per week (9.30 am to 12 pm) throughout Term 1, Term 2, Term 3, Term 4. The children and their teachers venture into the immediate local environment (located near a River, Natural Bushland, Waterfall, Historic Convent, and Urban Farm) to explore a range of both preplanned and spontaneous interdisciplinary learning experiences within the natural environment that encompasses Education for Sustainable Development, Climate Education, Indigenous Studies, Science: Biology, Geology, Geography; Mathematics; Literacy; the Arts; Engineering and Design; and the inclusion of Digital Technologies.

Long-Term Goals

The long-term goals of the Stepping Out Program demonstrate the overarching objectives and aims of the program over a year of teaching and learning. The aim is for the children to:

- Develop an understanding of the significance and importance of the local natural environment for the traditional owners of the land, the Wurundjeri people.
- Engage in experiential, hands-on, open-ended, discovery learning (Dewey, 1938) and play in a wide range of environments, such as parkland, bushland, grassland, riverbanks, fallen logs, and leafy treed spaces.
- Actively participate in interdisciplinary (mathematics, literacy, science, humanities, the arts, information and communication technologies) learning focusing on linking knowledge schemas (Splitter & Sharp, 1995; Waller, 2007) and supporting individual interests and habits of mind (Costa & Kallick, 2000).
- Engage in individual and collaborative focused observation, problem solving, decision-making, and critical reflection about points of individual and group interest in the environment (Davis, 2015; Scott, 2015).

- Engage in a range of physical experiences to support the building of personal strengths, confidence, and resilience in negotiating challenges in the natural world, including uneven terrain, steep inclines, and rock formations and logs (Kahn & Kellert, 2002; Kaplan & Talbot, 1983).
- Develop a set of values connected to nature (Kellert, 2002), including enacting respectful and caring behaviours towards the environment, following the "Seven Principles of Leave No Trace" (Wynne & Gorman, 2015) and communicating thoughts and ideas about identifying and problem-solving environmental problems (Palmer, 1998; Perkins, 2014) (Deans & Deans, 2018, p. 80).

Learning Intentions

On a term and weekly basis, purposefully designed and preplanned learning intentions were generated as a way of including child voice, big ideas (Perkins, 2014), and contextual topics. The weekly learning intentions respond directly to the interests of the children, changes in the natural environment, or specific local, national, or global initiatives. Examples of the diverse learning content during the Stepping Out Program include for the children to notice changes over time in the local environment through seasonal changes (Seven Seasons of Kulin Nation); develop knowledge of local flora and fauna; and become aware of human impact on the environment. The learning intentions are integrated into the Wall-less Classroom curriculum highlighted earlier in Table 5.1.

Stepping Out Program and the ESD Learning Domains

The ESD curriculum encourages teachers to connect to diverse pedagogies and approaches that are learner-centred, teacher-facilitated, and collaborative in nature. As noted by UNESCO (2012b) "ESD is expected to flourish when teachers use innovative pedagogical practices" (p. 86) which create curriculum that is sustainability-related, with flexible application and commitment by the teacher and the children to achieve learning outcomes. Learning domains specific to ESD in the early years include the cognitive, socio-emotional, and behavioural, all of which are comprised of specific objectives that lead to a child's holistic development. Children have diverse levels of knowledge and understanding between the age of 3 to 5 years and analyse and interpret information at different rates. As their development progresses, children begin to memorize details of the natural world that are necessary and relevant to their holistic growth and development in the cognitive, socio-emotional, and behavioural domains. Framing the children's learning to align with set objectives (Table 5.2) supports the child to communicate and process ideas in a systematic manner, moving through a range of educational objectives that are explicit, clear, and methodical in nature. Planning for set objectives within an ESD curriculum creates a student-oriented, learning-based, assessable outcome-focused

Table 5.2 Key indicators for ESD learning domains 3–5 Years

ESD Learning Domain	Cognitive	Socio-Emotional	Behavioural
3–4 years	Emerging pro environmental knowledge and understandings: label, list, explain & discuss	Emerging environmental values and awareness: listen, focus & feel	Emerging environmental actions & participation: follow, replicate, repeat
4–5 years	Established environmental knowledge and understandings: apply, discover, create & investigate	Established environmental values and awareness: respond, justify, solve	Established environmental actions & participation: re-create, implement, design & invent

framework where the teacher can observe and document the students learning (Anderson & Krathwohl, 2001).

To support the children's growth in the cognitive, socio-emotional, and behavioural learning domains, weekly experiences are prearranged to put into practice the Stepping Out Program long-term goals and learning intentions. The weekly teaching and learning experiences during the Stepping Out Program include for the children to:

- Participate in individual and/or collaborative drawing-tellings and journaling.
- Participate in dialogues with teachers and peers guided by thinking routines.
- Participate in mind-mapping discussions about the natural and built world, including identifying the features of the river, flora, and fauna and human-made structures.
- Photograph the natural environment/be photographed in the natural environment to inform the weekly photo collection and for subsequent reflective drawing/discussions in the classroom.
- Interpret the world around them through their five senses – hearing, sight, smell, taste, and touch.
- Engage in free, unstructured play and exploration in the local natural and built environments.
- Participate in expressive artmaking experiences (music, dance, painting, drama).

ESD and the Cognitive Domain

Providing children with opportunities to connect to the real world through an experiential and inquiry mode of teaching and learning (Dewey, 1938) gives children the "opportunity to plan and direct their own learning experience and pursue their own research interests" (Huchinson, 1998, p. 41). The notion of the teacher as facilitator is an important element in supporting children's cognitive capacities when connecting to ESD curriculum both inside and outside of the classroom. In the cognitive domain, children are supported to recognize and recall knowledge, which is built upon through a variety of interactions, experiences, and processes. The cognitive learning domain focuses on the formation of children's thinking, understanding, and knowledge skills and how children can better understand the environment and society. The interdisciplinary nature of teaching ESD in the early years emphasizes the process of learning as a two-way interaction between:

- the child and the environment,
- child and the curriculum,
- child and their peers, and/or
- child and their teacher.

Children aged 3–4 years are developing their emerging environmental understandings and knowledge, including their ability to list, label, explain, and discuss the features around them. This age group benefits from diverse sensory experiences, choice, open-ended questioning, focused prompts, and a clear guide during the Stepping Out Program. As the child matures to the age of 4–5 years, an established knowledge base and understanding of the environment has occurred, with children able to apply, discover, create, and investigate (Anderson & Krathwohl, 2001) matters of environmental importance and interest or concern. Children in this age group are beginning to understand the difference between the real and imagined; lead discussions; and apply previous knowledge to build new understandings (Figure 5.4).

ESD and the Socio-Emotional Domain

The socio-emotional domain includes the development of "skills that enable learners to collaborate, negotiate and communicate" (UNESCO, 2017, p. 11). The Stepping Out Program provides children with opportunities to build relationships, prosocial behaviours and attitudes, and behaviours that develop the self, an awareness of others, and the environment. Children's emerging growth in this area is fostered by periods of body stillness and balance, silent listening, deep discussions, shared conversations, thoughtful exploration, and quiet observation and noticing. Through collaborative experiences and consistent routines such as journal and walking partners, individual, small, and large group experiences, and one-on-one teacher–child engagement, children establish listening, thinking, and reasoning skills that are consistent with the socio-emotional domain. An ESD and Stepping Out curriculum encourages children to navigate different environments independently and with autonomy, and in turn builds their resilience and ability to cope

Figure 5.4 Cognitive learning domain photo examples.

throughout times of challenge. It is in this space where children mature their sense of awareness, response, value, and empathy towards each other and the environment and are observed developing their ability to actively participate, consider other points of view, take a personal position, and influence others with their growing knowledge of the world around them. In the 3–4-year-old age group children's emerging environmental values and awareness are developing and they are beginning to listen, focus, and feel during their time in the natural world, demonstrating a developing understanding of their role in the natural world and community. As the young child progresses through their development as a 4–5-year-old they demonstrate an established set of environmental values and awareness and an ability to respond, justify, solve processes and problems in the natural world and community. Examples of interactions with the natural environment in the socio-emotional domain include group experiences incorporating the five senses, mindful exploration, activities that support verbal and non-verbal development, and prosocial modelling while in the natural world (Figure 5.5).

82 Part II

Figure 5.5 Socio-emotional learning domain photo examples.

ESD and the Behavioural Domain

An ESD framed curriculum engages children in experiences that develop their action competencies, which are directly connected to the behavioural domain of learning. During the Stepping Out Program children are offered unlimited invitations to freely explore, critically observe and problem solve, and engage in multiple experiences that lead to a culture of individual and collaborative participation. The children spend time in dramatic and imaginative play experiences that develop their ability to reason, problem solve, negotiate, and communicate, all skills necessary for active citizenship (Figure 5.6). Further, the learner in the behavioural domain is beginning to plan, introduce, evaluate, and replicate activities that are related to the environment and the knowledge and attitudes they have developed within all three learning domains. Children between the ages of 3–5 years demonstrate emerging environmental action taking and participation, where they are observed to follow, replicate, repeat. As they develop into a 4–5-year-old, children present with an established awareness of environmental actions and participation, showing they ability to recreate, implement, design, and invent in scenarios connected to the environment and community.

Figure 5.6 Behavioural learning domain photo examples.

Children in both age groups are observed engaging in the natural environment and community with purpose and influence, repeating pro-environmental actions including nature exploration, hands-on participation, independent research, and eco skill development. To summarize or extend on the children's experience in the behavioural domain, the teacher forms reflections or plans for additional learning experiences that continue to progress children's abilities,

Table 5.3 Examples of children's learning during the Stepping Out Program in the cognitive, socio-emotional, and behavioural learning domains

---

Cognitive Learning Domain
- The child knows about water: where it comes from, where it goes, how it is used, its importance, and the cause and effect of pollution.
- The child understands human impact and the changing climate.
- The child understands how their choices can influence their level of impact on the natural environment.
- The child can understand the connection people have with the environment.
- The child can understand and identify the treats to biodiversity in local and global environments.
- The child can identify the characteristics of the local environment, including flora and fauna, geography, and biodiversity.
- The child can identify sustainable planning and building in the environment and community.

Socio-Emotional Learning Domain
- The child can identify their feelings, values, attitudes, and behaviours in response to the natural environment and their place in society (including empathy, care, respect, trust).
- The child demonstrates an ability to actively engage with their learning.
- The child can cooperate and collaborate with others to support further learning in ESD.
- The child can connect with the natural environment and local community and understand how-to live-in harmony with the natural world.
- The child understands that the natural environment is central to their sense of identity, wellbeing, and belonging.
- The child feels responsible for their environmental and social impacts.
- The child can influence others to engage in sustainable practices for the protection of the climate.

Behavioural Learning Domain
- The child can become an agent of environmental change at local and global levels.
- The child demonstrates their ability to collaborate with others to assess issues of environmental and societal concern.
- The child can effectively voice their opinions of environmental and societal concern.
- The child actively participates in research, discussions, and debates of environmental and societal concern.
- The child engages in climate-related discussions with questions, ideas, and actions.
- The child thinks of ways to reduce individual and collective impact in their everyday life and living.
- The child can design for sustainable, resilient environments and communities.
- The child recognizes that their voice matters, can create change, and influence others.

with a focus on equipping children with the skills necessary to achieve environmental stewardship and global citizenship.

Examples of the children's learning during the Stepping Out Program in the cognitive, social-emotional, and behavioural domains is presented in Table 5.3. Children require uninterrupted and regular periods of time in the natural world to develop their dispositions for learning (Carr, 2001; Claxton & Carr, 2004) and when this is supported children are observed taking an interest and being involved in the experience; gaining confidence to express a point of view, feeling, or behaviour; persisting with difficulty or uncertainty when in the environment and taking responsibility for thinking and action taking. Acknowledging children's voice is a focus within all ESD learning domains, with the development of a broad skill set that enables children to become active and informed citizens, able to explore their world as problem seekers, problem solvers, and action takers (Perkins, 2014).

Teaching and Learning in the Cognitive, Socio-Emotional and Behavioural Learning Domains

Experiences such as drawing-tellings (Wright, 2007a, b), journaling (Smith & Knapp, 2010), thinking routines (Ritchhart et al., 2011), mind-mapping, and teacher documentation are consistent and regular parts of the Stepping Out Program. These specific approaches further support children to become aware of their surroundings, specifically the natural and built worlds and the complex systems that exist within the environment and society. The child's voice and sense of agency are considered throughout the above strategies and connect to all three (cognitive, socio-emotional, and behavioural) learning domains. Assessment tools presented below allow the teacher to determine what level the child is performing at during the Stepping Out Program, where to take them to next, or how their individual learning style or interests could be integrated.

Tools for Teaching across the Learning Domains

Drawing-Tellings

The drawing-telling approach (Wright, 2007a, b) aims to engage children in a verbal and non-verbal reflective experience following their time on the Stepping Out Program. The children are provided with a clipboard, piece of A4 white paper, and a fine-line black pen and are asked to draw something they remember from their experience. The children are offered uninterrupted time to locate their thoughts, ideas, imaginings from their lived experience and time spent in the natural world. A one-on-one teacher–child period is offered to each child to document the narrative connected to their mark making and to acknowledge the children's voice and experience during the Stepping Out Program. The drawing-tellings are collected following their completion and are revisited with the teacher either as a group or individually and operate as

86 Part II

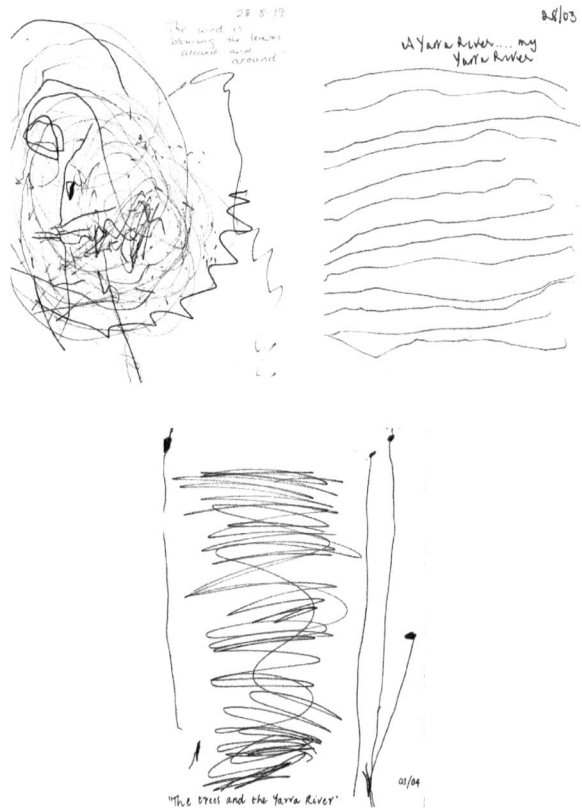

Figure 5.7 3-year-old drawing-tellings.

both formative and summative assessment pieces, enabling children to revisit their learning or project new learning. Consistent collections of drawing-tellings provide a clear insight into ESD and the Stepping Out Program and its power to "stimulate deep and abstract thinking, creative use of language, critical thinking, problem solving and personal agency" (Deans & Deans, 2018, p. 85). The drawing-telling experience is child-centred and inquiry-led, with the child independently representing their learning through non-verbal and oral symbolic meaning making and representation. Figures 5.7 and 5.8 present the drawing-telling experience for 3–4 and 4–5-year-old children.

Journaling

Journaling takes a scientific, research-based, and cooperative approach to the documentation of the children's ideas during or following the Stepping Out Program (Figure 5.9). The children are paired and provided with A5 journals, black fine-line pens and are asked to draw and describe their experience, a natural found

Figure 5.8 4-year-old drawing-tellings.

Figure 5.9 Journaling in pairs.

object, photos, or research content from the iPad, a memory, or vision. Similar to the drawing-telling process, children's words are collected by the teacher to gain an understanding of the children's thinking, with the teacher offering purposeful pausing and open-ended questioning throughout the experience. The process of journaling for young children engages the child through a scientific lens, providing them with a place to document their observations, investigations, and discoveries. The collaborative experience of journaling also offers time for peer-to-peer scaffolding, discussions, feedback, and relationship building and is a time when children can acknowledge and celebrate their experience in the natural world. Revisiting the journals during group time experiences also reinforces children's learning and supports further development in relation to children's "content knowledge, critical thinking and environmental stewardship" (Deans & Deans, 2018). The systematic collection of children's drawings and narratives in the form of journaling aims to show individual children's growth throughout

Figure 5.10 3-year-old journaling examples.

Empathy, Care, and Concern for the Environment 89

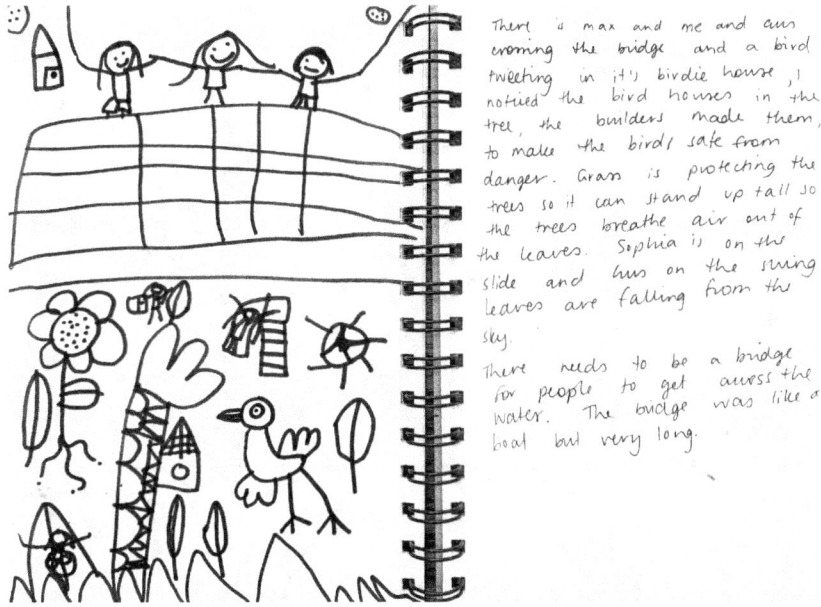

Figure 5.11 4-year-old journaling examples.

the program and is a powerful experience for the children, gaining awareness of their cognitive potential and voice. Figures 5.10 and 5.11 present the drawing-telling experience for 3–4 and 4–5-year-old children.

Thinking Routines

To gain further insight into the children's learning in the ESD cognitive domain, additional tools such as the thinking routine, "See, Think, Wonder" (Ritchhart et al., 2011) are utilized (Figure 5.12). The one-on-one teacher–child experience of the thinking routine, employed both inside and outside of the classroom, captures the children's level of vocabulary; ability to observe and notice; and capacity to wonder and imagine. Within the context of ESD, thinking routines have a significant role to play in gathering children's knowledge and understanding of the environment, their developing attitudes and behaviours, and growing ability to apply their experience to create solutions of environmental care and respect. This tool of learning and assessment also provides children with the skills necessary for effective verbal and non-verbal communication (listening, confidence, understanding, and performing) and self-assessment (cognition, critical thinking, and questioning). Completing the thinking routines in situ during the Stepping Out Program provides an accurate insight into the children's level of participation, knowledge, and reflective capacities. In the classroom, photographs are used to further prompt the child to remember and recall information. Both experiences are valuable tools for documentation and assessment.

Figure 5.11 (cont.)

Empathy, Care, and Concern for the Environment 91

This is a caterpillar and a chrysalis. I want to remember what I saw. I saw a bird in the sky with its friend. I found a little branch in the river. on top I saw a greysky. I like a rainy day. It's impressive.
3/5/21

Figure 5.11 (cont.)

92 Part II

Term 3

Learning in Nature Program: 'See Think Wonder' Thinking Routine

Birrarung

I see... the blue in the Yarra River, the sky, it's the reflection, it goes onto the river and makes it shiny and the sky goes onto the reflection and when it is really shiny it is a mirror.
I think... the Birrarung is beautiful because people come and look at it and they see ducklings, platypus and birds flying above, and trees blowing in the wind and canoeing people.
I wonder... who lives at the bottom of the river.

Figure 5.12 Thinking routines "See, Think, Wonder".

Empathy, Care, and Concern for the Environment 93

Term 3

Learning in Nature Program: 'See Think Wonder' Thinking Routine

Birrarung

I see... ripples, trees, the Yarra River, the sky, the clouds, sun, roots of the trees, leaves of the trees, reflections of the trees.

I think... I want to send a message with the words in my mouth, "the yarra river is beautiful." "the sky reflecting in the yarra river." "I feel happy."

I wonder... if a water always reflects like a mirror.
if the yarra river is drawing with the ripples.

Figure 5.12 (cont.)

Mind-Mapping

Group time experiences, such as mind-mapping (Figure 5.13), gather children's ideas and understandings that are connected to learning in, about, for, from, and with the natural world (Palmer, 1998). The mind-mapping experience occurs at either the pre- and post-program stage, on a weekly, monthly, or term basis.

94 Part II

Figure 5.13 Mind-mapping children's ideas captured by ELC teachers.

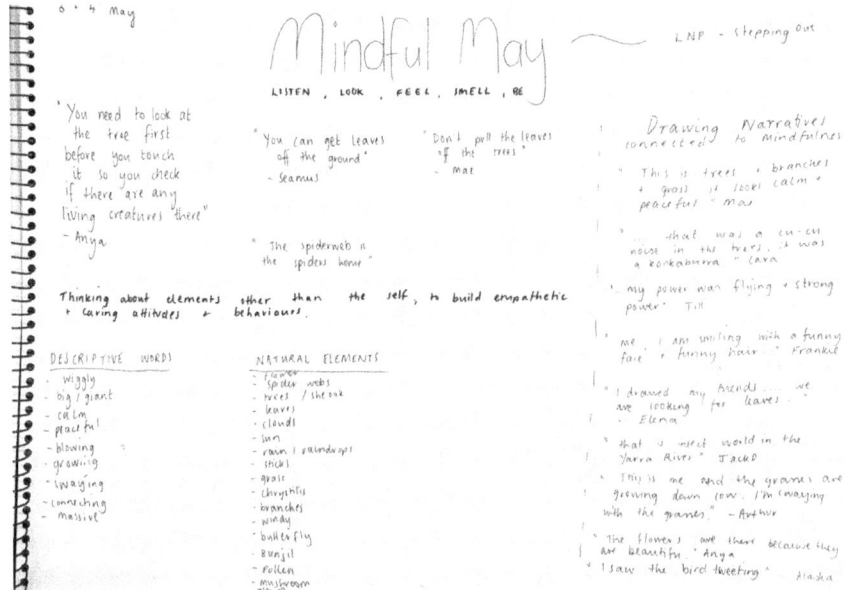

Figure 5.14 Teacher documentation: children's narratives and descriptive words.

A "big idea" or topic is employed as a central theme and is used to prompt children's thoughts; this includes listing, describing, applying, explaining, and creating knowledge. The mind-mapping process encourages the children to share descriptive vocabulary, make connections, reflect on experiences, and observe how big ideas form new and future learning or action taking.

Teacher Documentation

The Stepping Out Program prompts teachers to think about what to teach, how to teach, and how to assess learning in the natural environment. Figure 5.14 presents an example of the systematic and reflective capacities of the teacher in collecting, sorting, and presenting children's ideas, knowledge, reflections, and actions for further discussion and learning opportunities.

Concluding Remarks

This chapter provides an overview of the importance of ESD in the early years to foster a stronger sense of identity in children to see themselves as stewards of the Earth and building empathy to all living and non-living things. It draws attention to the development of a Wall-less Classroom that engages children through an Ecocentric Curriculum, creating opportunities for children to step out, find out, and speak out about matters of environmental concern and importance. An ESD Framework as a whole-of-school approach is also presented, to demonstrate how the SDGs can become mainstream and central to the early years curriculum. An outcome of a ESD early years curriculum, the Stepping Out Program is outlined in detail to highlight the need for careful planning and implementation of learning experiences that take children outside of the classroom and into the natural world and community to facilitate children's growth and development across the cognitive, socio-emotional, and behavioural learning domains. Additionally, this chapter highlights the importance of child's voice and action taking in response to matters of environmental and societal importance and the role of the teacher in facilitating child agency.

Take Home Messages

- Education for Sustainable Development (ESD) supports the development of children's lifelong learning skills.
- Children's prosocial, empathetic, caring, and respectful behaviours and attitudes are developed through a whole-of-school approach to ESD.
- An Ecocentric Curriculum highlights the important relationship between the child and the teacher in an ongoing process of stepping out, finding out, and speaking out about matters of importance in relation to the environment and society.
- Establishing a Wall-less Classroom with specific learning objectives supports the integration of ESD both inside and outside of the early years classroom.
- A Stepping Out Program designed specifically for children in the early years supports the development of eco knowledge, skills, and attitudes.
- Learning domains specific to ESD in the early years include the cognitive, socio-emotional, and behavioural, all of which are comprised of specific objectives that lead to a child's holistic development.
- The integration of cognitive, socio-emotional, and behavioural learning tools and experiences in a Wall-less Classroom and Stepping Out Program aim to connect children to the natural environment; support imaginative play; develop children's eco-literacy; engage children's senses; develop children's leadership skills, including confidence, flexibility, creativity, empathy, respect; encourage children's reflective capacities and provide opportunities for the child to voice their opinion around matters of environmental concern.

References

Anderson, L. W., & Krathwohl, D. R. (2001). *A taxonomy for learning, teaching, and assessing: A revision of Bloom's taxonomy of educational objectives'* New York: Longman.

Australian Children's Education and Care Quality Authority (ACECQA). (2016). Sustainability in children's education and care. Retrieved from https://wehearyou.acecqa.gov.au/2016/01/28/sustainability-in-childrens-education-and-care/

Australian Curriculum, Assessment and Reporting Authority. (2020). *The Australian curriculum: Cross-curriculum priorities – sustainability*. www.australiancurriculum.edu.au/f10-curriculum/cross-curriculum-priorities/ sustainability/

Australian Education for Sustainability Alliance (AESA). (2014). *Education for Sustainability and the Australian Curriculum Project: Final report for research phases 1 to 3*. Canberra: AESA.

Bruner, J. S. (1966). *Toward a theory of instruction*. Cambridge, MA: Harvard University Press.

Carr, M. (2001). *Assessment in early childhood settings: Learning stories*. London: Paul Chapman.

Claxton, G., & Carr, M. (2004). A framework for teaching learning: The dynamics of disposition. *Early Years, 24*(1), 87–97.

Costa, A., & Kallick, B. (Eds.). (2000). *Habits of mind*. Melbourne: Hawker Brownlow.

Davis, J., & Cooke, S. (1998). Parents as partners for educational change: The Ashgroe healthy school environment project. In B. Atweh, S. Kemmis,, & P. Weeks (Eds.), *Action research in practice: Partnerships for social justice in education*. London: Routledge.

Davis, J. M. (2015). *Young children and the environment: Early education for sustainability*. 2nd Ed. Victoria, Australia: Cambridge University Press.

Deans, J., & Deans, H. (2018). A 21st century pedagogy approach to environmental education in the early years. *International Journal of Research in Environmental Studies, 5*, 77–90.

Department of Education and Training (DET) (2016). *Victorian early years learning and development framework for all children from birth to eight years*. Victoria: National Education Access License for Schools (NEALS).

Dewey, J. (1938). *Experience and education*. New York: Collier Books.

Duhn, I. (2012). Making "place" for ecological sustainability in early childhood education. *Environmental Education Research, 18*(1), 19–29.

Hattie J. (2012). *Visible learning for teachers*. New York: Routledge.

Hutchinson, D. (1998). *Growing up green. Education for ecological renewal*. New York: Teachers College, Columbia University.

Kahn, P. H., & Kellert, S. R. (2002). *Children and nature: Psychological, sociocultural and evolutionary investigations*. Cambridge, MA: MIT Press.

Kaplan, S., & Talbot, J. F. (1983). Physiological benefits of a wilderness experience. In I. Altman and J. F. Wohlwill (Eds.), *Behaviour and the natural environment* (pp. 163–203). New York: Plenum.

Kellert, S. R. (2002). Experiencing nature: Affective, cognitive, and evaluative development in children. In P. H. Kahn, Jr. & S. R. Kellert (Eds.), *Children and nature: Psychological, sociocultural and evolutionary investigations* (pp. 117–151). Cambridge, MA: MIT Press.

Mayall, B. (2000). The sociology of childhood in relation to children's rights. *International Journal of Children's Rights, 8*, 243–259.

O'Brien, L. (2009). Learning outdoors: The Forest School approach' *Education 3–13, 37*(1), 45–60.

Palmer, J. A. (1998). *Environmental education for the 21st century: Theory, practice, progress, and promise*. London: Routledge Falmer.

Perkins, D. N. (2014). *Future wise. Educating our children for a changing world*. San Francisco, CA: Jossey-Bass.

Ritchhart, R., Church, M., & Morrison, K. (2011). *Making thinking visible: How to promote engagement, understanding, and independence for all learners*. San Francisco, CA: Jossey-Bass.

Rogoff, B. (1994). Developing understanding of the idea of communities of learners. *Mind, Culture and Activity, 1*(4), 209–229.

Scott, C. L. (2015). The futures of learning 3: What kind of pedagogies for the 21st century? Education research and foresight, working papers, 15. Paris: UNESCO.

Smith, T. E., & Knapp, C. E. (2010). *Sourcebook of experiential education.* New York: Routledge.

Splitter, L., & Sharpe, A. (1995). *Teaching for better thinking: The classroom community of inquiry.* Hawthorn, Victoria: Australian Council for Educational Research.

Sterling, S. (2001) *Sustainable education: Re-visioning learning and change.* Schumacher Briefing, 6. Totnes: Green Books.

Taylor, A. (2017). Beyond stewardship: Common world pedagogies for the anthropocene. *Environmental Education Research, 23*(10), 1448–1461.

United Nations. (1992). *Sustainable development.* United Nations Conference on Environment and Development. Agenda 21. Accessed online, at https://sustainabledevelopment.un.org/content/documents/Agenda21.pdf.

United Nations Educational, Scientific and Cultural Organization (UNESCO). (2012). *Education for sustainable development sourcebook.* Learning and Training Tools, 4. Paris: UNESCO.

United Nations Educational, Scientific and Cultural Organization (UNESCO). (2014). *Shaping the future we want: UN decade for sustainable development (2005–2014). Final report.* Paris: UNESCO.

United Nations Educational, Scientific and Cultural Organization (UNESCO). (2015). *Rethinking education. Towards a global common good?* Paris: UNESCO.

United Nations Educational, Scientific and Cultural Organization (UNESCO). (2017). *Education for sustainable development goals: Learning objectives.* Paris: UNESCO.

United Nations Educational, Scientific and Cultural Organization (UNESCO). (2019). *Framework for the implementation of education for sustainable development (ESD) beyond 2019.* Paris: UNESCO.

United Nations Educational, Scientific and Cultural Organization (UNESCO). (2020). *Education for sustainable development: A roadmap.* Paris: UNESCO.

Vygotsky, L. (1978). *Mind in society: The development of higher psychological processes.* Cambridge, MA: Harvard University Press.

Waller, T. (2007). The trampoline tree and the swamp monster with 18 heads: Outdoor play in the foundation stage and foundation phase. *Education 3–13, 35*(4), 393–407.

Warden, C. (2010). *Nature kindergartens and forest schools.* Crieff: Mindstretchers Ltd.

Wright, S. (2007a). Graphic-narrative play: Young children's authoring through drawing and telling. *International Journal of Educational Arts, 8,* 1–28.

Wright, S. (2007b). Young children's meaning-making through drawing and "telling": Analogies to filmic textual features. *Australian Journal of Early Childhood, 32*(4), 37–48.

Wynne, S., & Gorman, R. (Eds.). (2015). *Nature pedagogy.* Osborne Park, WA: Association of Independent Schools of Western Australia.

6 Children as Global Citizens
Children's Voices Expressed through Drawing, Painting, and Narrative

Introduction

Children around the world can be facilitated to make connections with diverse communities using a range of meaning-making processes with the purpose of expanding understandings of a range of 21st-century social and global challenges. The presentation of children's art through public exhibition has for the past five decades drawn attention to the capacity of young children to recognize the many social, political, and environmental challenges that local and global communities face. There has been recent interest by teachers in collating and presenting children's artworks and narratives as a way of acknowledging the voices of children; their thoughts, ideas, and feelings. Also, child art exhibitions provide a means of highlighting the powerful impact of contemporary pedagogical practice that locates the arts centrally in early childhood curriculum. Drawing on two case studies of long-term collaborations between colleagues in Australia, Italy, and USA, this chapter focuses on the value of arts-based teaching and learning, highlighting the importance of drawing, painting, and narratives as significant meaning-making and communication tools. It will also demonstrate how cross-cultural collaborative inquiry between teachers can support children to engage in active citizenship through learning that examines meaningful sociocultural content that stimulates sophisticated levels of thinking and reasoning as well as imaginative, creative, and aesthetically oriented problem solving.

Collaborative Global Partnerships through Child Art Exhibitions

Recognizing the global character of the lives of children in the 21st century, teachers of young children are beginning to broaden their definition of what constitutes quality pedagogy. The recognition and acknowledgement of young children as global citizens provides a unique opportunity for teachers to develop curricula that provide children with access to learning communities beyond the confines of their immediate preschool and local communities. Indeed, this is not a new idea, in their writings Twigg and Pendergast (2015) refer to a lecture delivered by Rudolf Steiner in Berne, Switzerland, in 1924, that alluded to the

DOI: 10.4324/9781003213147-9

role of education outside the classroom where children experience themselves as part of the world. The authors point out that some seven decades later in 1997 OXFAM in the UK described global citizens as being aware of the wider world, respecting and valuing diversity, willing to engage in collaborations designed to make the world a more equitable and sustainable place by encouraging contribution to the community at a local and global level. Also, prominent educational philosopher John Dewey (1938) advocated for first-hand experiential learning that was socially constructed and relied on the child's use of previous and prevailing lived experience to create new meanings and understandings. Dewey's philosophy emphasized the role of citizenship and democracy, recognizing that the individual grows and learns within society. He identified the importance of the development of self-knowledge, *inquiry-based learning*, and even self-directed and active participatory learning, noting that children should be prepared for the future by being supported by an adult who helped the child to become competent and contributing members of society.

Building on ideas around the social construction of knowledge Rogoff (1990, 1994) has identified the "cultural historical activity theory". This construct, places learning more deeply within the social, cultural, and historical context, highlighting the relationship between the impact of the context or environment, and psychologically based cultural practices in shaping learning (Rogoff, 1990; Wertsch, 1991). Embedded within is the idea of "community of learners" (Rogoff, 1994), which describes the active and meaningful participation of teachers and children in the learning process where the involvement in the three foci, namely, intrapersonal, interpersonal and cultural-historical-institutional influences, work together to support learning. It highlights the value of collaborative participation in shared experiences where each participant is valued for the knowledge, skills, and the experience they bring to the learning activity. By focusing on the dispositional elements of teaching and learning, experts and novices learn to cooperate, share their knowledge, understandings, skills, and feelings, motivate and support each other, and develop respect and responsibility in their relationships (Rogoff, 1998). The result is the development of individual and shared understandings, with the practices and artefacts that are derived from the collaborative experience providing evidence of this growth. Rogoff (1998) suggests that, within the idea of the community of learners, there is an attempt to equalize the assumed dichotomy of teacher-led and child-led approaches, thereby creating a collaborative learning model that supports a culturally valued approach to teaching and learning. As noted by the United Nations Convention on the Rights of the Child, General Comment No. 7 (UNCRC et al., 2006, p. 3), children grow and develop through relationship building:

> Through these relationships, they learn to negotiate and coordinate shared activities, resolve conflicts, keep agreements, and accept responsibility for others.

This powerful construct is centrally embedded in the view of the child as active global citizen who from an early age learns what is meant by accepting civic responsibility, especially in relation to developing awareness and values for ensuring harmonious relationships between people and protecting the earth and its flora and fauna. Twigg and Pendergast (2015) undertook a qualitative study of 25 children aged between 3.6 years and 6.4 years who were interviewed over an eight-month period, each on three occasions, reported and reinforced the idea that children's social experiences are memorable and important, they are aware of differences and similarities between children living in various countries around the world, and are capable of making thoughtful decisions about friendships based on social behaviour and judgements about sharing and saving resources. The implication of this research is that children are capable of understanding and learning through experiences that have a global focus rather than just application to matters that are of concern in their immediate local surroundings. Children are supported to develop a sense of awareness on how they can make things better, not just for those in their immediate circle or community but for the greater whole. That is, it is a worthwhile endeavour to engage children in activities that engender qualities of citizenship in the early childhood years. Such engagement provides a vehicle for developing empathy on a larger scale that is likely to have lasting effects as children develop throughout childhood into adulthood.

The notion of citizenship is now entrenched in educational theory in most countries of the world. For example, within the Australian context the national framework, Belonging, Being, and Becoming, The Early Years Learning Framework (EYLF) for Australia (Australian Government Department of Education Employment and Workplace Relations, DEEWR, 2009), describes children as becoming active and informed citizens. Whilst early childhood broadly provides the opportunity to develop understandings of what it means to be a global citizen, it is the arts that provide a vehicle through which children can communicate their thoughts, ideas, and feelings in relationship to a range of issues and contexts in both proximal and distal communities.

The Promotion of Child Voice through Art Exhibitions

One way to help broaden communities not only to recognize young children as citizens but also to pay attention to their ideas and thoughts is to promote the presentation of child voice through art via exhibitions. Child art is considered as a universal language which provides the opportunity for children to communicate insights, experiences, and ideas that are significant and meaningful to them. Interestingly the first children's art exhibition was staged in London in 1908 by Franz Cizek, who drew attention to the fact that children are not small adults who are imitators but rather creators in their own right (Malvern, 1995). Post-Second World War interest in what young children wanted to communicate through their art became apparent. Fuelled by the changing political idealism of the time, the art of children and adolescents was perceived to communicate honesty and sincerity, qualities that were highly valued during a time of upheaval and redevelopment. Ziegfeld (1955, p. 5) noted: "The art of young people … is a fresh examination and appraisal of the world, full of wonder and excitement and unsentimental affection".

The emotionally moving extensive collection of drawings created by the children of the Terezin Ghetto (1941–1945) and now displayed in the Jewish Museum in Prague (www.jewishmuseum.cz) provides testimony to the power of drawing and painting as a key to the importance of self-expression and a way of channelling emotions and understandings for children.

The renowned philosopher Loris Malaguzzi (1996), the founding director of the Reggio Emilia early childhood movement, spoke out strongly about the importance of a socially constructed experience where children and adults share the learning journey by first getting to know each other through questioning, problem solving, imagining, hypothesizing, and documenting. Such an approach led to the development of the internationally acclaimed children's art exhibition titled "The Hundred Languages of Children" which is viewed as having made a highly significant, educational, and social contribution to how the voices of young children can be given an opportunity to be presented within the broader community. This exhibition has toured the world extensively, exposing viewers to the complexity of the teaching and learning experience and the richness and sophistication of the children's thinking as expressed through their art. Malaguzzi believed in the importance of child art exhibitions as a way of recognizing children's contributions and culminating the teaching and learning process. He noted that "Children are like actors on the [stage]. They need to be seen, to be understood, and to have a relationship with what they do … to see what they have done and what others do" (Stevenson & White, 1995, p. 286). The sharing of collaborative learning partnerships between children and teachers through exhibitions enables an opportunity for audiences to critically reflect on children's holistic learning as well as the creativity–skills relationship which is displayed through graphic representations and accompanying documentation which systematically records the depth of the learning process. Through child art exhibitions the audience is invited into the intimate world of the child and teacher and challenged to consider their image of the child as learner and the dynamism of the teaching and learning process. Malaguzzi noted that the use of graphic representation by children "comes from a need to bring clarity … when they draw, they are not only making a graphic intervention but are also selecting ideas, and getting rid of excessive, superfluous or misleading ones" (Edwards et al., 1998, p. 66). Dewey (1938) described artmaking, or thinking in symbols, as one of the most sophisticated modes of thinking that brings into play a creative process that enables the outpourings of personal experience, thought, and imaginative problem solving. This ability to capture a personally meaningful moment through graphic symbolization sheds light on the young child's focus, interests, intention, mood, and emotions (Matthews, 1994; Trevarthen, 2004; Wright, 2007a, 2007b) opening another window into the nature of the child's experience. Drawing, when combined with verbal narration and often expressive gestures and vocalisms, affords a mutually beneficial integration of thinking and feeling modalities. Cox (2005) notes that "talk and drawing interact with each other as parallel and equally transformative processes" (p. 123) and as such these processes work effectively to help children crystallize their understandings of their lived experience.

Associazione L'Eta Verde

The ideas discussed previously have inspired early childhood teachers to investigate the viability of the establishment of cross-cultural partnerships designed with the specific purpose of enabling young children to engage in life-worthy first-hand experiential learning that expands understandings and excites expression of experience through drawing, painting, and narration. With the view that collaboration with organizations and like-minded colleagues provides a deep resource for professional growth and development, more than 20 years ago the University of Melbourne's Early Learning Centre (ELC) reached out to the Associazione L'Eta Verde (Association of the Green Age: www.verde-green. net/it/) which plays a significant role in the activities of the Italian Futures Organization, Club of Rome. Each year the association works with teachers locally and internationally who encourage young children and adolescents to research topics of concern to their current and future local and global environment. Specific topics are identified within a broad qualitative judgement of life-worthy learning, with the expectation that the projects emanating from the topics stimulate deep inquiry-based learning where children are encouraged to engage in problem solving "a range of strategies to address the issues, many of which take the form of visual images" (Page, 2007, p. 49). Perkins (2014, p. 52) has classified this type of learning into an accessible framework for teachers by noting that the learning content should have four essential criteria to achieve big understandings, namely the topic needs to be:

> Big in Insight: The understanding helps to reveal how our physical, social, artistic or other worlds work.

> Big in action: The understanding empowers us to take effective action professionally, socially, politically, or in other ways.

> Big in ethics: The understanding urges us toward more ethical, humane caring mindsets and conduct.

> Big in opportunity: The understanding is likely to come up in significant ways in varied circumstances. One might say, a little more playfully, big in comeuppance.

This move towards a broader view of what constitutes quality pedagogy is not merely methodological but also epistemological, having long-term ramifications for children's learning as they take their place as global citizens. It represents a way of helping children to understand and make sense of ideas, concepts, and real-life problems using the arts as a vehicle for the sharing of understandings. As Eisner (2002, p. 215) states:

> A lesson the arts teach – is that the choice of an approach to the study of the world is a choice of not only what one is able to say about the world,

but also what one looks for and is able to see. Methods define the frames through which we construe our world.

As described, the ELC has used child art exhibition as a method for disseminating the voices of children through their drawings, paintings, and narration to stimulate audiences to appreciate the voices of young children regarding matters that impact on global peace and environmental health. Diverse topics have been explored, many of which have been aligned with the theme identified by the United Nations which designates specific years and decades as occasions to mark events or topics to promote, through awareness and action, the objectives of the organization. Usually, it is one or more Member States that propose these observances, and the General Assembly establishes them with a resolution. On occasion, these celebrations are declared by the specialized agencies of the United Nations, such as UNESCO, UNICEF, and FAO, when they identify issues that fall within the scope of their competencies. Some of these may be later adopted by the General Assembly.

During the long relationship with Associazione L'Eta Verde ELC teachers have guided children to explore life-worthy learning topics around themes such as Children's Perceptions of the Future, First Nations, Oceans and Forests, Antarctica, Astronomy, Endangered Species, Soil, Indigenous Languages, Impact of Climate Change, and Peace and Trust, to name just a few. Each exhibition was developed through a long-term inquiry into the topic which included first-hand investigations with peers and teachers, children's drawings, paintings, and narratives, all of which worked together to highlight the transformative nature of a pedagogical approach where the emphasis is placed on enabling children to communicate their capacities to think, feel, and take action in ways that contribute to the common global good and in so doing enrich their own lives and the lives of others. Examples of drawings, painting and narratives are provided in Figures 6.1 to 6.4 below to exemplify the breadth of commitment towards communicating understandings of connection to place,

Figure 6.1 If I were a forest.

cultural heritage, spiritual connections to earth, and taking action as global citizens; with a group of children even going as far as writing a letter to the Prime Minister in defence of an old growth forest located within an hour's drive of their city and creating a book relating to the protection of iceberg landscapes in Antarctic.

> I'd wear my night goggles and
> count all of the Leadbeater's Possums
> I'd stop the loggers with my powers
> I'd plant more trees
> I'd protect my treasures left in me
> by Aboriginal people
>
> Maybe your heart is a star
> If the moon and the stars and the clouds are in the sky
> It is all light and I know that it is OK

The Iceberg's Heart

At the bottom of the big big world there is an iceberg called MELT. He had a blue heart as blue as the sea. His heart was deep down in his body of ice. One day he asked a group of penguins if they could dive into the ocean and find his heart. The penguins went searching deep and deeper at the bottom of the SNOW MOUNTAINS of the ocean they spotted a blue BLUE shiney love heart. They couldn't pick it up because Melts heart was made up of blue snow ice. It was frozen and heavy. Too heavy for them to pick it up. So after good thinking the penguins asked some friendly seals if they could help and flip it up with their strong tails but the seals couldn't do it, the heart was just too big. Both Penguins and Seals shooted back on the surface of the ocean and they told Melt: Your heart is just too heavy, we can't lift it up but we can tell you that your heart is as blue as the Sea and the Sky. It is covered with Diamond Dust ... and it is everywhere in the ocean. The iceberg called Melt liked what they said. He felt his heart shimmering. It made all of the Antarctica beautiful. Come and follow the adventures of Penguins and Seals as they search for Melt's HEART in the depth of Antarctica

-Original Story of The Iceberg's Heart created by ELC children as part of a centre-wide exploration of Antarctic for the L'Eta Verde Project

---

As can be seen from these examples, young children can be guided to use creative expressive activity to think about a range of complex social, emotional, cultural, and environmental issues. What is required is a teacher who is in partnership with children to identify life-worthy learning topics as a provocation

106 Part II

Figure 6.2 Maybe your heart is a star.

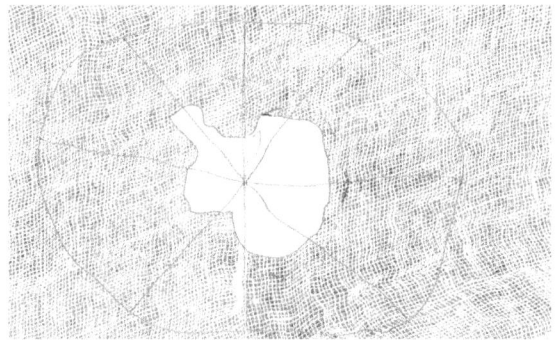

Figure 6.3 Children's drawing of the Heart of an Iceberg.

Figure 6.4 A story by children from the ELC: The Iceberg's Heart.

for deep inquiry. These teachers are required to understand the teaching and learning process to involve:

- a commitment to advance learning and understandings from surface to deep;
- active, careful listening;
- the acceptance of children's ideas as worthy contributions for the ongoing investigation;
- sensory-rich and aesthetically pleasing materials, resources, and associated provocations;
- enriched vocabulary;
- ongoing back-and-forth exchanges that involve questioning, hypothesizing, and problem solving.

As a central aim of education is to promote the child's ability to develop thoughts, ideas, and feelings, it should be noted that engagement with "big ideas" allows for individual expressive responses that invite children to pay close attention to the expressive features and possibilities that exist in the world around them.

The Interdependence Hexagon Project

Returning once again to the value of children's art exhibitions for the dissemination of children's responses related to significant themes evident in society, through a chance meeting with the founder of the Hexagon project at an InSEA[1] Conference held in Melbourne, Australia, teachers from the ELC enthusiastically embraced the opportunity to be part of this unique movement. As teachers around the world know, it always takes extra energy and commitment to be open to new relationships and ways of thinking about teaching and learning. For the ELC teachers this chance encounter opened a range of exciting possibilities about sharing children's thoughts and ideas through art and narration.

The Interdependence Hexagon Project (https://hexagonproject.org) is an International Arts Project which was founded in Pennsylvania in 2007. It seeks to provide opportunities for children, youth, and adults to engage in critical inquiry through the visual arts and to acquire the knowledge and understanding of local and global issues and interconnectedness and interdependency of diverse cultures and countries. Based on the Interdependence Movement, the Hexagon Project's main mission is to promote empathy, tolerance, and respect by giving voice to the ideas and messages of young people around the world through art created on hexagons, a symbol and metaphor of interconnectedness.

1 InSEA is the largest international community of artists and art educators dedicated to advocacy, networking, and the advancement of research and good practice in education through visual art in the world.

> The Hexagon Project uses the Hexagon as a metaphor for Interdependence and interconnectedness. As such, the hexagon is a composition of complex relationships, interdependent lines, like bonds of human connection. It maintains its own presence as a shape, symbol of light and life. Destined to be part of a whole – it becomes a splendid architectural element, forever expandable. Multiples attach and strengthen one another to become an infinite network of connections.
>
> (https://hexagonproject.org)

The longstanding themes of the arts program within the Hexagon Project include human rights, especially children's rights, rights to education, social equity and equality, multicultural diversity, empathy, peace, tolerance, respect, and understanding, local and global issues and environmental safety, conservation, and sustainability. Global conversations from participants including children all over the world are invited using the shape of a hexagon – or multiple hexagons – in any medium, including digital, to respond creatively to the many themes of interdependence and become part of an international movement to create a more civil, peace-minded, and just world. These artworks are then shared by local and global audiences through annual exhibitions in galleries, museums, and social media platforms. It hopes to inspire individuals to act ethically and responsibly at local, national, and global levels and contribute to a more sustainable and a peaceful global society.

With this inspirational platform in mind, teachers at the ELC have adopted the annual special theme as a provocation for in depth inquiry. They recognize that they need to give plenty of time for the exploration of the identified theme. As Malaguzzi notes, "the verbal discussion is certainly the coordinating fulcrum of negotiation within the group (Edwards et al., 1998, p. 66) and as such time is dedicated to discussing ideas, providing verbal explanations, and verbally engaging in back-and-forth exchanges. Teachers record these discussions, ensuring that all children's voices are included. The next step is to meet with small groups of children to start putting the ideas, thoughts, and feelings discussed into graphic representation, with teachers entering further dialogue with the children, asking them about the image that they have created. For example, teachers have used the hexagon as the central metaphor for interconnectedness to communicate children's concerns and actions around social justice, personal identity, connectedness, ecology, and environment. Over several years the ELC submitted hexagons drawn by the children and some years the children created 2D and 3D art (installations) that teachers photographed and embedded into hexagonal shape. Featured projects from 2015, 2019, and 2020 are presented here (illustrated in Figures 6.5–6.9).

> I made daily preparations throughout the running of the program (May–July) collected through children's stories, drawings, cards and reflective feedback by children, teachers, and families. I displayed hexagons (universal size) at the ELC and submitted up to 20 representing children's ideas from other classrooms.
>
> (ELC Teacher)

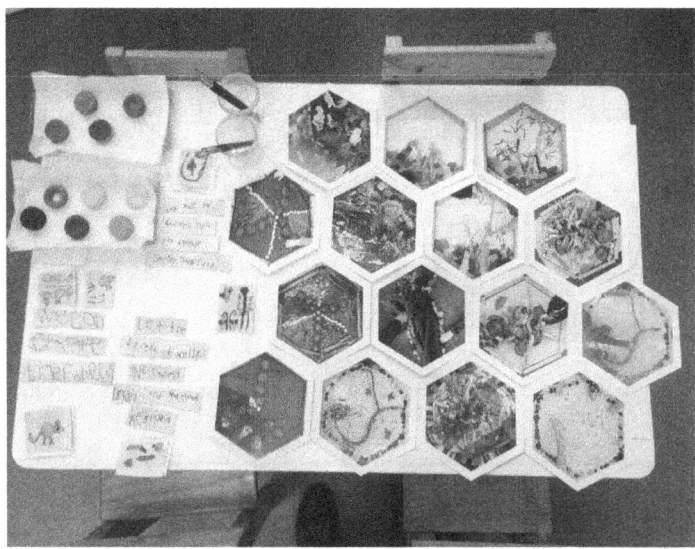

Figure 6.5 ELC Children's creation for the 2015 Hexagon Project on the theme of Natural Habitat.

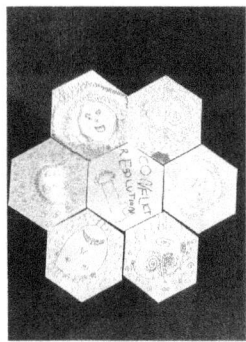

*Figure 6.6*a,b ELC Children's creation for the 2019 Hexagon Project on the theme of Transforming Conflict.

In 2015, ELC children participated in the Hexagon Project by building collaborative installations based on an ongoing environmental project about deforestation. Across five classrooms teachers collaborated with children to explore the identified theme, guiding their learning pathways, interests, and ideas. Such an approach created a ripple effect with each group of children and teachers identifying their own learning journey, such as secret pathways and patterns of the land, investigations of local grass species, observations of growth from the tiniest seed to the tallest trees, regeneration of the forest after logging, including

110 Part II

Figure 6.7 "Koalas need homes to live so they won't become extinct." – ELC Children's creation for the 2020 Hexagon Project on the theme of Diversity.

Figure 6.8 "Bees help plants grow and make honey." – ELC Children's creation for the 2020 Hexagon Project on the theme of Diversity.

Figure 6.9 The exhibition: the leather back turtle is endangered – ELC Children's creation for the 2020 Hexagon Project on the theme of Diversity.

ways in which actions by people can help to preserve the ancient forests. The children told a series of unique stories of the wonder of the local environment and the need for its protection and their stores were recognized by the judging panel as the most Overall Effective Interpretation of Interdependence at the Pre-K – Kindergarten level.

> The International Interdependence Hexagon Project is pleased to announce that the University of Melbourne's Early Learning Centre Children and teachers have been recognized for their dynamic and creative exploration of the natural forest – utilizing the HEXAGON as a lens, a frame, a habitat, a connecting metaphor for a collection of amazing forest creatures, textures, shapes, paintings, collages, interwoven understandings, messages and stories, stories, stories, stories about things questioned, things learned and things still to be curious about! What a creative display of learning – just beautiful! Thank you for seeing – and adapting and adopting the Project within your curriculum.
>
> (Hexagon Project, 2015)

In response to the 2019 theme of Transforming Conflict, a call to "promote global citizenship and enable young people to develop skill for civic literacy such as critical thinking and problem solving, peace building and personal and social responsibility", the ELC children were encouraged to be competent thinkers and communicators of their own emotions and the emotions of others, but also to express their capacity for critical reflection through artistic expression. The aim of the 2019 exhibition was to support children to develop peacebuilding skills and to communicate personal and social responsibility. They were invited to address other social, cultural, local, regional, national, and local issues that they were most concerned and passionate about. In Figure 6.6 are two examples from ELC children's creative artwork that represent their understandings of empathy and conflict resolution.

More recently the 2020 theme "Diversity" was explored by ELC children through the sub theme "Bio-DIVERSITY". Threatened, endangered, or vulnerable native flora and fauna (land and marine) were researched, including eucalypt tree, the koala, the dianella, the blue banded bee, and the leatherback sea turtle. The children studied biodiversity in Victoria, Australia and connected to the overarching curriculum red thread "International Year of Plant Health". Human impacts including land degradation and environmental changes such as bush fires and sea pollution were also explored.

> Learning from an early age to interact with care and kindness and to live in harmony with all living and non-living things is central to achieving eco-citizenship and global citizenship. Also critical is engaging children in a dialogue around diversity, community, spirituality, environment, and culture and how these key themes interact in positive or negative ways.
>
> (ELC Teacher)

Young children when provided with opportunities to explore their environment can develop attitudes, knowledge, and skills that they take with them into later life. Through the exposure to diverse ideas, environments, and experiences, including learning in the natural world and an arts-based curriculum, educators can intentionally foster growth and development of environmental literacy in children. This also helps cultivate pro-environmental behaviours and an appreciation of all life forms, human and non-human, as young children mature into adulthood.

Reflection on Children's Learning through the Hexagon Project

As noted, the mission of the Hexagon Project is to spread meaning of interdependence through school- and community-created hexagons. Themes of social justice, identity, peace, and environment are expressed, through the power of the arts, in an increasingly interconnected world. Involvement in the Hexagon Project allows children to participate as a community of learners to create individual hexagons which connect with thousands of others collected from around the world and in so doing deepen their knowledge about a range of topics on social action, activism, and education.

> I was instantly drawn to the complexity of messages communicated in a simple and effective way and the ways the Project inspired thousands of students around the world. All hexagons received by the organizers are exhibited and viewed by thousands in Scranton and via live stream.
> (ELC Teacher)

The resulting artwork is born not only out of a need to seek clarity about an idea but also out of an innate desire to express understanding within the realm of creative problem solving and aesthetically oriented decision-making. Over several years teachers have facilitated discussion and comment about coping and resilience amongst peers and siblings, aspects of inclusion where differences between people and cultures are explored, peace and trust amongst family, friends, and community and protection of the earth's resources. When guided by teachers into inquiries of this kind children can focus in on their personal lived experience and current understandings of essential themes that relate to their role as global citizens. Such engagement has inspired significantly elevated levels of critical thinking for children of such an early age. This is an example and an exemplar on transforming children's energies toward coexistence through collaboration, cooperation, and coming together to contribute to a movement which is making a difference by responding to local, regional, and global challenges that face our world.

Concluding Remarks

Children as active citizens are in local, national, and global worlds where culture, context and communication are all important. Through art and narrative children are provided with opportunities to engage in conversations about things that matter in their own lives and beyond. In many ways the child is the artist and author who generously shares his or her insights with the communities of teachers, parents, and children. Through exhibition the children's creative and expressive outcomes propel discussion and learning for others and can be viewed as evidence of children taking action about topics that have meaning to them, their families, and broader community members. Through child art exhibitions borders are crossed and as global citizens it is about the togetherness of an interconnected world community. This chapter has demonstrated how children's art creates opportunities to bring together diverse communities in a shared belief that art can communicate the lived experience of children from the early years and provide a powerful conduit for the expression of ideas, dreams, and visions for a better future for all.

Take Home Messages

- Children are capable of understanding and learning through experiences that have a global focus.
- Arts-based teaching and learning with a focus on children's narratives acknowledges the voices of children and their thoughts, ideas, and feelings to be heard.
- Children can make connections with their global peers using a range of meaning-making processes with the purpose of expanding understandings of a range of 21st-century social and global challenges.
- Projects in this chapter present ways to engage children in activities that engender qualities of citizenship in the early childhood years.
- Engagement in these projects provides a vehicle for developing empathy on a larger scale that are likely to have lasting effects as children develop throughout childhood into adulthood.

References

Associazione L'Eta Verde (2012). Association of the Green Age: www.verde-green.net/it/

Cox, S. (2005). Intention and meaning in young children's drawing. *Journal of Art and Design Education*, *24*(2), 115–125.

DEECD Department of Education and Early Childhood Development. (2009). *Victorian early years learning and development framework*. Melbourne: Early Childhood Strategy Division, Department of Early Childhood Development and Victorian Curriculum Authority.

DEEWR Department of Education, Employment and Workplace (2009). *Belonging, being and becoming: The early years learning framework for Australia*. Canberra: Commonwealth Copyright Division.

Dewey, J. (1938). *Experience and education*. New York: Collier Books.

Edwards, C., Gandini, L., & Forman, G. (Eds.) (1998). *The hundred languages of children: The Reggio Emilia approach to early childhood education*. Westport, CT: Ablex.

Eisner, E. (2002). *The arts and the creation of the mind*. New Haven, CT: Yale University Press.

Hexagon Project (2021). *Hexagon Project*. https://hexagonproject.org/about/

Malaguzzi, L. (1996) The hundred languages of children: Narrative of the possible, *Catalogue of the 'Hundred Languages of Children' exhibition, Reggio Emilia*. Comune di Reggio Emilia, Italy.

Malvern, S. B. (1995). Inventing "child art'" Franz Cizek and modernism. *British Journal of Aesthetics, 35*(3), 273–277.

Matthews, J. (1994). *Helping children to draw and paint in early childhood*. London: Hodder & Stoughton.

Page, J. (2007) Children's discourses of emotions: Rethinking citizenship. Unpublished doctoral dissertation, University of Melbourne, Victoria.

Perkins, D. (2014). *Future wise. Educating our children for a changing world*. San Francisco, CA: Jossey-Bass.

Rogoff, B. (1990). *Apprenticeship in thinking: Cognitive development in social context*. New York: Oxford University Press.

Rogoff, B. (1994). Developing understanding of the idea of communities of learners, *Mind, Culture and Activity, 1*(4), 209–229.

Rogoff, B. (1998). Cognition as a collaborative process. In D. Kuhn & R. Siegler (Eds.), *Handbook of child psychology*. 5th ed., Vol. 2, *Cognition, perception and language* (pp. 679–744). New York: John Wiley.

Stevenson, C., & White, M. (1995). Children's art exhibitions: The contexts and challenges. Children's *Environments, 12*(3), 285–289.

Trevarthen, C. (2004). Learning about ourselves from children: Why a growing human brain needs interesting companions. *Research and Clinical Centre for Child Development, 26*, 9–44. Annual Report 2002–2003.

Twigg, D., & Pendergast, D. (2015). Growing global citizens: Young children's lived experiences with the development of their own social world. *International Research in Early Childhood Education, 6*(1), 79.

UN Committee on the Rights of the Child, United Nations Children's Fund & Bernard van Leer Foundation. (2006). *A guide to general comment 7: Implementing child rights in early childhood*. The Hague: Bernard van Leer Foundation.

Vygotsky, L. (1978). *Mind in society. The development of higher psychological processes*. Cambridge, MA: Harvard University Press.

Wertsch, J.V. (1991). *Voices of the mind: A sociocultural approach to mediated action*. Cambridge, MA: Harvard University Press.

Wright, S. (2007a). *The arts: Young children and learning*. Hoboken, NJ: Pearson Education.

Wright, S. (Ed.). (2007b). *Children, meaning-making and the arts*. Belmont, Western Australia: Prentice Hall.

Ziegfeld, E. (1955). Art education/a world view. *School Arts, 54*(9), 5–9.

7 Friends on the Farm

Reciprocal Relationship Building with People with Special Needs

Introduction

Attitudes of bias towards disability and difference are deeply embedded in our culture and, for many early childhood professionals, the challenge of developing a curriculum that is inclusive and fosters positive attitudes and behaviours towards those who are different continues to stimulate debate.[1] Inclusion is seen as a universal human right and the aim is to embrace people with diverse backgrounds and needs within the community. Key concepts include equity, participation, belonging, and the recognized and valued contribution of all people (Cologon, 2014). The notion of inclusion in early childhood context is based on the recognition of individual needs and the celebration of difference and for early childhood professionals it is helpful to broaden this definition to include the idea of the removal of barriers to learning for all teachers, children, and families (Connors & Stalker 2010).

Postmodern theory, with its emphasis on "uncertainty, complexity, diversity, subjectivity, multiple perspectives and temporal and special specificities" (Dahlberg et al., 1999) provides a platform from which teachers can promote and construct inclusive pedagogies suitable for early childhood settings; pedagogies based on beliefs and practices that acknowledge social justice, fairness, and human rights. It has been argued that high-quality inclusive education is a matter of instructional practice and meaningful social integration (Love & Horn, 2021). These authors suggested that inclusive education can be organized to take place within early childhood programs.

Going hand in hand with inclusive pedagogy is the connection to sociocultural theory where learning is understood to be influenced by relationships between people, contexts, actions, meanings, communities, and cultural histories (Edwards, 2003), and is concerned with meaning making and inquiry processes that occur on three interacting planes of influence: the intrapersonal (i.e. the individual child), interpersonal (interactions among social partners),

---

1 An earlier version of this chapter appeared in *UNESCO e-journal*, 1(4) under the same title and is reproduced with permission. www.unescoejournal.com/wp-content/uploads/2020/01/1-4-3-dean.pdf

and community/institutional (contextual) (Rogoff, 1990). Construction of knowledge is seen to be influenced by active participation in real-life situations within communities and a paradigm shift in educating children is the emphasis on lived experience (Rogoff et al., 2018). Nimmo (2008) draws our attention to the need to involve our youngest citizens in democratic life as both "participants and contributors" and for teachers to consider more complex possibilities for practice by including diverse cultural and social perspectives. Undeniably the environment plays a key role in teaching and learning. The curation of a supportive and inviting environment by early childhood teachers based on a culture of rights and inclusive belonging and contribution can cultivate a sense of confident, competent, and resilient citizenship in young learners (McAnelly & Gaffney, 2019).

Linking inclusive practice, socio-constructivist theory, and arts-based teaching and learning may be considered uncharted territory for some early childhood professionals. However, in the case of community arts projects, a nexus between these ideas is uncovered; one that is both accessible and capable of integrating a diverse range of participants in collective and collaborative creative processing. Involvement in the arts can be considered as a form of "cultural communication" whereby individuals of different ages or cultures, as well as those with disabilities, can come together in an atmosphere of mutual respect to honour the differences that exist. The idea of communities of practice in the arts has been gaining attention worldwide in the field of early childhood education. This is a new way of thinking about the place of art and play in the lives and education of young children, with an emphasis on the lived experience of being a child and the excitement of creating and playing with meaning in social settings, and in dialogue with materials, peers, and adults (Schulte, & Thompson, 2018).

Traditionally the arts have been recognized for their capacity to enhance the wellbeing of individuals by providing a means of expression – sometimes a means for which there may not be words. For example, recent literature in early childhood research has advocated for the use of arts-based inquiry as aesthetic approaches to generate data which illuminate the perspectives of young children who experience disability (Cologon et al., 2019). The arts are also seen as essential vehicles for "personal and collective improvement" (Okuyama, 2001) and contribute to the soul of the community by representing the link to internal thinking processes that allow for the expression of thoughts, ideas, and emotions. Arts within the community are concerned particularly with providing opportunities for expression of social minorities or sub-cultures; whether for people with disabilities to support communication and expression, for disadvantaged people to express needs, for minority groups to sustain and reinterpret their cultures, or for young people to make sense of their lived experience. Such opportunities contribute to the establishment of social cohesion by bringing individuals together in neutral spaces where friendships can develop in an atmosphere of partnership and cooperation.

This chapter, drawing on research into inclusive and reflective practice, attempts to demonstrate the impact of a community arts program as a vehicle for successful reciprocal relationship building between a group of preschool children and adults with disabilities. It examines the nature of the "lived experience" of the participants with the support of journal extracts and presents an insight into what was felt and learned throughout the project. The chapter concludes with some questions for teachers and other community members who share an interest in community arts projects.

The Background to the Project

"Friends on the Farm" was a funded[2] community arts project that was designed to support the ideas of social inclusion and citizenship through participation (Nimmo, 2008) by bringing together a group of 4- and 5-year-old preschool children and a group of adults with disabilities, to explore relationship building in a community context, this being an inner-city Children's Farm (Figure 7.1). The rationale for the project was based on the idea that participation between these diverse groups would pave the way for the recognition of difference, similarity, and diversity, for the establishment of new forms of "talk" that incorporated inclusive language and action and provided opportunities for relationship building that was authentic and meaningful for all participants.

This rationale was premised on a commitment to real-life experiences that reflected principles of human rights, social justice, and inclusion rather than exclusion (Gunn et al., 2004). Of relevance were the guiding principles that underpin the Victorian State Disability Plan 2002–2012 that promotes the principles of Equality, Dignity and Self-Determination, Diversity and Non-Discrimination (Victorian Government, 2002). This plan articulates the vision that people with a disability should be able to live and participate in the life of the community with the same rights, responsibilities, and opportunities as all other citizens. It also outlines a vision for local communities; one that advocates for people to have a sense of belonging, to be valued for the contributions they make to the community, to have individual rights respected, and to be able to act if discriminated against. Most importantly, the plan promotes the idea that individuals should be able to contribute to community with a shared sense of responsible citizenship through participation in all aspects of community life.

During the planning stage of the project, teachers, disability development staff, and artist/teachers met regularly to establish goals and program content, discuss teaching strategies, and address how the physical needs and safety of the children and adults would be met, especially about wheelchair and walking frame access. To ensure that meaningful relationships had every chance to develop it was agreed that the program would aim to meet criteria identified by Nimmo (2008), namely:

---

2 This project was funded by the City of Yarra, local council in Victoria, Australia.

Figure 7.1 Children and adults with special needs engaging in Friends on Farm.

   Intimacy: Will the relationships between participants include care and concern?
   Continuity: Will the relationships be developed through opportunities for multiple contacts over time?
   Complexity: Will the relationships have the potential to engage the participants' curiosity and imagination?
   Identity: Will the relationships offer the participants insight into their sense of place and belonging?
   Diversity: Will the relationships stretch the participants' understanding of human diversity?
   Reciprocity: Will the relationships strengthen the teachers', disability development staff, and artists' image of the participants?

The "Friends on the Farm" project could be categorized within the genre of phenomenological enquiry with the systematic record keeping and ongoing critical reflection between the teachers, artist/teachers, and the disability development staff providing an opportunity to uncover the heart of the experience itself and gain insight over time into the developing relationships and collaborative learning. The project was documented using descriptive methods (Patton, 1990) with teachers, artists, and disability development staff taking on the role of participant observers who did not attempt, "to classify, compare groups, explain, predict or make judgments" (Hawke, 1993, p. 10) but instead aimed to broadly identify the key recurrent themes (Burns, 1994) and "essences of shared experience" (Patton, 1990) that were indicated by the child and adult responses. In line with Schön's (1983) ideas associated with "reflection-in-and-on-action" the program leaders became deeply engaged in the experience, finding time for ongoing individual and collaborative critical reflection (Larrivee, 2005), a process that involved a week-by-week review of the program and a reshaping and rebuilding of the teaching and learning approaches based on the evaluation.

Journal notes, program plans, written observations, participant art products, and photographic and video documentation informed the critical analysis.

About the Participants

The "Friends on the Farm" Project brought together a diverse group, including

- 20 children, aged 4–5, attending a long day preschool in inner city Melbourne, Australia, and their three teachers,
- 15 adults with varying physical and intellectual disabilities enrolled in a creative arts program offered by the Northern Metropolitan Institute of TAFE, Melbourne, Australia,
- Five disability development staff,
- Three artist/teachers, and
- Two Children's Farm staff.

The project was undertaken over six months, with the group meeting once a week for two hours at an inner-city Children's Farm, which was within short walking distance of both the preschool and the TAFE art studio. Ethical principles of voluntary participation and informed consent were followed, with participants being given the opportunity on a weekly basis to either agree or not to agree to attend the sessions.

More about the Children and their Teachers

The teachers of the preschool children were committed to actively addressing diversity issues in their program and as the participating children were from socially and culturally homogeneous backgrounds and had very limited exposure to people with disabilities, it was considered particularly important to try to incorporate opportunities for the group to experience relationship building with different types of people from a range of racial and cultural backgrounds, with varying abilities, ages, and lifestyles (Figure 7.2). During the planning phase of the project the teachers found time to share their personal beliefs and values about inclusive education with each other and it was not unexpected that they all wanted to ensure that ideas surrounding the discourse associated with social justice, human rights, and inclusive education were honoured. There was a perceived need to go further than reading books and displaying posters as a way of acknowledging difference. They were especially interested in moving away from a standardized curriculum and scheduling to designing an authentic learning program that took the children into the context of neighbourhood and community, where a safe level of risk taking would expand understandings of the diversity that exists in their world and have a positive impact of their sense of competence and identity (Nimmo, 2008). Expanding learning beyond the classroom was also seen to be a way of impacting the wellbeing of the children and responded to recent ideas about the importance of connecting young

Figure 7.2 Friends on Farm activity.

children to the social capital of the neighbourhood (Coleman, 1988; Schaefer-McDaniel, 2004).

In line with socio-cultural perspectives of learning (Vygotsky, 1978; Rogoff, 1990; Dahlberg et al., 1999) the idea of engaging the children on a regular basis over an extended period with a group of adults with disabilities was seen to offer unique opportunities for all participants for cognitive, social, and emotional interchange.

The aim was for children and adults to actively participate in a range of shared arts-centred inquiry processes designed to stimulate relationship building and the co-construction of knowledge. As Wells (2001, p. 179) states, "knowledge building takes place between people doing things together" and this project provided concrete access to a "real life" situation where multiple perspectives were recognized and where the acts of listening to both familiar and unfamiliar voices and modelling open and accepting behaviours provided appropriate ways to empower all participants in a dignified celebration of difference.

More about the Adults and the Disability Development Staff

It is widely recognized that people with a disability currently face many inequalities and barriers to participating in the life of the community. However, the Victorian State Disability Plan (Victorian Government, 2002) outlines a whole of government and whole of community approach to disability that is based on human rights and social justice. The Victorian Government's vision for the future at the time was that: "By 2012, Victoria will be a stronger and more inclusive community – a place where diversity is embraced and celebrated, and where everyone has the same opportunities to participate in the life of the community, and the same responsibilities towards society as all other citizens of Victoria" (Victorian Government, 2002, p. 7).

Figure 7.3 Artmaking creations.

The 15 adults who participated in the "Friends on the Farm" project were enrolled in a creative arts program offered by the Northern Metropolitan Institute of TAFE on one day a week in a restored historic building located in the same street as the preschool. The program was designed to provide participants with opportunities for learning, development, and growth through explorations in visual art, music, and performing arts, and it achieved the added benefit of bringing people of mixed abilities together to participate in a community activity (Figure 7.3).

The uniquely human behaviour of artmaking maximized opportunities for individual expression, creative problem solving, collaboration, and friendship building, and the disability development staff worked as a strong and sensitive team to establish a collective creative spirit, address individual needs, and to achieve positive outcomes for all participants.

Artistic Community-Based Projects

The idea of involving artists in community projects has begun to garner positive attention over the past few years, with several documented projects (Junk Theory, 2006; In the Zone, 2006; Associazione L'Eta Verde, 2012; Hexagon Project, 2021) demonstrating that art projects and projects using artistic strategies can serve as a means by which a community can consider and examine its identity. The "Friends on the Farm" project was led by a group of talented artist/teachers with diverse skills and experience of working in a community arts environment. Together they designed a program that was both environmentally sensitive and accessible and engaging for both adults and children.

The aim was to help individuals to discover their personal talents, whatever their age or level of skill or ability and to ensure that the four central principles of community arts, namely, inclusion, mutual respect, process and consensus, and generosity of spirit were honoured (Ontario Arts Council, 1998). A range of approaches, including opening and closing group rituals, mutual exchanges of knowledge and skills, small and large group collaborations and sharing were used to acknowledge individual efforts and outcomes, to reinforce relationships, and to enable individuals to discover their own talents, whatever their level of skill or ability.

The Children's Farm

Both the preschool and the adult art facility were located within easy walking distance of an inner-city working Children's Farm where a sensory-rich natural environment provided a wide variety of opportunities for artistic explorations. The farm also offered a neutral neighbourhood and community space where both groups could meet to share the joys and challenges associated with being in close contact with animals and the working life of the farm. The farm was a place where the play/work dichotomy was openly addressed. In each two-hour session, time was set aside for completing farm work such as collecting eggs and feeding animals, for shared art activities, and for free play. Participation in shared community work was seen as significant in the process of relationship building and in the construction of meaningful group identity, with active engagement in tasks providing participants with direct sources of information about a wide range of real-life situations. Making art in a collaborative situation provided a shared focus that supported connectivity and empathy while free play stimulated excitement, enthusiasm, and a "joie de vivre" that was contagious, especially for the adults who had had little exposure to the playful exuberance of young children.

The Art Program

The program took place in various locations around the farm. The farm barn became the place where the group gathered for its greeting and farewell rituals and at times it was used as a designated space for drawing or sculpture creation. From one week to the next participants were introduced to a range of spaces, including the horse-riding area, the goat and sheep paddock, the kitchen garden, the duck pond, and the open field, where different artmaking opportunities provided an opportunity to experience the differing aesthetic qualities of each location (Figure 7.4).

Taking an ecologically sensitive approach, the artist/teachers planned:

- Clay slab drawing with sticks
- Clay and "other found things"– construction
- Clay impressions of found objects
- Clay texture buttons
- Individual observational drawing of animals, buildings, and people
- Group drawings
- Sand and small stone drawing

Figure 7.4 Nature-inspired art-making.

- Greasy wool constructions
- Stick and clay constructions
- Feather collage

Singing, chanting, and body percussion naturally found their place in the session format and the chant:

> Hi, hi we're down on the farm
> We're going to meet our friends here
> Friends on the farm

was generated during the first session and became the catchcry for the opening and closing rituals for the entirety of the project.

The Journal – Reflecting-in-and-on-Action

The teachers, disability support staff, and artist/teachers recorded their impressions of the weekly events as they naturally occurred in a shared electronic journal. This recording was based on remembered observations of the responses of the participants to the program and to each other, as well as personal thoughts, feelings, assumptions, motives, and decisions made in relation to the program and its development. Thus, the notion of reflective practice was deeply embedded in the project design, with ongoing review and analysis informing the planning, implementation, and evaluation of the program. The complete process of reflecting-in-and-on-action allowed those contributing to the journal to experience surprise, puzzlement, or sometimes confusion in a situation that was both unique and somewhat uncertain. Early in the project entries such as the following indicated that some children and adults were experiencing feelings of uncertainty regarding their involvement:

> As we met our friends some of whom were bound by the constraints of the wheelchairs and who were making excited spontaneous sounds there were wide-eyed stares from the children. "S" said that she felt nervous and when I tried to unpack that with her, she was unable to clarify why she felt that way.
>
> (Teacher Participant)

> Personally, I felt that the experience was confronting and very intense. I had to dig deep to role model appropriate behaviour and to respond to the situation in as a relaxed a way as possible.
>
> (Artist/teacher participant)

> To be honest I felt a little unsure of myself but felt adamant that this was a great project and that given time we would see the children (and ourselves) growing more and more comfortable and confident in this new and unfamiliar context.
>
> (Disability development participant)

Such transparent disclosure points to a deep level of reflection on the phenomenon experienced and, over time, journal entries such as those described below, generated by one artist/teacher and a disability development staff member, began to create a picture of growing relationships and positive shared experience:

> WOW what a session. It seemed as though we were in the midst of a creative surge. Children were moving around from place to place, gathering, acting as messengers, making, talking, brainstorming sharing and collaborating. A distinctly different feel to the previous weeks, and I believe we are now feeling and seeing the true spirit of collaboration and acceptance. There were so many light bulb moments:
>
> - Excited feather gatherers
> - Singing our chant
> - Discovering the banana tree bark,
> - Laughing about our long hair as we placed the banana tree bark over our heads
> - Discovering how quickly we can make a sculpture
> - Clay, sticks and leaves… what a great combination
> - John's chicken drawing
> - The excitement of finding that you can indeed draw a chicken
> - V's chicken song
> - The quiet moment when Victoria started to sing
> - M and J standing together to display their drawings

> The greatest joy comes from the company and enthusiasm of the little children. It is uncommon for adults with intellectual disabilities to have an opportunity to engage directly with young children. This is an amazing experience for our students.
>
> (Disability development staff participant)

Another positive outcome of engaging with ongoing critical reflection was that teachers were empowered to address several challenging issues to do with finding ways to describe disability to young children. The following journal entry by one of the children's teachers stimulated discussion between teachers which subsequently led to the building of new understandings of how to talk to children about disability:

> A parent has asked me to provide words to talk about adults with disabilities. His daughter referred to one of our adult friends as a funny man. This was not a disrespectful description, but we need to talk about appropriate words that acknowledge difference and are respectful.
>
> (Teacher participant)

Involvement in the "Farm Art and Friends" project placed teachers in an unfamiliar and challenging situation that required ongoing and sensitive management. As each week passed and participants became more familiar with each other, any fears or uncertainties that were present earlier were, over time, allayed, as is evidenced by the following journal entries:

> It seems that the ritual of meeting, greeting, and saying our farewells in the circle keeps us feeling bonded. There is no shyness now, in fact, the children seem to want to move into the centre of the circle to share their ideas or dances. The adults demonstrate enjoyment of the children's performances, and the spontaneous singing is a lot of fun. The song, "always look on the bright side of life" appeared out of the blue and somehow encapsulated the joy and positivity of our shared experience. It would be great to follow it up with another chorus.
>
> (Artist/teacher participant)

> I came away from today's session with a feeling that for these participants their memories of the farm will be forever shaped by the creative explorations and new friendships that were made during these weeks.
>
> (Disability development staff participant)

The Outcomes of the Lived Experience

"Friends on the Farm" was an innovative and ambitious community arts project that produced a myriad of positive outcomes. In the first instance there can be no doubt that the project achieved its goal of the establishment of reciprocal respectful relationship building between two diverse groups of people. By bringing the children and adults together in an environmentally pleasing and neutral space, friendships had the chance to be established and to thrive. There were many recorded examples of children and adults showing care and concern for each other and over time the two groups merged naturally into one with a new sense of group identity clearly apparent. Knowledge and understandings about inclusion and diversity were expanded and by the end of the project there was a generalized acceptance of the existence of multiple views of reality, including an acceptance that difference does exist but so too do similarities.

The experience of collaborative artmaking provided multiple opportunities for individual and group communication and expression, with all participants having the chance for creative processing that was imbued with all the excitement, vigour, magic, colour, symbolism, feeling, metaphor, and creativity that the arts have to offer. Art products were enthusiastically produced week after week and at the conclusion of the project many were selected for presentation in a community art exhibition that celebrated the achievements of the children and adults. It was clear that involvement in the creative arts stimulated curiosity and imagination and resulted in individual empowerment, with participants demonstrating confidence and enthusiasm for both the making and the sharing of art and art products. Understanding, empathy, and social inclusiveness were also evident as children and adults respectfully acknowledged each other's skills, abilities, and art products. The "end of session sharing" was a time when the group gathered with a strong sense of community identity to recognize achievements and to respect and celebrate the nature of the unique shared lived experience. The sharing of art products seemed to bolster the morale of the group and created a unity and a level of social solidarity that was unexpected.

The challenge of engaging young children and adults in a community arts project began with a commitment to inclusive education and to the theory surrounding the social construction of knowledge. The "Friends on the Farm" project honoured the idea that learning is socially and culturally situated and mediated, with active engagement in collaborative arts activities focusing the participants beyond the "self" to others'.

Teachers, disability support staff, and artist/teachers successfully employed a range of scaffolding techniques or "guided discovery" (Wright, 2003) to encourage both peer group and individual learning that was considered purposeful and age appropriate. The relationships between the children and the adults developed in line with the principles of reciprocity and a strong sense of agency became apparent, with both children and adults demonstrating their "two-way" capacity for creative thinking and problem solving.

A significant legacy of the project was the publication of the book titled *Farm Art and Friends* University of Melbourne, 2007which presents through photographs and participants' artworks, an insight into the experience of this inclusive community as they shared relationship building "down on the farm". The catchcry chant "Hi, hi we're down on the farm" is used to introduce the "friends" and the farm animals and as each page is opened the reader is presented with images and photographs that capture and communicate the essence of the "lived experience" of this remarkable community arts project. The book has been produced with a CD-ROM that offers teachers and parents a guide to building inclusive communities.

Concluding Remarks

This chapter has surveyed a unique and innovative community arts project that successfully addressed the tenets underlying inclusive education by providing opportunities for a group of young children and adults with disabilities to explore relationship building through artmaking. Wegner (1996) draws our attention to the fact that a community's practice does not just come into being but rather is a result of a community's history, shared knowledge, skills, values, and beliefs. In the "Friends on the Farm" project, children, adults, teachers, disability development staff, artists, and farm staff brought a shared commitment to inclusive practice as well as their individual talents to jointly explore diversity and difference. The adoption of practitioner reflection-in-and-on-action enabled all project participants to discover new and meaningful ways of relating to each other and helped to build and establish relationships over time. Some questions remain unanswered, however. Did the teachers adequately address the questions around difference that were generated by the children? Did the children and the adults with disabilities feel the benefits of community arts practice as presented? What sense did they make of the experience, their interactions with each other, and the processes in which they engaged? Was the joint experience as collaborative as has been described, given the limitations of verbal exchange? These questions warrant further consideration.

The program presented here hopes to provide inspiration for those willing to address inclusive education through reflective practice in their own communities. Readers can take note of, and possibly replicate, the way this project evolved organically out of its own community, drawing on local sensibility to spread awareness of diversity and inclusion. The message is clear: our communities can benefit from connecting diverse groups by allowing artmaking to facilitate communication, expression, and mutually respectful relationship building. Community arts projects and the use of artistic teaching and learning strategies can serve as a means by which communities can develop and examine their identity, providing a fresh perspective on responsible citizenship that is coloured by tolerance, empathy, and understanding.

Take Home Messages

- Inclusive practices can be taught in the early childhood setting by providing exposure to diverse groups of individuals.
- An arts-based program provides unique opportunities for both children and adults with special needs to benefit.

- Regular early childhood activities can be used with a range of groups, both adult and child.
- Activities can be collaborative, paired, or group, or engaged as parallel activities where each group is able to learn from and share outcomes with others.

References

Associazione L'Eta Verde (2012). Association of the Green Age: www.verde-green.net/it/

Burns, R. (1994). *Introduction to research methods*. 2nd Ed. Melbourne: Longman Cheshire.

Coleman, J. S. (1988). Social capital in the creation of human capital. *American Journal of Sociology*, 94 (special supplement), 95–120.

Cologon, K. (2014). Better together! Inclusive education in the early years. In K. Cologon (Ed.), *Inclusive education in the early years: Right from the start* (pp. 1–26). South Melbourne: Oxford University Press.

Cologon, K., Cologon, T., Mevawalla, Z., & Niland, A. (2019). Generative listening: Using arts-based inquiry to investigate young children's perspectives of inclusion, exclusion and disability. *Journal of Early Childhood Research, 17*(1), 54–69.

Connors, C., & Stalker, K. (2010) Children's experiences of disability: Pointers to a social model of childhood disability. In J. Rix (Ed.), *Equality, participation and inclusion*, Vol. 1: *Diverse perspectives*. 2nd Ed. London: Routledge.

Dahlberg, G., Moss, P., & Pence, A. (1999). *Beyond quality in early childhood education and care: Postmodern perspectives*. London: Falmer Press.

Edwards, S. (2003). New directions: Charting the paths for the role of sociocultural theory in early childhood education and curriculum. *Contemporary Issues in Early Childhood, 4*(3), 251–265.

Gunn, A., Child, C., Madden, B., Purdue, K., Surtees, N., Thurlow, B., & Todd, P. (2004). Building inclusive communities in early childhood education: Diverse perspectives from Aotearoa/New Zealand, *Contemporary Issues in Early Childhood, 5*(3), 293–307.

Hawke, D. (1993). Phenomenography as a research approach in art education. *Journal of the Australian Institute of Art Education, 17*(1), 7–13.

Hexagon Project. (2021). *Hexagon Project*. https://hexagonproject.org/about/

In the Zone. (2006). www.vichealth.gov.auContent.aspx?toopicID=575

Junk Theory. (2006). www.australiacouncil.gov.au/news

Larrivee, B. (2005). *Authentic classroom management: Creating a learning community and building reflective practice*. Boston and London: Pearson Allyn & Bacon.

Love, H. R., & Horn, E. (2021). Definition, context, quality: Current issues in research examining high-quality inclusive education. *Topics in Early Childhood Special Education, 40*(4), 204–216. https://doi.org/10.1177/0271121419846342

McAnelly, K., & Gaffney, M. (2019). Rights, inclusion and citizenship: A good news story about learning in the early years. *International Journal of Inclusive Education, 23*(10), 1081–1094.

Nimmo, J. (2008). Young children's access to real life: An examination of the growing boundaries between children in childcare and adults in the community. *Contemporary Issues in Early Childhood, 9*(1), 293–307.

Okuyama, M. (2001). *An artist's-educator's role in community arts: Integrating people of diverse backgrounds and ages*. Ottawa: National Library of Canada.

Ontario Arts Council. (1998). *Community arts book: Another vital link.* Toronto: Ontario Arts Council.
Patton, M. (1990). *Qualitative evaluation and research methods.* Newbury Park, CA: Sage.
Rogoff, B. (1990). *Apprenticeship in thinking: Cognitive development in social contexts.* Oxford: Oxford University Press.
Rogoff, B., Dahl, A., & Callanan, M. (2018). The importance of understanding children's lived experience. *Developmental Review, 50,* 5–15.
Schaefer-McDaniel, N. J. (2004). Conceptualizing social capital among young people: Towards a new theory, *Children Youth and Environments, 14*(1), 140–150.
Schön, D. (1983). T*he reflective practitioner: How professionals think in action.* New York: Basic Books.
Schulte, C. M., & Thompson, C. M. (2018). *Communities of practice: Art, play, and aesthetics in early childhood.* Cham: Springer.
The University of Melbourne's Early Learning Centre. (2007). *FARM ART & FRIENDS* (Abbotsford, VIC : University of Melbourne's Early Learning Centre, 2007), CD-ROM.
Victorian Government, Department of Human Services. (2002). *Victorian state disability plan 2002–2012.* Melbourne: Disability Services Division.
Vygotsky, L. S. (1978). *Mind in society: The development of higher psychological processes.* Cambridge, MA: Harvard University Press.
Wegner, E. (1996). Communities of practice: The social fabric of a learning organization. *Health Forum Journal.* Online at www.hhnmag.com/thfnet/th960401
Wells, G. (2001). The case for dialogic inquiry. In G. Wells (Ed.), *Action talk and text: Learning and teaching through inquiry* (pp.171–194). New York: Teachers College Press.
Wright, S. (2003). *Children, meaning making and the arts.* Frenchs Forrest, NSW: Pearson Prentice Hall.

8 Building Intergenerational Connections

The Social and Emotional Benefits of Intergenerational Programs

Introduction

Since the Industrial Revolution, many societies have seen a significant shift in relationships as a result of increased life expectancy and more people spending time in age-segregated institutions. With modern people living in an increasingly age-segregated society, there is less opportunity for meaningful interactions across age stratifications. Intergenerational programs have been growing in practice and interest around the world and programs have been piloted in the United States, Europe, and the United Kingdom to combat the growing social challenge of ageism. There is also growing research being done in the Asia-Pacific communities on how nonfamilial intergenerational programs reduce age stereotyping and increase the wellbeing of both youth and older adults. Some benefits include positive impact on children's perceptions of older adults and the ageing process. Furthermore, children who engage in intergenerational programs are more positive about older people when they have frequent and regular contact with them. The chapter provides a comprehensive coverage of the programs that relate to young people working with the elderly. One example of processes and program outcomes is considered.

This chapter introduces one intergenerational program developed and conducted at a preschool in Melbourne, Australia. The program has been implemented by several teachers on multiple occasions and was designed to run in a flexible format over a period ranging from four weeks to a year. The program content includes narrative and storytelling, historical/cultural reminiscing, show and tell, shared reading, fine arts and literacy, with a significant role for music, games, and gardening. Additional components of the program that are considered include parent engagement, through parent information evenings and throughout the program parents were provided with updates. Reciprocal visits and tours, such as residents taking the children on a tour of their environment and the children taking the neighbours on a tour of their environment, were also considered an important feature of the program.

At the end of each visit the children participated in a reflective drawing-telling. They were asked to draw something they remembered from their experience. Different formats of program delivery are also considered.

DOI: 10.4324/9781003213147-11

The Need and the Opportunity

As the average life expectancy increases the global population is ageing and the number of people over 60 years old is expected to double by 2050 (Bongaarts, 2009). There are an increasing number of people living in old age residential settings, with up to 40% never receiving visitors, so these aged-care home residents face loneliness and isolation (Yaxley, 2017). Intergenerational programs have been one approach to tackle and prevent negative attitudes to the elderly developing from an early age. Typically, programs have involved bringing together children in the preschool setting with the elderly in neighbourhood settings. The key goals of such programs have been to develop empathy along with other social emotional indicators, such as emotional competence and self-regulatory skills, described in the literature. It was clear when we examined the growing body of literature in this field that the findings are not always conclusive (Jarrott & Savla, 2016; Lineweaver et al., 2017; Okoye, 2004; Robinson et al., 2015; Thompson & Weaver, 2016). Nevertheless, because the negative attitudes and stereotyping of old people, such as seeing them as sick, tired, and ugly, is considered to begin at an early age (Cuddy et al., 2005; Levy, 2009; Robinson & Howatson-Jones, 2014; Gilbert & Ricketts, 2008), early learning educational settings provide a unique opportunity to develop empathy through intergenerational programs.

Research over the last four decades has found that intergenerational programs can benefit the social and emotional development of participants in the early years. Since the 1970s when intergenerational programs were first developed to stimulate engagement between older citizens and their younger counterparts, the benefits of these programs both for the individuals and the community have been reported (Kuehne & Melville, 2014; Martins et al., 2019). The programs have been instrumental in helping to develop positive attitudes towards older adults (Newman, 1997), while fostering intergenerational connectedness (Santini et al., 2018) as well as providing a way of encouraging collaboration between assisted living facilities and early child education centres (Lux et al., 2020). Furthermore, there are reciprocal benefits for both children and adults (Femia et al., 2008; Kamei et al., 2010; Yasunaga et al., 2016). Overall, intergenerational programs can provide opportunities for children to develop social emotional competencies that are associated with behaviour, self-regulation, and empathy, as well as having a greater familiarity with and subsequent acceptance of older adults and demonstrating an increase in prosocial behaviours.

Across the Globe

There is ready acknowledgement that linking generations and utilizing intergenerational programs provides a way forward. Nevertheless, the idea remains relatively novel around the globe. Culture and intergenerational programming are clearly interlinked. Whilst the programs take various formats in different locations, such as United States, Sweden, Singapore, Malaysia,

Thailand, Philippines, China, Hong Kong, Vietnam, Japan, and Korea, there is a general organizational structure which includes utilizing intergenerational shared sites in which multiple generations receive ongoing services and/or programming at the same site (Thang et al., 2003). Overall, in the Asian context intergenerational programs have been found to be an effective intervention, such as those in Korea in a play-based program that were found to improve health-related quality of life, loneliness, and depression among older adults and learning-related social skills among preschool children in the community (Choi & Sohng, 2018).

In 2019 a television series "Old People's Home for 4 Year Olds" was shown on the national Australian broadcaster (ABC), based around a unique social experiment where a group of elderly aged-care home residents were brought together in their residential setting with a group of preschoolers, to see whether this intergenerational contact could improve the health and well-being of the older people, thus helping them to lead happier and healthier lives (Hulsman et al., 2019). As in the Asian studies the experiment worked, with an elaborate range of health indicators demonstrating the outcomes for the elderly participants. Whilst there were no measures of how the children benefited, it was clear from the visual images that they enjoyed the experience. The program was so popular that in 2021 a second series was developed and screened that took a group of independently living older adults to join a group of lively 4-year-olds in an intergenerational preschool experience that focused on connection and friendship. Clearly there is an interest in how young people interact with the elderly for the benefit of engaging the elderly persons in talk and play. But the benefit was also clear for the 4-year-olds as they developed social emotional competence through intergenerational activities. As the six-week 2021 program concluded there were numerous wellbeing and health benefits recorded for the older cohort and quite significantly the 4-year-olds showed a tangible increase in prosocial behaviours.

The Evidence

Concern about the elderly is not something new but as the population ages in Western communities there is a growing awareness of the loneliness being experienced and the benefits of providing stimulation and engagement. With the focus on developing empathy and social emotional skills in young children, various formats and approaches to intergenerational programs have been developed and researched over the past four decades. In 2020 a systematic review of literature[1] was undertaken to see what we could learn about the social emotional benefits and outcomes from intergenerational programs (Banks, 2020). The systematic review selected and critically assessed the available literature in

---

1 A systematic review is a review of a clearly formulated question that uses systematic and reproducible methods to identify, select and critically appraise *all* relevant research, and to collect and analyse data from the studies that are included in the review.

the field to determine whether the outcomes from intergenerational programs contribute to the development of the SEL competences. As outlined in Chapter 3, social emotional competencies are about developing skills to manage intrapersonal and interpersonal experiences effectively. There is a particular focus on developing the five core competencies outlined by CASEL, namely, self-awareness, self-management, social-awareness, relationship skills, and responsible decision-making.

The systematic review involved searching four databases in 2020: Scopus, Education Research Complete, Education Resources Information Centre, and PsycINFO. The search terms used were designed to capture a broad range of references. The search terms were "intergenerational program" and ("young children" OR "early childhood" OR "early years"). Out of 359 publications there were 13 publications that were included which were in English, research rather than chapters in books, and had a focus on social emotional competence outcomes.

Unlike the storytelling and data gathering in the television productions that brought intergenerational programs to public attention, the 13 studies in the systematic review of the literature were rigorous. Only one of the five qualitative findings found that there was little change in children's perceptions of older adults before and after intergenerational program participation (Bertram et al., 2018). Other studies found that children provided more positive perceptions of older adults after participation in the intergenerational program, compared to prior to participating in it. For example, Holmes (2009) and Freeman and King (2001) reported that intergenerational program participation resulted in an increase in children's empathy towards older adults and children's sensitivity to the needs of older adults. Three studies reported that participation in an intergenerational program led to increased engagement and interactivity between children and older adults (Freeman & King, 2001; Lux et al., 2020; St John, 2009).

Overall, children who participated in an intergenerational program had higher levels of empathy compared to children who did not participate in an intergenerational program. Three studies found that participation in an intergenerational program resulted in more positive perceptions of older adults and higher levels of social acceptance (Dellmann-Jenkins et al., 1986; Femia et al., 2008; Heyman et al., 2011).

Two studies found an increase in the quantity of intergenerational interactions as intergenerational programs progressed (Detmer et al., 2020; Jarrott & Smith, 2010). Two studies produced findings which indicated that participation in an intergenerational program resulted in increased prosocial behaviours, including sharing, helping, cooperating, and following classroom rules (Dellmann-Jenkins et al., 1991; Rosebrook, 2002).

Most of the studies were based on practical considerations and are thus small in scale. For example, the much-cited Femia et al. (2008) quasi-experimental single time-point design study of 34 children aged 6–8 years who had previously attended an intergenerational day care program when they were 3–6 years old were compared to children who had attended a single-generation program when they were 3–6 years old on several variables. Data were collected from interviews, drawings, and a variety of measures including attitudes toward older adults, social acceptance of older adults, and distance empathy, a behavioural test, and behaviour regulation. They found that children from the intergenerational program had higher levels of social acceptance, higher levels of empathy, a greater willingness to help older adults, greater levels of behaviour self-regulation, and more positive attitudes towards older adults, compared to children who participated in the single-generation program.

Whilst every study did not report positive findings, overall the results pointed to the benefit of such programs. Furthermore, given the challenges of doing research that includes both the elderly and 4-year-old children, the research is often secondary to the implementation of the program and the enjoyment and perceived benefits of the participants. This too was the approach at the Early Learning Centre, where the programs focused on the benefits to the participants rather than on the evaluation alone.

Theoretical Underpinnings

There are several key theoretical underpinnings of the programs. Contact theory, as outlined in Chapter 3, is the major theory that has over time focused on overcoming prejudice and improving relationships between two races or groups of people with the principle that repeated contact was likely to achieve the best outcomes. Contact theories provide an important framework to inform the development of intergenerational programs.

Both for Vygotsky (1962) and Barbara Rogoff (2003) (see Chapter 1) learning is viewed as a social process and the adult can understand the child's needs and assist in the learning. Indeed, the adult can scaffold the child's learning as they complete their art or finish a puzzle. Rogoff (2003) describes a community of learners, which is most apt when describing learning in an intergenerational program as sometimes it is the child who is teaching the adult. Additionally, these programs are focused on building relationships, creating an environment where there is joy when the children and older adults get together.

Modelling

Social learning is modelled in a variety of ways including video-modelling, role-modelling, conversations that break down each progressive step in reaching a resolution, and opportunities for play where children can experiment, explore, and build social skills within a range of environments. This is a crucial part of children's development when supporting their social skills. The domain uses both verbal and non-verbal communication, expressive and receptive language, concentration and attention, self-regulation, executive function, planning and sequencing development.

Empathy and Intergenerational Program (IGP)

When it comes to the development of empathy in intergenerational programs, researchers have convincingly demonstrated that children need to exercise care and patience, which sometimes means delaying gratification as they think about the needs of other people. For example, one program which involved one 45-minute session with the children using music, teamwork, cooking, arts, and crafts increased preschool children's prosocial and empathic behaviours, as they assisted, helped, or provided support to the older adults aged 63–95 years old without being asked by teachers after just five sessions (Hayes, 2003). In Femia et al.'s 2008 study children who had previously participated in a pre-school intergenerational program were more likely to express empathy towards older adults than children without this experience, as measured by parent, teacher, and self-report.

The Intergenerational Program at ELC

Teachers at the Early Learning Centre at the University of Melbourne have engaged in the teaching and evaluation of such programs over several years as a way of overcoming the negative stereotypical views of the elderly and to teach empathy within the school setting. Children usually participated in approximately five sessions of the program conducted over two school terms. The aged-care facility, whose residents were known as "neighbours" to the children, was located in close proximity to the ELC. It accommodated 75 adults between the ages of 65 and 100 years of age. Two classes of 20 children visited the setting for one hour, with each class visiting on alternate weeks with two lead teachers and one support teacher from the ELC (Stirling, 2020). There was a focus on establishing respectful social connections, with collaborative activities between the old and the young participants (see Figure 8.1).

The program was underpinned by the belief that through the intergenerational experience it was possible to teach young children to experience the perspective of the other and to learn about the world of the elderly.

The values of respect, kindness, sharing, care, patience, politeness, and cooperation were embedded within the program. A series of learning experiences and planned activities involving music, discussions, show-and-share, visual art, and gardening promoted partnership and a responsive engagement between the children and neighbours. Such interactions supported the building of connections and belonging.

Child Preparation and Engagement

Prior to the commencement of the program, within the classroom environment children engaged in:

- Group discussions about the neighbours and older people in general (some were knowledgeable, and others were less so);

136   Part II

Figure 8.1 A child sharing his favourite book with one of the neighbours and handing her a cup of tea.

- Watching a video about the neighbours;
- Children shared knowledge and experiences of their immediate grandparents;
- Children listened to the picture book *Wilfrid Gordon McDonald Partridge* by Mem Fox as a point of reference; and
- Walked by and referenced the residential setting during an excursion.

The Activities

The program activities included playing bingo, gardening, storytelling, singing, and music performances. The sessions were usually a mix of structured and unstructured activities. For example, teachers would implement a structured game like bingo, with children and neighbours working together to win. As the game was unfolding the teachers would encourage conversations between the children and the residents. On some occasions there were reciprocal visits, with children able to show their activities in a "show and tell" format, and on some occasions, they would display what they were doing in the playground (see Figure 8.2). Sometimes the teachers just observed the interactions from the sidelines. There were opportunities for social skills and politeness training, with the children required to rehearse what they would say when greeting the neighbours or leaving them at the point of departure.

There were also activities around reminiscing and sharing about the past. For example, "Rebecca [a neighbour] gave a presentation to the children about how she was a doctor and about how at university the lecturer had told her that she was taking the place of a man … and the children were outraged". There were photos of the neighbours in the classroom. When the neighbours told stories of going to work in the olden days the children were captivated and repeated the stories. Table 8.1 outlines the program that was delivered in 2019.

Figure 8.2 Children invited the neighbours to visit the ELC community.

Table 8.1 Sample of activities for each of the focus areas in the 2019 IGP program

Focus Area	IGP sessions	Objectives / Learning experiences
Community & Wellbeing	Who are we?	Familiarize themselves with the rules and expectations associated with excursions. Experience being in the local community with their families and teachers. Example: Teacher reading children the story of Wilfred Gordon McDonald Partridge before walking them over to the aged-care facility and introducing themselves to the neighbours for a meet and greet.
	Who are our neighbours?	Interact and communicate positively with the elderly residents, through conversations, humour, and musical experiences. Photograph each other and share narratives. Draw native animals for a bingo set. Example: Children and neighbours playing bingo together; children singing happy birthday to one of the neighbours who turned 83.
Communication & Community	Acknowledging the rights of women (International Women's Day)	Reflect on experiences through partnership drawing-telling. Develop awareness of differences and similarities amongst people. Example: Children listening to and engaging with narratives and conversations of neighbours' experiences around the rights of women in the past, comparing the present, and hopes for the future.

(continued)

Table 8.1 Cont.

Focus Area	IGP sessions	Objectives/ Learning experiences
	Collaborative communities through drawing and storytelling	Continue to experience positive interactions and communication with the residents at the aged-care facility, through conversations and storytelling.
		To invite neighbours at the residence to ELC, guiding them through our learning environment.
		Example: Seven neighbours visited the ELC. The class sang songs to the neighbours and one of the neighbours sang the Collingwood footy song. The children engaged in regular outside play while the neighbours watched. One student kicked a soccer ball to a neighbour. The class sang some more songs, thanked the neighbours for coming, and said goodbye.
	Collaborative communities through music and shared activities	Shared morning tea.
		To celebrate neighbours' birthday through singing and card-making.
		To engage in singing and choir performance – an introduction to Winter Solstice song repertoire.
		To explore rhythm, beat, tempo, and lyrics of "True Colours" (by Cyndi Lauper) and "Blue Suede Shoes" (Elvis Presley).
		Example: Children visited the neighbours to deliver a hand-drawn birthday card for one of the neighbours. The teacher read out the messages in the card to everyone.
		The lifestyle coordinator of the residence took the students through to the chapel and one of the caretakers showed the students the organ. The class practised their choir songs with the residents in the audience.
Learning & Sustainability	Growing seeds/ music	To participate in the digging, planting, watering, and care of broad bean seeds/sprouts and nasturtiums.
		To participate in singing and choir performance, performing the Winter Solstice song repertoire within the chapel located next to the residential facility.
		To invite neighbours to be audience members for a choir performance to celebrate Winter Solstice.
		Example:
		Together, everyone planted broad beans in the garden and picked the sunflowers that children from last year planted.
		The neighbours were invited to attend the kindergarten's Winter Solstice Concert. After the performance, the students went up to each neighbour and thanked them for coming.

An earlier version of this table appeared in Kirsh (2019).

The curriculum was designed using place-based pedagogies to facilitate deep understanding of the local community including

- to freely explore natural and built environments;
- to pay weekly visits to the residence to connect with the local community and foster relationships between the children and residents within the age-care facility; and
- to participate in gardening program, collaborative art and murals, games and recall memories/share life experiences.

Because there are generational changes over time, exploring technology, cultural, and societal changes through the perspective of "when I was 4 years old", storytelling, and reflective sharing were key components of the program. There were child contributions during group-time that highlighted key themes or stories shared during the program; and drawing-tellings that reflected children's learning in domains of:

- Identity – building confidence to enter new and unfamiliar places, an awareness of the rights and needs of others, a capacity to self-regulate, engage, and respond to social relationships/interactions;
- Community – building a sense of place within an environment outside of the ELC and home;
- Wellbeing – reading and responding to the emotional climate of the needs of self and others;
- Learning – drawing skill and learning from the key themes presented and discussed during this time; and
- Communication – using non-verbal and verbal language and communication means to interact with teachers, peers, senior residents, and staff at the residence.

What we Found

When the program was evaluated in 2019 (Kirsh et al., 2021) children who participated were also asked about their experience and enjoyment of the program. As would be expected, some children were excited whilst others were anxious. With time, all but two of the children became at ease and comfortable and described the program as interesting.

When the researchers reflected on the program three main themes appeared to explain its success:

- singing songs;
- learning from each other: and
- forming relationships.

Most of the children's responses indicated that they had enjoyed the program and mentioned singing songs to the neighbours and/or playing games with them. Each session began and ended with a performance by the children. The teacher reported that residents "love the singing with the children". It was clear this was the most memorable and enjoyable aspect of the program for both parties. Children enjoyed learning the "back stories" of the neighbours such as the tales of their early days. So much so that they wanted to ask questions of the residents about their childhood. The teacher observed that the children were learning history, such as talking about a horse and cart when the children were reading a story about horses, as well as learning social skills, particularly politeness. One child commented that they learned to be "kind". One parent commented that the children had learnt about death as they wrote cards to the neighbours when one of the residents died during the year.

Both the residents and the children commented that they enjoyed making friends. The children saw themselves as citizens of a community around them as they learned some historical contexts. Consequently, the program appears to be able to create meaningful relationships between the preschool children and the aged-care residents, even in a short time frame.

Children commented for example that, "I like seeing Lily and I like seeing Nancy" (pseudonyms), "we like our neighbours", and "how lovely they are". Children reported having fun with the neighbours and enjoyed seeing and visiting them. This was echoed by the teacher, who noted the children demonstrated "a greater competence in approaching the neighbours for conversation ... increasing confidence in their relationships in the space and with the neighbours". These relationships were just as important to the residents, who relished the companionship according to the teacher; "seeing the children is like being able to see their own children" (Kirsh et al., 2021). The teacher indicated that the neighbours also benefited from the companionship and singing. Children taught the neighbours what they had been learning in the curriculum and offered the opportunity to compare and discuss changes in technologies and social relationships over time.

Positive attitudes towards older people were associated with both cognitive and affective empathy, suggesting that an increased ability to take the perspective of others and share in other people's emotional experiences is associated with less ageism and discrimination. It may be that, by increasing empathic behaviours, it is possible to reduce negative stereotypes in society more broadly (Petkova, 2015; Schwalbach & Kiernan, 2002).

Others too have reported that exposure to older people and diversity may be related to the ability to better empathize and take other people's perspectives, resulting in less negative attitudes (Bales et al., 2000; Femia et al., 2008; Lloyd et al., 2018), and may influence the development of positive coping styles, perhaps because older adults tend to use adaptive coping strategies themselves (Aldwin et al., 1996; Birkeland & Natvig, 2009; Choi & Sohng, 2018). For example, children who saw their grandparents once a month or more had more positive attitudes towards older people with higher cognitive and affective empathy (see Chapter 3), and the converse was true, in that children who had least exposure to older people had the most negative attitudes.

Impact on the Neighbours

The teachers also observed and talked to the neighbours about their experience of the program. They observed the interactions between the children and neighbours and how this impacted their overall mood. During one of the sessions, a neighbour was overheard saying "I enjoy them coming, they make me feel younger."

At the conclusion of each residential visit, the children reflected on their experience through drawing-tellings, with the teacher recording their ideas and thinking. Many of the significant events were brought back into discussion within the classroom group-times.

In addition to developmental observation and curriculum reflection, children were:

- Observant of members in their community;
- Focused on relationship building;
- Prompted to share experiences/memories of older members of their families;
- Aware of respectful practices (i.e. shaking hands, greetings);
- Connected to the environment through their enjoyment of playing bingo and the gardening program; and
- Able to manage their emotions and self-regulate when entering spaces predominately filled with adults.

The shared site program provided a sense of joy for both groups. Particularly for children who did not have grandparents there was the opportunity to meet a range of people that they may otherwise not have had the opportunity to meet. The focus was on the building of relationships.

Teacher's Reflections

The program had an impact on the teachers and indeed their responses had an impact on the child participants. For one teacher, visiting the residential setting for the first time was confronting as she had had limited experience interacting with older adults and the teacher was particularly apprehensive about responding to residents who had severe and visible dementia. The teachers had not received formal training in the numerous issues associated with working with the elderly so for them it was the support of other teachers that provided the modelling. This then had an impact on the children's experience. For example:

> You have to often hide your fears, you have to show confidence because the children feed off your energy and at the end of the day, if you're fearful or showing a lot of reservation, they pick up on it as well.

Another teacher commented:

> Entering this space was a new experience and having a colleague leading this program allowed me time to familiarize myself with the routines and structures when implementing this program. Each child required a different amount of guidance and support to contribute. Recognizing these needs was a challenge but having two other participating staff allowed flexibility and fluidity to implement activities, lead discussion and support individual or small groups of children. Having consistent residents participating in the program allowed children and myself to build relationships and have comfortable conversations.

Concluding Remarks

Whilst it was possible to evaluate student outcomes through evaluation with parents and teachers it was also possible to do that through the students' own drawing-tellings. It was clear that the teachers achieved personal change and derived benefits. The teacher commented that she had developed a greater competence in approaching the neighbours for conversation – even just approaching the residence she was more confident and chattier. She had become more aware of the elderly and those with mobility issues in public spaces. To sum it up, one teacher who had run the program over several years commented:

> The program has pushed me to advocate for this program and by that, I mean, speaking up for the program to colleagues to ensure that it is being continued. The program has also pushed me to share these experiences at conferences when public speaking was not my forte but because I am passionate about it and I wanted to make sure that I could try and spread the word as much as possible as one could about the program. It has a huge impact on the residents, and they tell me about their lives, even though I don't have much time to talk to them I am mostly busy with the kids. When there are moments that the residents open up to us and I can see that it is important for them to have visitors because some of them haven't seen family members for years and I don't know if they get visitors. Made me reflect on my own life and that I should spend more time with my parents, and they are not even that old, but they are grandparents now and I don't see them that much. The program challenges me to reflect and think about the institutionalization of the young and the old in our society and makes you think about what you can value in this life.

Take Home Messages

- Key theoretical underpinnings of intergenerational programs include contact theory and social learning theory.
- Learning outcomes are reflected in prosocial practices.
- Equity and diversity – exploring self and difference through self- and other-portrait drawings using varying art materials; exploring gender equity through storytelling, a senior resident's perspective (International Women's Day); and sharing stories from home and experiences (show and tell).
- Gardening – collaboratively planting, watering, and harvesting edible kitchen garden; participating in observational drawings and shared mealtimes.
- Music, singing, and performance – singing and performing ELC repertoire of songs; collaborative participation of the music specialist program.
- Generational changes through time – exploring technology, cultural, and societal changes through the perspective of 'when I was 4 years old', storytelling, and reflective sharing.

References

Aldwin, C., Sutton, K., Chiara, G., & Spiro, A. (1996). Age differences in stress, coping, and appraisal: Findings from the Normative Aging Study. *Journals of Gerontology: Series B, 51*(4), 179–188. https://doi.org/10.1093/geronb/51B.4.P179

Bales, S., Eklund, S., & Siffin, C. (2000). Children's perceptions of elders before and after a school-based intergenerational program. *Educational Gerontology, 26*(7), 677–689. https://doi.org/10.1080/03601270050200662

Banks, J. (2020). Promoting social and emotional learning in early childhood through intergenerational programming: A systematic review. Unpublished master's thesis, University of Melbourne.

Bertram, A. G., Burr, B. K., Sears, K., Powers, M., Atkins, L., Holmes, T., Kambour, T., & Kuns, J. B. (2018). Generations learning together: Pilot study for a multigenerational program. *Journal of Intergenerational Relationships, 16*(3), 243–255. https://doi.org/10.1080/15350770.2018.1477402

Birkeland, A., & Natvig, G. (2009) Coping with ageing and failing health: A qualitative study among elderly living alone. *International Journal of Nursing Practice, 15*, 257–264. https://doi.org/10.1111/j.1440-172X.2009.01754.x

Bongaarts, J. (2009). Human population growth and the demographic transition. *Philosophical Transactions of the Royal Society B: Biological Sciences, 364*(1532), 2985–2990. https://doi.org/10.1098/rstb.2009.0137

Choi, M. J., & Sohng, K. Y. (2018). The effect of the intergenerational exchange program for older adults and young children in the community using the traditional play. *Journal of Korean Academy of Nursing, 48*(6), 743–753. https://doi.org/10.4040/jkan.2018.48.6.743

Cuddy, A., Norton, M., & Fiske, S. (2005). This old stereotype: The pervasiveness and persistence of the elderly stereotype. *Journal of Social Issues, 61*(2), 267–285. https://doi.org/10.1111/j.1540-4560.2005.00405.x

Dellmann-Jenkins, M., Lambert, D., & Fruit, D. (1986). Old and young together: Effect of an educational program on preschoolers' attitudes toward older people. *Thomas Childhood Education, 62*(3), 206–212. Retrieved from: https://eric.ed.gov

Dellmann-Jenkins, M., Lambert, D., & Fruit, D. (1991). Fostering preschoolers' prosocial behaviors toward the elderly: The effect of an intergenerational program. *Educational Gerontology, 17*(1), 21–32. https://doi.org/10.1080/0360127820170103

Detmer, M. R., Kern, P., Jacobi–Vessels, J., & King, K. M. (2020). Intergenerational music therapy: Effects on literacy, physical functioning, self–worth, and interactions. *Journal of Intergenerational Relationships, 18*(2), 175–195. https://doi.org/10.1080/15350770.2019.1670318

Femia, E. E., Zarit, S. H., Blair, C., Jarrott, S. E., & Bruno, K. (2008). Intergenerational preschool experiences and the young child: Potential benefits to development. *Early Childhood Research Quarterly, 23*(2), 272–287. https://doi.org/10.1016/j.ecresq.2007.05.001

Freeman, N. K., & King, S. (2001). Service learning in preschool: An intergenerational project involving five–year–olds, fifth graders, and senior citizens. *Early Childhood Education Journal, 28*, 211–217. https://doi.org/10.1023/A:1009538708148

Gilbert, C., & Ricketts, K. (2008). Children's attitudes toward older adults and aging: A synthesis of research. *Educational Gerontology, 34*, 570–586. https://doi.org/10.1080/03601270801900420

Hayes, C. (2003). An observational study in developing an intergenerational shared site program: Challenges and insights. *Journal of Intergenerational Relationships, 1*(1), 113–132. https://doi.org/10.1300/J194v01n01_10

Heyman, J. C., Gutheil, I. A., & White–Ryan, L. (2011). Pre–school children's attitudes toward older adults: Comparison of intergenerational and traditional day care. *Journal of Intergenerational Relationships, 9*(4), 435–444. https://doi.org/10.1080/15350770.2011.618381

Holmes, C. L. (2009). An intergenerational program with benefits. *Early Childhood Education Journal, 37*(2), 113–119. https://doi.org/10.1007/s10643

Hulsman, B., Mason-Campbell, J., Bibb, S., & Arwell-Lewis, B. (Producers). (2019). *Old People's Home for 4 Year Olds* [Television series]. Red Arrow Studios International.

Jarrott, S., & Savla, J. (2016). Intergenerational contact and mediators impact ambivalence towards future selves. *Intergenerational Journal of Behavioural Development, 40*, 282–288. https://doi.org/10.1177/0165025415581913

Jarrott, S. E., & Smith, C. L. (2010). The complement of research and theory in practice: Contact theory at work in nonfamilial intergenerational programs. *The Gerontologist, 51*(1), 112–121. https://doi.org/10.1093/geront/gnq058

Kamei, T., Itoi, W., Kajii, F., Kawakami, C., Hasegawa, M., & Sugimoto, T. (2010). Six–month outcomes of an innovative weekly intergenerational day program with older adults and school–aged children in a Japanese urban community. *Japan Journal of Nursing Science, 8*(1), 95–107. https://doi.org/10.1111/j.1742

Kirsh, E. (2019). *Singing Songs and Making Friends: An Intergenerational Program in the Early Years*. Unpublished master's thesis, University of Melbourne.

Kirsh, E., Frydenberg, E., & Deans, J. (2021). Benefits of an intergenerational program in the early years. *Journal of Early Childhood Education Research, 10*(2), 140–164.

Kuehne, V. S., & Melville, J. (2014). The state of our art: A review of theories used in intergenerational program research (2003–2014) and ways forward. *Journal of Intergenerational Relationships, 4*, 317.

Levy, B. (2009). Stereotype embodiment: A psychological approach to aging. *Current Directions in Psychological Science*, *18*, 332–336. https://doi.org/10.1111/j.1467-8721.2009.01662.x

Lineweaver, T., Roy, A., & Horth, M. (2017). Children's stereotypes of older adults: Evaluating contributions of cognitive development and social learning. *Educational Gerontology*, *43*(6), 300–312. https://doi.org/10.1080/03601277.2017.1296296

Lloyd, K., Devine, P., & Carney, G. (2018). Imagining their future selves: Children's attitudes to older people and their expectations of life at age 70. *Children & Society*, *32*, 444–456. https://doi.org/10.1111/chso.12289

Lux, C., Tarabochia, D., & Barben, E. (2020). Intergenerational program perceptions and recommendations: Perspectives from teachers, children, residents, and staff. *Journal of Intergenerational Relationships*, *18*(2), 196–213. https://doi.org/10.1080/15350770.2019.1665609

Martins, T., Midão, L., Martinez Veiga, S., Dequech, L., Busse, G., Bertram, M., McDonald, A., Gilliland, G., Orte, C., Vives, M., & Costa, E. (2019). Intergenerational programs review: Study design and characteristics of intervention, outcomes, and effectiveness. *Journal of Intergenerational Relationships*, *17*(1), 93–109. https://doi.org/10.1080/15350770.2018.1500333

Newman, S. (1997). History and evolution of intergenerational programs. In S. Newman, C. R. Ward, T. B. Smith, J. O. Wilson, & J. McCrea (Eds.), *Intergenerational programs: Past, present, and future* (pp. 55–80). London: Taylor & Francis.

Okoye, U. (2004). Knowledge of aging among secondary school students in southeastern Nigeria. *Educational Gerontology*, *30*, 481–489. https://doi.org/10.1080/03601270490445096

Petkova, G. (2015). An analysis of children's attitudes toward older adults. *Trakia Journal of Sciences*, *13*(1), 533–540. https://doi.org/10.15547/tjs.2015.s.01.094

Robinson, S., & Howatson-Jones, L. (2014). Children's views of older people. *Journal of Research in Childhood Education*, *28*(3), 293–312. https://doi.org/10.1080/02568543.2014.912995

Robinson, T., Zurcher, J., & Callahan, C. (2015). Youthful ideals of older adults: An analysis of children's drawings. *Educational Gerontology*, *41*, 440–450. https://doi.org/10.1080/03601277.2014.983372

Rogoff, B. (2003). *The cultural nature of human development*. Oxford University Press.

Rosebrook, V. (2002). Intergenerational connections enhance the personal/social development of young children. *International Journal of Early Childhood*, *34*(2), 30–41. https://doi.org/10.1007/bf03176765

Santini, S., Tombolesi, V., Baschiera, B., & Lamura, G. (2018). Intergenerational programs involving adolescents, institutionalized elderly, and older volunteers: Results from pilot research–action in Italy. *BioMed Research International*, *2018*, 1–14. https://doi.org/10.1155/2018/4360305

Schwalbach, E., & Kiernan, S. (2002). Effects of an intergenerational friendly visit program on the attitudes of fourth graders toward elders. *Educational Gerontology*, *28*(3), 175–187. https://doi.org/10.1080/036012702753542490

St John, P. A. (2009). Growing up and growing old: Communities in counterpoint. *Early Child Development and Care*, *179*(6), 733–746. https://doi.org/10.1080/03004430902944882

Stirling, S. (2020). Embedding SEL within curriculum: Partnership with communities. In E. Frydenberg, J. Deans, & R. Liang (Eds.), *Promoting Well-Being in the Pre-school Years* (pp. 141–162). Abingdon: Routledge.

Thang, L., Kaplan, M., & Henkin, N., 2003. Intergenerational programming in Asia: Converging diversities toward a common goal. *Journal of Intergenerational Relationships*, 1(1), pp. 49–69.

Thompson, E., & Weaver, A. (2016). Making connections: The legacy of an intergenerational program. *Gerontologist*, 56, 909–918. https://doi.org/10.1093/geront/gnv064

Vygotsky, L. (1962). *Thought and Language*. Cambridge, MA: MIT Press.

Yasunaga, M., Murayama, Y., Takahashi, T., Ohba, H., Suzuki, H., Nonaka, K., Kuraoka, M., Sakurai, R., Nishi, M., Sakuma, N., Kobayashi, E., Shinkai, S., & Fujiwara, Y. (2016). Multiple impacts of an intergenerational program in Japan: Evidence from the research on productivity through intergenerational sympathy project. *Geriatrics & Gerontology International*, 16, 98–109. https://doi.org/10.1111/ggi.12770

Yaxley, L. (2017, October 25). Up to 40 per cent of aged care residents get no visitors, minister Ken Wyatt says. *ABC News*, Retrieved from www.abc.net.au/news/2017-10-25/aged-care-residents-suffering-from-loneliness,-ken-wyatt-says/9085782.

Part III

9 The COPE-Resilience Program

A Guide to Successful Connections Building Activities at Early Childhood Programs

COPE-R in Action: Each day brings something new ... when we are doing COPE-R, we are doing it over weeks but [the program] goes longer because it's constantly present in the classroom. You can see the child being unpolite, you can see who is expressing empathy towards another. It is like you've developed this sixth sense of what's going on in the classroom through a COPE-R lens you see what you didn't see before. Every time an opportunity arises, we stop and look at that very specific thing that just happened in the classroom and try to incorporate COPE-R activities, knowledge and reflections straight away. It has become more and more meaningful each year. As a teacher I kept adding my own elements and just fit in into the curriculum as I go. I would never go through a year without having COPE-R.

(Teacher's reflection)

Introduction

At a very young age, children learn and develop within a web of connections within their families, communities, culture, and place. Positive, responsive, and consistent relationships help young children to flourish by providing a supportive and growth-promoting environment for them to feel secure enough to play, explore, learn, participate in, and contribute to their communities. This supports children to build an authentic sense of identity and agency that they have the ability and capacity to make a difference in the world by participating in their communities, as illustrated in Part II of this book. Besides family members, early childhood educators are often a significant part of many children's web of connections. This chapter illustrates with practical tools and examples how educators in an early childhood environment can play an important role in modelling and supporting children to understand the emotions of self and others by facilitating approaches to help children to express emotions and through developing healthy strategies to regulate them. These all contribute to cultivating a successful preschool experience – an environment that supports building empathic capacity, empowers a positive sense of community in young children, and enhances their sense of belonging and enabling lifelong learning.

DOI: 10.4324/9781003213147-13

A Less Discussed Area in Implementing Early Childhood SEL Programs: The Role of the Teacher

With the growing emphasis on social emotional learning in education and the importance of building foundational skills in the early years, there are many preschool Social and Emotional Learning (SEL) programs being developed. Most of these preschool SEL programs focus on building foundational social skills such as emotion regulation, respectful communication skills, social awareness and promoting prosocial behaviour such as empathy, kindness, and gratitude (Flook et al., 2015). Although the content, including activities and resources for teachers, that constitutes a SEL program in a preschool setting is important, a less discussed topic in this arena is the paramount role that educators play and their capacity to follow specifically designed programs whilst scaffolding children's learning throughout the process of implementation. Literature in character strengths development, for example, has indicated that adult modelling is an essential process for young children to learn and develop their own character strengths and this is especially relevant for early childhood educators because they are often the first non-family adults who regularly interact with young children (Smith, 2013; Kokoszka & Smith, 2016; Park, 2004; Steen et al., 2003). It is evident that early childhood educators who regularly practise socialization of character strengths with young children and who are competent at engaging with them have better success in nurturing these attributes in young children (Haslip et al., 2019).

It is well accepted in the literature relating to child development, early education, and parenting, that children learn by imitating adults. When it comes to implementing a SEL program within the early childhood setting, attuning to the process is as crucial as the delivery of content and activities. Educators and teachers have a pivotal role by, first, creating a safe environment for teaching and learning to occur and, second, by enacting and modelling the SEL concepts through their daily interactions with children. One commonality across successful implementation of such program is the purposeful weaving of the SEL program into the school day and embodying SEL concepts moment-by-moment (Caselman, 2007; Miyamoto et al., 2015; Rafaila, 2015). Researchers have noted a strong connection between early years teachers' embodiment and implementation of SEL curriculum and the development of social and emotional competence of young children (Burdelski, 2010; Dachyshyn, 2015; Rosenthal & Gatt, 2010). Teachers' and educators' embodiment of SEL curriculum simply means making aspects of social emotional competence tangible and visible through their direct and implicit instructions and interactions with young children. This includes the way emotions are cultivated and expressed throughout the daily activities using different forms of arts; how empathic behaviours are being modelled and delivered; how productive coping and problem-solving skills are encouraged and facilitated; positive reinforcement to shape effective communication behaviours through positive reinforcement; and most importantly, how elements of what is being taught in the SEL program are enacted through a stable and secure relationship that the teacher or educator has with the child, as this relationship has been shown in research to directly influence SEL outcomes (DeMeulenaere, 2015; Havighurst et al., 2010). For example, children can learn helpful coping skills not only through direct teaching, such as using visual tools such as the Early Years Coping Cards (Frydenberg & Deans, 2011), but also through modelling by adults and the interactions they have with adults and other children in their lives (Frydenberg et al., 2021).

Cultivating Empathic Capacity: Quality of Educator–Child Relationship Matters

As highlighted in Chapter 3, for many young children and their families, their early childhood setting is a community. The relationships children make in the early childhood setting with the educators and their peers is a critical aspect for building a "sense of community". Being part of a community strengthens children's sense of identity and, through positive relationships with other people in the community, builds resilience and friendships, which all contribute positively to their development. Early childhood literature has long emphasized the interconnectedness of relationships, play, and environments in influencing children's learning and development. For example, Kirk and MacCallum in their study (2017) identified that, when these three elements work synergistically, that is, together, they enhance the potential of each other in providing an optimal supportive environment for children's social and emotional development. The warm relationships, for example, create safe emotional environments, which in turn encourage children to play and interact with each other and their teachers. As teachers come to understand the children more by observing how children play together, their relationships are further enhanced, and it helps to increase the potential for conceptual understandings on prosocial behaviours for children (Kirk & MacCallum, 2017). Early childhood settings provide a unique developmental context and environment in which daily activities including play can become increasingly more complex and sophisticated for young children, which further strengthens relationships and creates safe environments that are rich in creativity and encourage exploration. Consequently, these elements work cohesively together to reinforce the teacher's support of children's social and emotional development, and the degree to which this support is provided also increases with the growing sophistication of the relationship, environment, and play. Thereby the community and context grow together with the holistic and continuous social and emotional development of the child.

The quality of the teacher–child relationship matters as it can encourage or discourage the development of young children's character strengths and related prosocial traits and skills such as love, kindness, and forgiveness (Hyson & Taylor 2011; Shonkoff & Phillips 2000; Pianta, 1997). Teachers who intentionally create secure attachment relationships in the preschool setting help create confident learners. Preschool children who have developed secure attachment/ relationships with their teachers are found to be more self-confident in the preschool setting and more successful learners in that environment (Bergin & Bergin, 2009). Moreover, the secure bond between the teacher and child also facilitates school readiness, with increased academic, language, and social competencies among 4-year-olds, as these children tend to have more enhanced cognitive abilities (Howes et al., 1998; Mashburn et al., 2008; Birch & Ladd, 1997; Commodari, 2013).

Children can learn how to be kind, caring, empathic, and prosocial in a community that espouses these characteristics. There are specific ways that early childhood educators can nurture warm relationships with children, such as listening and conversing in a thoughtful and attentive way; consciously and intentionally monitoring their personal feelings and responding to children with sensitivity; modelling empathetic behaviour by interacting in emotionally supportive ways with children, particularly for those who may need extra assistance socially (Flynn & Schachter, 2017; Hyson & Taylor, 2011; Priest, 2007).

Creating a Community of Prosocial Learners and Fostering Skills Development

Humans thrive in communities where they have a strong sense of belonging. This is the same for children. Thus, being a member of a warm and supportive classroom community can promote children's prosocial development. Swick (2005) suggested that by the age of 4 children can understand that others have different ideas and viewpoints, including different feelings about oneself and about others. Young children also start to develop more meaningful friendships at this age and are more likely to use prosocial behaviour when they are with other children than with adults (Eisenberg et al., 2006). Wanting to play with their friends motivates young children to behave in prosocial ways because other children may not want to play with them unless they cooperate, help solve problems, and engage in flexible give and take (Hyson & Taylor, 2011). Children who spend time with peers who are sophisticated in their prosocial skills are likely to become more prosocial themselves as they learn to adopt the more helpful, caring norms of their peers over time (Eisenberg et al., 2006). Teachers can identify everyday opportunities for children to have the time and space to interact with each other through intentional pairing and grouping children for different activities. For example, they can scaffold the development of the less prosocial children by pairing them with the more capable ones. Teachers can also use positive guidance strategies during daily interactions between children and thus promote prosocial behaviour by helping children first become more aware of their own needs and feelings and then become aware of the feelings of others (Barry, 2011). Children who learn to cope with their own negative feelings are better able to tune in to and help others who are distressed.

Another key role early childhood educators can play in a classroom context to cultivate empathic skills is by demonstrating and modelling those skills. Many studies have shown that children are more likely to notice and imitate aspects of adult behaviour, including prosocial actions if the adult (i) is warm, nurturing, and responsive; (ii) is clear about the kind of behaviour they expect; and (iii) uses induction as a discipline strategy, that is, pointing out the reasons for rules or the effect of one's behaviour on others (Hyson, 2004; Hyson & Taylor, 2011; Eisenberg et al., 2006). In everyday interactions, teachers can utilize different classroom activities, such as morning meetings and / or circle time, to foster empathic and prosocial behaviour in children. Besides the use of positive behaviour guidance systems that focus on teaching prosocial skills, reading storybooks to young children to exemplify moral and prosocial behaviour is another valuable tradition in early childhood classrooms, particularly when the characters portrayed are human rather than anthropomorphized animals (Kersey & Masterson, 2013; Larsen et al., 2018).

In summary, early childhood teachers play an important role in developing empathy and caring skills in young children and help them to be more responsive, enjoy closer friendships with their peers, and work more collaboratively with others to solve problems (Griggs et al., 2009). Empathetic children can understand the feelings of themselves and of others and therefore respond more readily to help those in need (Marshall & Marshall, 2011). They also grow up to have more healthy social relationships and achieve better academically in the long term (Denham, 2005; Masterson & Kersey, 2013; McKown & Gumbiner, 2009).

The ideal teacher classroom approaches are exemplified as appropriate in each of the Community Connections Programs described in Part II of this volume. In the next section one additional example is provided to illustrate how the above suggestions and recommendations for teachers have been put into practice and documented in an early childhood classroom context.

Theory in Action: Process of Socialization and Embodiment of COPE-R

To illustrate how theory is translated into action the example of one SEL Program titled COPE-Resilience (Frydenberg et al., 2021) and its implementation in an early childhood setting (the Early Learning Centre (ELC) in Melbourne, Australia) is documented here. The role of the educator/teacher in building young children's sense of community and belonging is augmented as children are engaged with meaningful connections that support the development of social and emotional understandings, particularly around caring and empathy for self, others, and the world they live in.

The COPE-R Program

COPE-R is a theory-rich and evidence-grounded child-centred programme of social and emotional learning activities appropriate for children aged 4–8 years, with modifications for 3-year-olds (see Table 9.1 for program outline). It is designed to be used flexibly in various early learning contexts, enabling program directors, educators, teachers, and facilitators – including those who

Table 9.1 COPE-R sessions: objectives and learning experiences

COPE-R sessions	Aims objectives	Learning experiences
Session 1 CARE	The *teacher* to discuss feelings Engage in role play and focused observation on body language The *children* to identify and be aware of emotions in self and others	*Provocation* *Group discussion* How do we care for others and ourselves? Can we be feeling detectives? Can we name good feelings that make our bodies happy and relaxed? Can we name bad feelings that make our bodies feel hard and shaky? Can you draw a picture when you were caring for yourself or someone else? Role playing good feelings or bad feelings Drawing-tellings that depict good feelings or bad feelings or both
Session 2 OPEN COMMUNICATION	The *teacher* and *children* brainstorm the qualities of open communication Emphasis placed on seeing, hearing, listening, and sensing	Guided drawings to show what is needed to achieve open communication Use of Early Years Coping Cards Body language/posture to show what it is to be a good listener Role-plays and drawing-tellings to show open communication
Session 3 POLITENESS	The *teacher* and *children* to show what is politeness with a focus on the teacher's verbal and physical reactions	*Group discussion* on politeness *Provocation* What does it mean to be polite? Use of Early Years Coping Cards to stimulate discussion Create a list of words that indicate politeness Create a mandala of silence with stones and shells Drawing-tellings that depict polite caring behaviour

Table 9.1 Cont.

COPE-R sessions	Aims objectives	Learning experiences
Session 4 EMPATTHY	Children introduced to empathetic behaviour through role-play scenarios and discussing real-life experiences with people and communities, resources, and world issues	Group discussion on what it means to be empathic and share
Provocation
How do other people see us if we don't share? What can we share with others?
Develop the noise level chart
Drawing tellings that depict showing care and concern for self for others
Session 5 REVIEW	Teacher and children review learnings from previous sessions And cross-reference knowledge across all of the curriculum	Create a bank of words that communicate care, concern, and empathy
Children to choose word that resonates most with them and write them on a tag and hang on the care and respect tree
Japanese tea ceremony to enact sharing, open communication, politeness
Create a poster as a reminder of caring and sharing in their classroom
Singing songs
Sharing final thoughts and celebrating new knowledge

An earlier version of this table appeared in Deans et al. (2017).

work with children of diverse backgrounds – to select activities that best suit their setting.

The COPE-R program aims to:

1. Develop children's knowledge and skills in recognizing their own and other's feelings and emotions.
2. Encourage children's ability to be resilient through use of positive coping strategies.
3. Increase children's knowledge and use of prosocial and empathic behaviours towards each other, such as caring and sharing.
4. Enhance children's empathy towards the environment, animals, and diverse people.

From Activities to Implementation – Flexibility and Teacher's Wisdom

We outline the process that the educators have utilized and adapted when implementing COPE-R at the ELC. This illustrates the process by which adults can help children develop more empathetic skills by consciously and intentionally monitoring their personal feelings, modelling empathetic behaviour, responding to others with sensitivity, and by using positive guidance strategies (Kirk & MacCallum, 2017).

Creating a Safe Teaching and Learning Environment

In a safe environment, children are able to learn more effectively. The COPE-R teacher creates an environment that is accepting and warm, where positive relationships are encouraged (see Figure 9.1). For example, they start the day with circle time where all children sit down and look into each other's faces and greet each other with respect before the teacher introduces the topic or concept for the day.

The teacher has commented that "The introductions have been really important. It's amazing what children remember from every class introduction. Every time we have a COPE-R meeting there is excitement, and it's telling me the children are enjoying being in the sharing circle."

Another important aspect in curating a safe environment is setting "ground rules" with the children. This can help them understand what acceptable behaviour is, such as listening quietly when someone is speaking, speaking nicely to one another, being respectful to one another, looking after one another:

> It's almost as if you see something that is not visible, but it's actually there such as a child ignoring another child, or a child walking in and sneakily going to do something. You sort of see those things straight away.
>
> (Teacher feedback)

Figure 9.1 Circle time: Tuning in to ourselves to start the day.

The COPE-Resilience Program 157

*Cultivating Foundational Relation Skills and Fostering Ways
for Expressing Emotions*

As outlined in Chapter 2 and Chapter 3, empathy is described as individuals being able to understand and interpret the behaviour of others, anticipate what someone else might do, and feel what others are feeling, and then respond to them. The establishment of empathetic behaviours is important for the development of moral reasoning and overall prosocial development. Mortari (2011) has reported that young children (4 to 7 years of age) are not only competent thinkers and communicators about their own emotions and the emotions of others, but they also have the capacity for deep reflection, and develop complex arguments around emotions when given conversational prompts and guided by more competent partners.

An important foundational skill for children to develop is understanding emotions and empathy. The COPE-R teacher chooses from a selection of activities that are intended to help build the foundational understanding of emotions for children. For example, the Feelings Explorer activities ask children to become a "Feelings Explorer", and engage in activities where they can think, explore, research, and discover social emotional skills. This understanding is the building block for each of the COPE topics. The COPE-R teacher also revisits these foundational skills with children, such as what feelings look like and noticing feelings in others, prior to the commencement of each of the sessions. Teachers of COPE-R also emphasize their use of feeling words when implementing COPE-R so it becomes commonplace for children to hear and use the language of coping.

Modelling and Developing Empathic Behaviours

As highlighted earlier in this chapter, young children imitate the behaviours of adults, so it is important for adults to model appropriate behaviours, by

Figure 9.2 Children's artwork to exploring different feelings.

158 Part III

Figure 9.3 Children's art creation demonstrating empathy towards nature.

focusing on modelling empathy and prosocial behaviours – not just in one or two lessons but throughout the program and have it embedded as part of the expected behaviour at the early learning centre. Educators and teachers use their discretion to highlight and incorporate empathy into the daily activities and curriculum (Figure 9.3). For example, the teacher who runs COPE-R mentioned that:

> When we engaged in the "threatened species day" we talked about empathy towards all the animals, so when an opportunity like that arises, we stop the group and use COPE-R to even tackle environmental issues so COPE-R becomes integrated into everything we do.

Class discussions use visual prompts such as the Early Years Coping cards (Figure 9.4), which provide images of situations for children to help them explore their feelings, the feelings of others, and what they might do in the different situations presented.

Encouraging and Facilitating Productive Coping, Problem-Solving Skills

Role-play provides children with an opportunity to experience and practise the social emotional skills being explored in the program, individually, in pairs, and in small groups. Role-play requires active involvement from the children and their educators.

Developing empathy and prosocial behaviours can take time, especially when learning to take the perspective of another. During the implementation of COPE-R, teachers readily identify opportunities during the day to help children practise their skills. For example, if there is conflict in the playground, ask each child how their behaviour has affected the other and how the other may be feeling. Using these opportunities, teachers can

Figure 9.4 Early Years Coping cards: getting hurt/feeling sad.

encourage independent problem solving rather than solving the problem for the child.

> When I go outside, I always say, "Be kind to one another and every living thing" so just reminding them often so that they go out to play feeling strong. Or I might speak to individual children who are often disruptive and say, "today, can you feel that some children are a little bit down, they're a little bit sad", "could you keep an eye on them, and just be there for them". So I reverse the roles, and I empower the children who are having problems and I put them in a position where they can look after each other.

Shaping Effective Communication Behaviours through Positive Reinforcement

Teachers who run the COPE-R have found that using specifically labelled praise (indicating what it is you are praising) is the best feedback for children as it specifically tells the child which behaviours are preferred and appropriate and allows them to learn the exact behaviour to be repeated. Labelled praise is more than just saying "good job"; identify the behaviour that is being approved, for example, "Good job! I really liked how you helped your friend find the pencils". It is highly recommended that labelled praise be provided regularly when empathic and prosocial behaviours are observed.

> Introduce the concepts and reinforce them every time, so children know what is coming. There are always ongoing discussions, either at an individual, small group or big group level about respect, not just for each other but for the environment and the materials in the classroom. It is the circle time that generates most of the powerful understanding … of anything that we do.

160 Part III

Figure 9.5 Children's drawing: How to care for the environment.

Weaving SEL into the School Day and Embodying SEL Concepts Moment-by-Moment

One of the most essential elements that teachers of COPE-R have focused on is the use of different approaches and art modules, such as body movement, drawings, poetry, and songs etc., to encourage children to revisit the learning content in the program and celebrate their individual and group understandings (Figure 9.5). For example, Figure 9.6 shows a group of children engaging in a mindfulness-based activity of cloud and star gazing in one of their excursions to connect with nature.

Seeking Ongoing Feedback and Reflection from Children

In the context of classroom teaching, it would be appropriate for teachers to encourage children to use words and drawings to process and reflect on their emotions associated with lived experience. Teachers who run the COPE-R have also utilized different art forms including drawing-tellings to elicit learning reflection from children. Drawing has been identified as one of the preferred modes of expression for children in the early childhood years (Burkitt et al., 2005; Dockett & Perry, 2005) and, as such, offers a non-threatening means of collecting meaningful feedback from children and giving voice to children. Through children's drawings, we can also develop an insight into how children make meaning of their lived experience (Cameron, 2005; Scott Frisch, 2006; Wright, 2007a, 2007b).

The COPE-Resilience Program 161

Figure 9.6 Mindful in May excursion: cloud and star gazing.

Figure 9.7 Children drawings: what kind of heart do you have?

At the conclusion of each COPE-R session, children are given the opportunity to express their understandings of emotions and social behaviours by being invited to draw something they had remembered from the session. The teacher moves throughout the group, giving one-on-one time to enable individuals to share their drawings and to add a descriptive narrative. Figure 9.7 is an example of how the visual record created by each participating child at the conclusion of COPE-R session involved the children in the immediate identification and revisitation of thoughts, feelings, images, and actions experienced during the session.

From the teachers' journal notes, children's drawing-tellings, and collaborative posters, it is evident that children were able to learn and use a wide range of emotive words to describe their "good/pleasant feelings that make our bodies happy and relaxed". These included: *joyous, silly, surprised, loving, caring, trusting, friendly,* and *sunny*. They also identified a corresponding list of words that described "hard/unpleasant feelings that make our bodies hard or shaky and jelly-fish like". These included: *grumpy, sad, cross, annoyed, going bananas, bored, mad, frustrated, scatty,* and *having a yellow minute.* By the ongoing process of scaffolding the use of feelings words and allowing space and time to process these learnings, children are encouraged to embrace their personal responsibility for naming emotions, and to enthusiastically engage in collaborative discussions about social emotional issues. For example, one child's drawing-telling communicated deeply felt emotion*:*

> When I felt sad, my friends came around me and they said, "let's go and play together". I wasn't crying, but I felt like crying; my eyes felt sad. When I was sad, it felt like there was a dark sun in the sky. When my friends came to talk to me, it felt like the sun was shining in the sky again.

Helping Children Appreciate the Emotions of Self, Others, and Spaces

As noted by Berrol (2006), feeling empathetic is understood to have its roots both in the brain and in the body, with scholars Feshbach and Feshbach (2009) and Hoffman (2000) identifying that, in order to share and respond to another person's physical and emotional experience, the child needs to first experience it him/herself. One of the ways that teachers of COPE-R used to facilitate appreciation of emotions in children is curating a collaborative learning experience through creating a poster that represented *listening with your whole body*. The resultant collaborative drawing (Figure 9.8) of a "good listener" depicted a person listening with his brain (*open brain*) eyes (*clear, bright and focused*), ears, whole body (*calm and tall*), and heart (*gentle, especially when a person is sad or angry*). One child said, "listening is more than just hearing, it's concentrating with your whole body; you need to listen to your friends with your whole body".

Expanding and Extending Learning of Empathy

The concept of empathy can be viewed as the building block for relationships because it refers to an individual's capacity to understand and even embody the perspectives, needs, and intentions of others (Gallese, 2003). The children's focused engagement in the COPE-R program highlights their capacity to question not just what they know about care between and for humans, but also their perception of care between humans and the environment. For example, in some of the drawing-tellings, children were able to represent and explain their involvement in the care of their friends, the immediate environment, and the world:

> When you care, you look at someone and listen.
>
> I am caring for my sister. She is learning to walk and I use my hands to make her feel strong.

Figure 9.8 Children's drawing of listening with the whole body.

My dad felt like not going to work one day. He works very hard. I made him a vegemite sandwich and a cup of coffee to help him feel better. After his breakfast, he felt better.

164 *Part III*

> To share, you must be kind and listen to a person, and ask for something in a nice way.

The children also expressed wishes for a more sustainable and peaceful future, for example:

> We should melt all the guns and turn them into beautiful things.
> We should connect all the waters of the world.
> Every human is precious.

Creating your own Connections Building Activities

There are many ways that early childhood educators and teachers can utilize their creativity to build classroom activities that cultivate empathic capacity in young children and build a community of prosocial learners. Some of these activities can be led by adults/teachers whilst providing opportunities also for children to direct their own activities.

Example of an Adult-Led Activity in COPE-R

On the topic of appreciation for and sensitivity to one's surroundings, teachers extended the reach of children's social emotional understandings to include the appreciation for the emotion of spaces. The teacher led the children into the development of a "voice level chart" (see Figure 9.9), with colours selected by the children to correspond to voice levels: white being the softest, whispering sound, blue being soft and normal, green being an optimal loud sound, orange being very loud but not alarming, and red being the shouting, angry sound. The significance of silence was also identified in the teacher-researcher journal notes as being important, with children engaging in meditation and creating soft, quiet, peaceful spaces in the playroom.

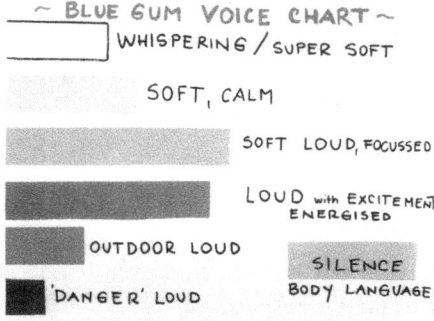

Figure 9.9 Voice level chart.

Figure 9.10 Children's creation of hand mandala.

Example of a Child-Led Activity in COPE-R

Teachers can prepare aesthetically pleasing and open-ended play materials, such as stones, crystals, and glass to stimulate children to express their social and emotional connections. For example, in the COPE-R program, the children took the initiative to develop collaboratively a hand mandala using natural objects (Figure 9.10).

International Adaptation

The COPE-Resilience program has also been adapted and trialled with a Taiwanese preschool population in Taiwan. Overall, it was found that even in culturally contrasted environments, the implementation achieved beneficial outcomes for both the teachers and the children.

Concluding Remarks

This chapter illustrates the essential capacity of the teacher–child relationship which can be intentionally cultivated in the early childhood educational context to foster empathetic skills development of young children. The COPE-R teacher illustrates the processes and methods used to consciously support children to monitor their personal feelings, modelling empathetic behaviour in their daily activities. The case examples also illustrate how, in everyday interactions, teachers can teach young children to respond to others with sensitivity using positive guidance strategies. Many art forms, including children's drawing-tellings, poetry, songs, and collaborative work can be used when designing activities to help shape and cultivate an empathic community of prosocial learners. These activities can be both adult-guided activities and child-guided. When children engage with their community, it creates a sense of belonging to something bigger than themselves. Building community connections through an early childhood program also promotes a positive sense of identity through the interactions they have with others while developing social and other skills which are crucial for lifelong success.

Take Home Messages

- The teacher can personally learn and benefit through the teaching of social emotional skills.
- Teachers are role models and model the skills as part of their everyday practice
- All COPE-R approaches can be incorporated into any Community Connection programs.
- The development of empathy and prosocial practices are key learning outcomes for children who participate in social emotional programs such as COPE-Resilience.
- Approaches to the teaching of social emotional skills can be readily incorporated into Community Connections programs.

References

Barry, M. (2011). *The forgiveness project: The startling discovery of how to overcome cancer, find health, and achieve peace.* Grand Rapids, MI: Kregel Publications.

Bergin, C., & Bergin, D. (2009). Attachment in the classroom. *Educational Psychology Review, 21*(2), 141–170.

Berrol, C. (2006). Neuroscience meets dance/movement therapy: Mirror neurons, the therapeutic process and empathy. *The Arts in Psychotherapy, 33*(4), 302–315.

Birch, S. H., & Ladd, G. W. (1997). The teacher–child relationship and children's early school adjustment. *Journal of School Psychology, 35*(1), 61–79.

Burdelski, M. (2010). Socializing politeness routines: Action, other-orientation, and embodiment in a Japanese preschool. *Journal of Pragmatics, 42*(6), 1606–1621. https://doi.org/10.1016/j.pragma.2009.11.007

Burkitt, E., Barrett, M., & Davis, A. (2005). Drawings of emotionally characterised figures by children from different educational backgrounds. *International Journal of Art and Design Education, 24*(1), 71–83.

Cameron, H. (2005). Asking the tough questions: A guide to ethical practices in interviewing young children. *Early Child Development and Care, 175*(6), 597–610.

Caselman, T. (2007). *Teaching children empathy, the social emotion: Lessons, activities and reproducible worksheets (K-6) that teach how to "step into other's shoes".* Chapin, SC: YouthLight Incorporated.

Commodari, E. (2013). Preschool teacher attachment and attention skills. *Springer Plus, 2*(1), 1–12.

Dachyshyn, D. M. (2015). Being mindful, heartful, and ecological in early years care and education. *Contemporary Issues in Early Childhood, 16*(1), 32–41. https://doi.org/10.1177/1463949114566756

Deans, J., Klarin, S., Liang, R., & Frydenberg, E. (2017). All children have the best start in life to create a better future for themselves and for the nation. *Australasian Journal of Early Childhood, 42*(4), 78–86. http://doi:10.23965/AJEC.42.4.09

DeMeulenaere, M. (2015). Promoting social and emotional learning in preschool. *Dimensions of Early Childhood, 43*(1), 8–10.

Denham, S. A. (2005). The emotional basis of learning and development in early childhood education. In B. Spodek (Ed.), *Handbook of research in early childhood education* (pp. 85–103). Mahwah, NJ: Lawrence Erlbaum.

Dockett, S., & Perry, B. (2005). Children's drawings: Experiences and expectations of school. *International Journal of Equity and Innovation in Early Childhood, 3*(2), 77–89.

Eisenberg, N., Fabes, R. A., & Spinrad, T. L. (2006). Prosocial development. In W. Damon & R. Lerner (Eds.), *Handbook of child psychology*, Vol. 3: *social, emotional, and personality development* (6th Ed., pp. 647–702). Hoboken, NJ: Wiley.

Feshbach, N. D., & Feshbach, S. (2009). Empathy and education. In J. Decety & W. Ickes (Eds.), *The social neuroscience of empathy* (pp. 85–98). Cambridge, MA: MIT Press.

Flook, L., Goldberg, S. B., Pinger, L., & Davidson, R. J. (2015). Promoting prosocial behavior and self-regulatory skills in preschool children through a mindfulness-based kindness curriculum. *Developmental Psychology, 51*(1), 44. https://doi.org/10.1037/a0038256

Flynn, E. E., & Schachter, R. E. (2017). Teaching for tomorrow: An exploratory study of prekindergarten teachers' underlying assumptions about how children learn. *Journal of Early Childhood Teacher Education, 38*(2), 182–208.

Frydenberg, E., & Deans, J. (2011). *The early years coping cards*. Melbourne: ACER Press.

Frydenberg, E., Deans, J., & Liang, R. (2021). *Young children's social and emotional learning: The COPE-Resilience program*. Abingdon: Routledge.

Gallese, V. (2003). The roots of empathy: The shared manifold hypothesis and the neural basis of intersubjectivity. *Psychopathology, 36*(4), 171–180.

Griggs, M., Gagnon, S., Huelsman, S., Kidder-Ashley, P., & Ballard, M. (2009). Student–teacher relationships matter: Moderating influences between temperament and pre-school social competence. *Psychology in the Schools, 46*(6), 553–567.

Haslip, M. J., Allen-Handy, A., & Donaldson, L. (2019). How do children and teachers demonstrate love, kindness and forgiveness? Findings from an early childhood strength-spotting intervention. *Early Childhood Education Journal, 47*(5), 531–547.

Havighurst, S. S., Wilson, K. R., Harley, A. E., Prior, M. R., Kehoe, C. (2010). Tuning in to kids: Improving emotion socialization practices in parents of preschool children. Findings from a community trial. *Journal of Child Psychology and Psychiatry, 51*, 1342–1350. http://doi:10.1111/j.1469-7610.2010.02303.x

Hoffman, M. L. (2000). *Empathy and moral development: Implications for caring and justice*. Cambridge: Cambridge University Press.

Howes, C., Hamilton, C., & Philipsen, L. (1998). Stability and continuity of child–caregiver and child–peer relationships. *Child Development, 69*(2), 418–426.

Hyson, M. (2004). *The emotional development of young children: Building an emotion-centered curriculum*. New York: Teachers College Press.

Hyson, M., & Taylor, J. L. (2011). Caring about caring: What adults can do to promote young children's prosocial skills. *Young Children, 66*(4), 74.

Kersey, K., & Masterson, M. (2013). *101 principles for positive guidance with young children: Creating responsive teachers*. Upper Saddle River, NJ: Pearson Higher Ed.

Kirk, G., & MacCallum, J. (2017). Strategies that support kindergarten children's social and emotional development: One teacher's approach. *Australasian Journal of Early Childhood, 42*(1), 85–93.

Kokoszka, C., & Smith, J. (2016). Fostering character education in an urban early childhood setting. *Journal of Character Education, 12*(1), 69–74.

Larsen, N. E., Lee, K., & Ganea, P. A. (2018). Do storybooks with anthropomorphized animal characters promote prosocial behaviors in young children? *Developmental Science, 21*(3), e12590.

Marshall, L., & Marshall, W. (2011). Empathy and antisocial behaviour. *Journal of Forensic Psychiatry & Psychology, 22*(5), 742–759.

Mashburn, A. J., Pianta, R. C., Hamre, B. K., Downer, J. T., Barbarin, O. A., Bryant, D., et al. (2008). Measures of classroom quality in prekindergarten and children's development of academic, language, and social skills. *Child Development, 79*(3), 732–749.

Masterson, M. L., & Kersey, K. C. (2013). Connecting children to kindness: Encouraging a culture of empathy. *Childhood Education, 89*(4), 211–216.

McKown, C., & Gumbiner, L. (2009). Social-emotional learning skill, self-regulation, and social competence in typically developing and clinic referred children. *Journal of Clinical Child and Adolescent Psychology, 28*(6), 858–871.

Miyamoto, K., Huerta, M. C., & Kubacka, K. (2015). Fostering social and emotional skills for well-being and social progress. *European Journal of Education, 50*(2), 147–159.

Mortari, L. (2011). Thinking silently in the woods: Listening to children speaking about emotion. *European Early Childhood Education Research Journal, 19*(3), 345–356. http://dx.doi.org/10.1080/1350293X.2011.597966

Park, N. (2004). Character strengths and positive youth development. Annals of the *American Academy of Political and Social Science, 59*(1), 40–54.

Pianta, R. C. (1997). Adult–child relationship processes and early schooling. *Early Education and Development, 8*(1), 11–26.

Priest, C. (2007). Incorporating character education into the early childhood degree program: The need, and one department's response. *Journal of Early Childhood Teacher Education, 28*(2), 153–161. https://doi.org/10.1080/10901 02070 13667 23.

Rafaila, E. (2015). The competent teacher for teaching emotional intelligence. *Procedia: Social and Behavioral Sciences, 180*, 953–957. https://doi.org/10.1016/j.sbspro.2015.02.253

Rosenthal, M., & Gatt, L. (2010). "Learning to live together": Training early childhood educators to promote socio-emotional competence of toddlers and pre-school children. *European Early Childhood Education Research Journal, 18*(3), 223–240.

Scott Frisch, N. (2006). Drawing in preschools: A didactic experience. *International Journal of Art and Design Education, 25*(1), 74–85.

Shonkoff, J. P., & Phillips, D. A. (Eds.). (2000). *From neurons to neighborhoods: The science of early childhood development (Report of the National Research Council).* Washington, DC: National Academies Press.

Smith, C. A. (2013). Beyond "I'm sorry": The educator's role in preschoolers' emergence of conscience. *Young Children, 68*(1), 76–82.

Steen, T. A., Kachorek, L. V., & Peterson, C. (2003). Character strengths among youth. *Journal of Youth and Adolescence, 32*(1), 5–16.

Swick, K. (2005). Preventing violence through empathy development in families. *Early Childhood Education Journal, 33*(1), 53–59.

Wright, S. (2007a). Graphic-narrative play: Young children's authoring through drawing and telling. *International Journal of Education and the Arts, 8*(8), 1–28.

Wright, S. (2007b). Young children's meaning-making through drawing and "telling": Analogies to filmic textual features. *Australian Journal of Early Childhood, 32*(4), 37–48.

10 Community Connections

In an open carpeted space in the Early Learning Centre (ELC) children dance, sing, engage in dramatic enactment, and even practise yoga. Staff and visitors also gather to discuss ideas and to learn from each other. The space is known as Boorai – The Children's Art Gallery and it is here that the ideas and thoughts of children as expressed through their art and narratives are displayed for the enjoyment of children and adults. The exhibits change frequently, reflecting the thematic learning focus of the ELC program at a given period of time.

Bringing it Together

This volume on community connections in the early years has been written in three sequenced components. Part I outlines a range of foundational educational and psychological theories that have informed the programs in this volume, and which would be relevant to consider when designing early years educational programs. Part II details the theories in action, creating a community of learners through inquiry-based learning. Whilst four programs are detailed there, countless others have been implemented in the context of engaging children with their communities, some of these are presented, albeit briefly, in this final chapter as we bring it all together and present our programs as exemplars, developed in a particular setting at a particular point of time with potential for adaptation in different settings. Theoretically, there is an infinite range of possible ways to connect an early childhood educational setting with its community base. Ultimately, through such programs the aim is to provide a stimulating, meaningful educational experience that builds the capacity of children to develop life skills that enable them to contribute to their communities as active citizens.

Children's rights, their voices, their words, and their ideas are at the front and centre of all exemplars provided in this volume, as they should be in any early childhood educational program. Such programs are also in a positive psychology framework, with both classical theories of cognitive growth and socio-cultural theories of development, along with more recent approaches that highlight the development of empathy in communities.

DOI: 10.4324/9781003213147-14

As noted throughout the text, social emotional learning (SEL) in the context of early childhood education highlights the focus on the development of children's personal and social capabilities so that they can become productive members of their communities. Developing attitudes as well as knowledge and skills is an important dimension in the educational journey. SEL programs have gained traction as critical components of the educational curriculum in many parts of the Western world and are also gaining traction in Eastern communities such as Singapore, Taiwan, and Hong Kong SAR. As part of meeting curriculum requirements, the teaching of emotion language and self-regulation are key skills to be learned.

Contact theory underpins the bringing together of two groups with the key outcome of them developing understanding and reducing the likelihood of the development of prejudice. But more significantly, the development of empathy is a core foundational emotional skill that can be fostered through programs involving community connections. There are several aspects to the development of empathy, with emotional empathy being developed in the preschool years whilst cognitive empathy continues to develop into the school years. Equipping children with communication skills such as politeness, courtesy, and the development of prosocial skills are also highly desirable learning outcomes.

Chapter 4 details the important part the arts play in early years' education. It focuses particularly on the multiple arts-related modalities that are utilized in early childhood whilst teaching empathy and social emotional development. The linking of children's play with the arts is not new but a universal educational tool that can be applied in all contexts, particularly in early childhood education. Given the importance of the arts in developing and expanding children's creative and imaginative horizons, it is an ideal vehicle to link with any number of approaches that bring children closer to their communities and engage them to help deal with existing and emerging challenges. In the chapter on the arts the concept of *perezhivanie* is introduced to focus on the meaningful relationship between children's emotions, thinking, and their environments. That concept, articulated by Lev Vygotsky, highlights the capacity to bring children as participants on a social emotional journey. The classical educational scholar Dewey (1934) emphasizes that learning from life, or in other words, first-hand experience, is a powerful educational tool that links cognition and emotion. Through engagement with wide-ranging sensory and perceptual experiences as well as through semiotic meaning making through the child's representations, expressed in their personal art forms, there is a capacity to learn from and contribute to the life of a community. This is most clearly illustrated in Chapter 5.

Part II provides some detailed examples of four programs as an illustration of what is possible. Each educational setting draws upon what is accessible, what is consistent with the requirements of the curriculum, and the resources of the setting. In the experience of the authors the focus has been on the development of empathy for all persons and for the environment as the consistent underpinning and purpose of our programs. For example, in a program that focused on social inclusion the children at the ELC were engaged with adults with various intellectual and physical disabilities. They met once a week with staff from both communities present to explore visual and performing arts together, with the purpose of relationship building and the breaking down of barriers. A second program sought to break down the barriers of ageism between 4–5-year-old children and elderly citizens living in a residential community. In both communities the arts-based programs along with gardening, community singing, and storytelling became key shared activities.

In the chapter by Harriet Deans on sustainability and the environment (Chapter 5) there is considerable detail on the curriculum as it unfolds week by week. Also, this chapter details the specific approaches to instruction and experience in the early childhood setting. A whole of school approach is always desirable where possible, as it is a way of bringing the school community, parents, teachers, and children on the journey. The role of the teacher as a facilitator is detailed. Learning goals and intentions, both long-term and short-term, are considered in the weekly planning and design of the program. Furthermore, Chapter 5 outlines six instructional domains that benefit learning outcomes, namely the cognitive, social emotional, thinking routines, mind-mapping, drawing-tellings and behaviours. These are not discrete approaches but interrelated. Nevertheless, the descriptions of each highlight the ways in which the reader can make use of them for any facet of their early childhood curriculum. Each is an important approach that contributes to a child's development in the educational context.

Some would argue that facilitating cognitive development is the key role of education. Children at 3–4 years of age develop their understanding of their environments and in the educational setting strategies include listing, labelling, discussing, explaining of what they see, with teachers providing prompts and open-ended questioning. With progression to 4–5 years, children mature and their ability to explore, investigate, and articulate advances. As in most aspects of education it is possible to build on prior knowledge or learnings.

Without discounting the importance of cognitive development, others might argue that the social and emotional aspects of education are all important. It is the aspect of education that focuses on relationships and prosocial aspects of behaviour where the goal is contribute to good citizenship throughout the lifespan. Children often walk together and work with partners or in groups. Social skill development is a feature of learning about the environment. Caring for the environment can translate into the development of empathy. Where there is a focus on mindfulness that can be readily incorporated into the stepping out program.

In the process of advancing both cognitive and social emotional domains, certain approaches are used. Thinking routines are used to facilitate skills to observe and describe. Demonstrating environmental care and respect contributes to social emotional development that is transferable to different contexts. Thinking about problems and articulating solutions, sometimes individually and at other times through discussion that may be conducted in small or large groups with a teacher facilitator, advances both cognitive and social skill development.

Since the arts are a strong feature of early childhood education, particularly visual representations of experiences or imaginings, drawing-tellings are used to engage children to recall and draw on what they had seen or done. The drawings are followed by a one-on-one engagement by the teacher as interlocuter with each child, helping to capture their verbal descriptions of their drawings or any other way they want to describe their experience. All aspects of language development, critical thinking, and problem solving can be utilized as part of the interaction. Both journaling and drawing-tellings provide data for formative and summative evaluation of children's development. There is an opportunity for both oral and non-oral data gathering.

Journaling can be done individually or in pairs, as illustrated in Chapter 5. Children recall their experiences and can use words that are collected by teachers or draw what they recall – they use objects that they found or research they do with iPads. There is a systematic collection of material by the teacher that can be drawn upon or followed through on a subsequent occasion.

Mind-mapping is an approach that takes a "big idea" topic as a theme, such as for example the weather, and asks children to apply, create, and share knowledge. Links are made in ways that connect the information which can then be mapped. Children respond to the connections and question and answer exchanges can occur in the classroom or beyond.

Finally, in both the traditional and the wall-less classrooms behavioural outcomes can be observed and measured. Children's play and practices in the environment provide evidence of progress and development. What a child does provides evidence of development and learning as well as opportunities for engagement and teaching.

The International Focus

As part of the international focus of connecting children with communities outside their home country relationships were established outside the classroom and beyond the national borders. For example, as part of the multiple Associazione L'Eta Verde Projects themes have been explored that generally coincide with an International Year of, for example, Trees and Forests, Oceans, Astronomy, or which focus on Polar Research and the COVID Pandemic in 2021. The projects that are produced are then shared across the global communities. Modern technology makes that readily possible, whether in a visual or auditory format. The Hexagon Project was another such program that emanated from contact with the United States educational community. That project draws on six-sided figures that can interconnect and metaphorically represent interdependence. Themes around topics like biodiversity and conflict have been explored but theoretically any number of contemporary socially relevant issues can be explored, and the visual arts provide an ideal vehicle.

One of the early projects that moved beyond the familiar world of the children's early childhood setting was the reaching out to the researchers located in ice-bound Antarctica. For the project relating to polar research, the ELC Director contacted the station leader at Casey Station in Antarctica. He was able to produce mp4 files and, in that way, children could ask questions of the experts and vice versa. A children's book was one of the outcomes; created as part of a centre-wide exploration of Antarctic. This project demonstrated how teachers can guide and support beyond the classroom learning to achieve unexpected and memorable outcomes.

In Part III the Cope Resilience Program (COPE-R) (Frydenberg et al., 2021) featured stories to show the connection between theories, activities, and social emotional learning, with the main focus on building connections and relationships – with self, others, the world, the environment. Whilst that program featured as a core SEL program it stimulated enquiries that supported relationships of a high order and skill building. Such programs can be incorporated into any community relationships activity, with elements such as caring, sharing, gratitude, and politeness being some of the universally desirable topics that are tackled in that program.

An additional project that was undertaken was a result of a collaboration between a teacher and a glass artist. The glass artist introduced the children to the art of glass blowing and then proceeded to use the children's ideas and drawings as stimulus to produce glass sculptures. Visiting a glass artist provided an opportunity for the children to experience the role of the artist in his studio. The underlying concept of this unique program was based on the facilitation of making connections between a drawing design and the creation of a glass object. In this project the children drew their ideas, and the teacher wrote narratives that explained the ideas behind the drawing. The glass artist then used the children's drawings and words, combining and integrating the ideas and transforming the two-dimensional designs into a three-dimensional glass sculpture.

A collaboration of this kind produces many concrete outcomes including high-level thinking, creative processing, and expressive communication for all involved. One significant public exhibition, "Step gently on this earth and this sky", highlighted the processes and products of this innovative approach to community-based learning.

Another program that was integrated with the Associazione L'Eta Verde and Interdependence Hexagon Projects mentioned in Chapter 6 and also within the "stepping out – finding out – speaking out" curriculum presented in Chapter 5, focused on the children's in-depth journey investigating a range of ecological outcomes of human impact on the health of the environment, including the local Yarra River, the critically endangered Leadbeater's Possum, and the ancient Mountain Ash trees that stand in Toolangi State Forest, close to the City of Melbourne.

These initiatives were developed in collaboration with teachers, children, families, artists, and scientists. Through the participation of a diverse range of people powerful outcomes were achieved. In the case of a community visit to Toolangi Forest, children were inspired to write to the Prime Minister of Australia at the time, articulating their concerns about the ongoing logging of the forest and the impact on the Leadbeater's Possum.

One teacher commented

> all the teachers from the ELC visited Toolangi Forest and engaged in a science session, we showed the short film to all the ELC children to see if they would embrace the plight for the critically endangered Leadbeater's Possum, that was a powerful and emotional hook that inspired everyone and provided an opportunity for each child to become a keeper of the green Earth.
>
> This project taught us how to become active citizens and advocate for all living things that need our voices and both the children, and the teachers were empowered to step out of the everyday curriculum and speak out by contacting the Prime Minister and the Parliament.
>
> These two years have been the most powerful years of my teaching and the sheer inspiration, power and beauty discovered through them never left me.
>
> The children who were involved in this project proceeded to school where they shared it with others and one of them became a main organizer and leader of the March for Climate Change. She collaborated with Gretta Thurnberg and opened our exhibition "Greening Melbourne" in 2019.

The Challenges of 2020–2021

The year 2020 provided new challenges for teachers, children, and families. COVID-19 being particularly dangerous for the elderly meant that, for example, the intergenerational program turned its efforts to remote connections. Teachers also had to reconsider different approaches to engaging children in remote learning. Projects such as singing, letter writing, video face-time messaging were trialed and were used as ways to maintain connections between children and the community throughout the pandemic. There were times when the children were challenged to retain the level of attention and interactivity in the non-face-to-face mode with community participants.

In response to the requirement for online learning teachers thought creatively about how children's lived experience could be communicated beyond the classroom. For example, as part of the Associazione L'Eta Verde 2021 Macro Problem, a video[1] was produced that communicated Australian children's responses to COVID-19.

---

1 University of Melbourne Early Learning Centre L'Eta Verde 2021: https://vimeo.com/544802266

To first establish the context, in Australia the first confirmed case of COVID-19 was on 25 January 2020. Australian borders were closed to all non-residents on 20 March 2020. Social distancing rules were imposed on 21 March 2020. A second wave of infections emerged in Victoria during May and June 2020. From 23 July 2020, "face coverings" in Metropolitan Melbourne and Mitchell Shire became mandatory whenever residents left their homes. On 2 August 2020, a state of disaster was declared, and Metropolitan Melbourne was moved to Stage 4 restrictions. A curfew across Melbourne from 8 pm to 5 am was imposed and a 5 km (3.1 mile) radius restriction was added. The Australian Government's COVID-19 vaccination program began in Victoria, Australia on 22 February 2021. The children at the University of Melbourne's Early Learning Centre reflected on their experience of COVID-19 and the strict lockdowns. Poetry, musical composition, drawing, and painting were arts-based methods used to tell their story.

Drawing Masks

World Health Organization recommended that, as a key measure to suppress transmission and save lives, masks should be used as part of a comprehensive "Do it all!" approach including physical distancing, avoiding crowded, closed, and close-contact settings, good ventilation, cleaning hands, covering sneezes and coughs, and more (Figures 10.1, 10.2).

Drawings-Tellings

Children were supported to cope through play and discussion about emotions. For instance, children were provided with the opportunity to express their feelings in a safe place (see Figures 10.3 a & b). To help young children have some sense of control and safety, adults were encouraged to have conversations about being part of a community and to care for each other.

Figure 10.1 ELC children's drawings of wearing masks.

176 Part III

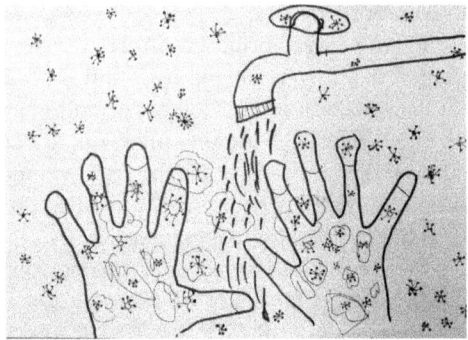

Figure 10.2 ELC children's drawings of washing hands.

Figure 10.3a ELC children's drawing-tellings during the pandemic.

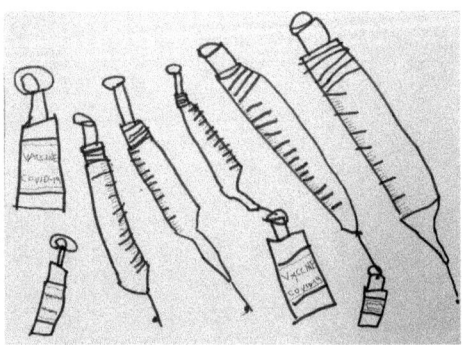

Figure 10.3b ELC children's drawing-tellings during the pandemic.

Community Connections 177

Figure 10.4 Children's drawing for *Then and Now: Out of the Birdcage*.

Poetry

A vimeo was produced with the poetry and children's work which was sent to Associazione L'Eta Verde (see Chaper 6). It was a true collaboration between all members of the ELC community, including teachers, children, and parents.

> *Then and Now: Out of the Birdcage*
> When COVID arrived
> we felt trapped
> like a bird in a cage
> It arrived fast
> Like a storm
> at the speed of a cheetah or a leopard 100 KMS
> The world was quiet
> and silent
> and whispering
> and tiptoeing
> and the birds loved it that way.
> We felt like inside a volcano
> And we measured time in visits.
> We stopped seeing
> People we love.
> We stopped travelling
> And got locked in other countries
> For one hundred years or longer.
> We walked masked up and with
> clean and squeaky hands
> and noticed every flower
> and every leaf

> Now we feel safer
> and braver
> and happy
> We flew out of bird cages
> and we feel free.
> Feel free

Final Remarks

This book has presented a wide range of pedagogical approaches that support children's development and self-concept as an active citizen within community. It has highlighted innovative approaches that teachers have adopted to inspire children and families as well as themselves. As described in Chapter 3, ongoing and post evaluations within early childhood programs through multiple formats are important as they allow teachers and educators to reflect on how their programs have unfolded, what factors supported success, and what ideas for future planning and implementation could be considered to improve learning outcomes. For example, in 2021 when we evaluated the environmental project in Chapter 5, we found that children's emotional expression (a negative coping strategy), externalizing behaviour, internalizing behaviour, and total difficulties decreased throughout the program (McNamara, 2021). We found that the quantitative results using validated measurement tools were confirmed in the main by the qualitative responses of children with their drawing and verbal descriptions, as well as the affirmations made by both parents and teachers describing their children's learnings and actions. The tried-and-true concepts and activities described in this book demonstrate that it is possible to increase prosocial behaviour, attention to emotions, and the use of positive coping strategies in young children, while cultivating a powerful sense of connection to their communities as well as being global citizens who have a solid foundation to build a sustainable future for themselves and others around them. We trust that this volume contributes to that endeavour.

References

Deans, J., Liang, R. & Frydenberg, E. (2016). Giving voices and providing skills to families in culturally and linguistically diverse communities through a productive parenting program. *Australasian Journal of Early Childhood, 41*(1), 13—16.

Dewey, J. (1934). *Art as experience*. New York: Capricorn Books.

Frydenberg, E. (2015). *Families coping*. Melbourne: Australian Council for Educational Research.

Frydenberg, E., Deans, J., & Liang, R. (2021). *Young children's social and emotional learning: The COPE-Resilience program*. Abingdon: Routledge.

Gulliford, H., Deans, J., Frydenberg, E., & Liang, R. (2015). Teaching coping skills in the context of positive parenting within a preschool setting. *Australian Psychologist, 3,* 219. https://doi.org/10.1111/ap.12121" https://doi.org/10.1111/ap.12121

McNamara, N. (2021). Social and emotional learning through an environmental education program: An evaluation of the Learning in Nature Program. Unpublished master's thesis, University of Melbourne.

Thomson, S., Frydenberg, E., Deans, J., & Liang, R. (2015). Increasing wellbeing through a parenting program: Role of gender and partnered attendance. *Australian Educational and Developmental Psychologist, 32*(2), 120–141.

Index

Abecedarian Project 5
active citizenship 58–60
adult–child relationship 26
affective empathy 33, 34, 35, 44
age-segregated institutions 130; *see also* intergenerational programs
agency 10
Allport, Gordon 32
apprenticeship 14
arts 3, 6, 7, 15, 49, 170; active citizenship 58–60; Associazione l'Eta Verda 103–7, 172, 174; child art exhibitions 99–102, 107, 113, 170; children's voices 56–8, 60; community arts projects 117, 121, 125, 127; disabilities and 116, 117, 127; drawing-tellings 85–6, 85–6, 160, 161, 172, 175–77; glass blowing 173; Interdependence Hexagon Project 107–12; playful artistic meaning making 49–51, 60; semiotic meaning making 55–6; significance of arts education 52–4, 60
Associazione l'Eta Verda 103–7, 172, 174
attachment relationships 151
attachment theory 10, 22–3, 24, 27, 40
Australia: Code of Ethics of Early Childhood 6, 57; curriculum 20, 27, 53; Early Years Learning Framework (EYLF) 49, 51, 101; intergenerational programs 132; Victorian State Disability Plan 117, 120
Australian Curriculum, Assessment and Reporting Authority (ACARA) 17, 19
Australian First Nations 8, 32

Bandura, A. 23
Baron-Cohen, S. 35

behavioural domain 83, 84, 85
Berrol, C. 162
Better Beginnings, Better Futures program 5
biodiversity 13
Bioecological Systems Theory 10–11
Borden, Esta 31
Bowlby, John 22, 40
Brackett, Marc 23, 25
Bronfenbrenner, U. 10, 15, 40
Bruner, Jerome 52
bullying 35

caring 35
Chicago Child-Parent Centers 5
child art exhibitions 99–102, 107, 113, 170
child development 10
children's voices 56–8, 60, 171; art exhibitions 101–2, 170
Chronosystem 19
circle time 156
citizenship 58–60, 100, 101, 112, 113, 116
Cizek, Franz 101
co-construction of knowledge 71
Code of Ethics of Early Childhood Australia 6, 57
cognitive development 12–13, 14, 171
cognitive domain 79–80, 84, 85
cognitive empathy 33, 34, 35, 44
collaborative learning 100, 102, 126
Collaborative for Academic Social and Emotional Learning (CASEL) 17, 18, 19, 27, 31, 133
communicative behaviours 159
communication skills 38
communities of practice 116
community 151

community arts projects 117, 121, 125, 127
community connections programs 5–9, 14, 22, 26, 31; conscience 35, 37–8; contact theory 32–3, 44; empathy 33–5, 39–40, 41, 44; empathy in action 35–7; foundational emotional skills 33–9; open communication 38; politeness 39; program implementation 43–4; prosocial skills 31, 33, 35, 41, 42–3; social learning 40–2; teacher's role 39–40
community of learners 7, 100
compassion 37
concrete operational stage 12
conflict resolution 111
Confucianism 39
Connery, C. 55
conscience 35, 37–8
construction of knowledge 116
contact theory 32–3, 44, 134, 170
cooperation 32
COPE-Resilience program (COPE-R) 23, 25, 149, 153–5, 173; adult-led activities 164; child-led activities 164, 165; connection building activities 164–5; embodying concepts moment by moment 160; fostering ways of expressing emotions 157; foundational relation skills 157; helping children appreciate the emotions of self, others, and spaces 162; international adaptation 165; learning empathy 162–3; modelling and developing empathic behaviours 157–8; ongoing feedback and reflection 160–2; positive reinforcement of effective communication behaviours 159; productive coping, problem-solving skills 158–9; safe teaching and learning environment 156; voice level chart 164; weaving SEL into the school day 160; embodying concepts moment by moment 160
coping skills 158–9
COVID-19 pandemic 174–8
Cox, S. 60
cultural historical activity theory 100
cultural holidays 41
cultural norms 35

Danesi, M. 55
databases 133
Deci, E. L. 24

developmental psychology 49–50
Dewey, John 53, 59, 100, 102, 170
dialogic pedagogy 23
disabled young adults 32, 115–17, 171; arts and 116, 117, 127; Friends on the Farm 117–127
diversity 8, 116
drawing-tellings 85–6, 160, 161, 172, 176–78
Durlak, J. A. 19–20

Early Learning Centre (ELC), University of Melbourne 6, 8, 77, 103, 104, 107, 108, 109, 110, 134, 171, 175; Boorai-Children's Art Gallery 169; intergenerational program 135–42, 171
Early Years Learning Framework (EYLF) 49, 51, 101
ecocentric curriculum 68–70, 71, 72, 77, 96
Ecological Systems Theory 10–11, 15
Education for Sustainable Development (ESD) 7–8, 67–8, 96; behavioural domain 83, 84, 85; cognitive domain 79–80, 84, 85; definition 68; drawing-tellings 85–6, 85–6; ecocentric curriculum 68–70, 71, 72, 77, 96; journaling 87–88, 87, 89, 89–91; learning domains 78–85, 96; learning intentions 78; learning objectives 72–7; long-term goals 77–8; mind-mapping 95, 94; socio-emotional domain 80–2, 84, 85; Stepping Out Programs 72, 77–85, 96; teacher documentation 95, 95; teacher's role 71–2; thinking routines 89, 89, 92–3; wall-less classrooms 70, 71, 72–7, 96
Eisenberg, N. 42
Eisner, Eliot 50, 52, 53, 54, 103
emotional intelligence (EI) 10, 24–5, 34, 41, 42
emotional skills 33–9
emotional understanding (EU) 36–7
empathy 8, 10, 33–5, 39–40, 41, 44, 111, 113, 170, 171; COPE-R 167–8, 162–3, 166; intergenerational programs 131, 132, 134, 135; quality of educator-child relationship 151–2, 153
empathy in action 35–7
engagement 7
environment 3, 5, 8–12, 14, 35, 36, 67, 69–96; see also Education for Sustainable Development
executive functioning 13
Exosystem 10

182 *Index*

Fabes, R. A. 42
families 7, 10, 38, 41, 42–3, 71
Femia, E. E. 133
Feshbach, N. D. 162
Feshbach, S. 162
First Nations programs 8, 32
forgiveness 38
formal operations stage 12
Freeman, N. K. 133
Friends on the Farm 117–127
friendships 22, 24, 33, 41
Froebel, Friedrich 49

glass blowing 174
global citizenship 100–2, 112, 113
global partnerships: Associazione L'Eta Verde 103–7, 172, 173, 174; child art exhibitions 99–102, 107, 113; Interdependence Hexagon Project 107–112, 172, 174
Goleman, Daniel 24, 34, 42
Gray, G. 18, 19
guided discovery 126

Hexagon Project 107–12, 172, 174
Hoffman, M. L. 162
holistic well-being 9
Holmes, R. 133
Hong, Euny 39
Howe, T. R. 24

inclusivity 8, 115, 116, 126, 127
inquiry-based learning 100, 115
Intent Community Participation 14
Interdependence Hexagon Project 107–12, 172, 174
intergenerational programs 32, 130, 171; across the globe 131–2; ELC 135–42; empathy 131, 132, 134, 134; evidence 132–5; modelling 134; need and opportunity 131; theoretical underpinnings 134, 143
intergroup contact 33
international focus 20–1, 107–11, 165, 172–4
IQ 42
Italian Futures Organization 103

journaling 86–7, 87, 88, 89–91, 123–5, 172

King, S. 133
Kirk, G. 151

Korea: intergenerational programs 132; *nunchi* 39
Kremenitzer, J. 42

language development 25–6, 40
learning domains 78–85, 96
learning environments 5, 7
life expectancy 131
lived experience 116, 125–7

MacCallum, J. 151
Macrosystem 10
Malaguzzi, Loris 57–8, 102, 108
mandalas 164, 165
masks 175
Mayer, J. D. 24, 42
meaning making 49–51, 55–6, 99, 115
Mesosystem 10
meta-analysis 32
metacognitive skills 24, 26
Microsystem 10
mind-mapping 93–5, 94, 172
mindfulness-based activity 160, 161, 171
modelling 134, 150, 152
Montessori, Maria 49
moral reasoning 35, 157
Mortari, L. 157
Mother–Child Home Program 5
multidimensional thinking 51–2, 60

New Zealand curriculum 20, 27
Nimmo, J. 116, 117
nunchi 39

older adults 130; *see also* intergenerational programs
open communication 38

parents 10, 13, 21, 22, 23, 24, 34, 37, 38
Pendergast, D. 99, 101
perezhivanie 51v2, 170
Perkins, David 14, 15
Perry Preschool Program 5
personal best 24
Pettigrew, Thomas 32, 33
Piaget, Jean 12–13, 31
play 7, 22, 26; artistic meaning making 49–51, 60; *perezhivanie* and multidimensional thinking 51–2
poetry 177–8
politeness 39
Positive Education 9–10
positive psychology 9, 10, 15, 169

positive reinforcement 159
postmodern theory 115
pre-operational stage 12
prejudice 134
problem-solving skills 158–9
Process-Person-Context-Time (PPCT) model 11
program implementation and evaluation 43–4
Progressive Education Movement 53
prosocial behaviours 5, 31, 33, 35, 41, 42–3, 131, 133, 151; creating a community of prosocial learners 152–3

quantitative results 178

reflection-in-and-on-action 118, 123–5, 127
Reggio Emilia philosophy 58
relational skills 39
relationship building 22
relationships 7
rights of the child 6
Rogoff, Barbara 13–14, 15, 40, 59, 100, 134
role models 43, 44, 166
role-play 158
Rousseau, Jean-Jacques 49
RULER program 23, 25
Ryan, R. M. 24

Salovey, P. 24, 42
scaffolding 13, 43, 126, 152
Schön, D. 118
self-awareness 18, 19, 27
self-determination theory 24, 40
self-directed learning 100
self-management 18, 19, 27
self-regulation 10, 22, 23–4, 26, 40, 131, 134
Seligman, Martin 9
semiotic meaning making 55–6
sensorimotor stage 12
sensory explorations 54
sensory-rich learning environments 8
Slade, P. 49
Smith, C. A. 37
social awareness 18, 19, 27
social construction of knowledge 100
social emotional learning (SEL) 17–19, 26, 31, 40–2, 170; attachment theory 22–3; Australia and New Zealand 20, 27; basis for early years curriculum 20–2; benefits 19; building strong foundations 19–20; emotional intelligence 24–5; Europe and beyond 21–2; intergenerational programs 133; role of language 25–6; self-regulation 23–4; teacher's role 150–1, 165–6; United Kingdom 20–1, 27
social management 18, 19
social skills 25
socio-constructivist theory 71
socio-cultural perspectives 120
socio-cultural theory of development 13–14, 40
socio-emotional domain 80–2, 84, 85
special needs see disabled young adults
Spinrad, T. L. 42
Steiner, Rudolf 99–100
Stepping Out Programs 72, 77–85, 96
sustainability 3, 8, 68, 71, 75, 78, 108, 138, 171; see also Education for Sustainable Development
Swick, K. 152
symbolic representations 54, 58–9, 60, 102

teachers 7, 8, 12, 23, 24, 32, 37, 38, 39–40, 56; Education for Sustainable Development (ESD) 71–2, 95, 95; intergenerational programs 141–2; philosophy and values 41, 42; program implementation and evaluation 43–4; quality of educator–child relationship 151–2; role models 43, 44, 166; social and emotional learning programs 40, 150–1, 165–6
thinking routines 89, 92–3
Toolangi State Forest 173–4
Twigg, D. 99, 101

UK Curriculum 20–1, 27
UNESCO 67, 68, 69, 78, 80
United Nations 104
United Nations Convention on the Rights of the Child (UNCRC) 6, 15, 56, 100

voice level chart 164
Vygotsky, Lev 13, 15, 25, 40, 41, 43, 50, 51, 134; *perezhivanie* and multidimensional thinking 51–2, 170; semiotic meaning making 55

wall-less classroom 70, 71, 72–7, 96
Weare, K. 18, 19

Wells, G. 120
Wheelwright, S. 35
Whitebread, D. 26
Wright, S. 59
Wurundjeri people 8, 77

Yarra River 173

Ziegfeld, E. 101–2
zone of proximal development (ZPD) 13, 14